ANTHROPOLOGY &
EGALITARIANISM

Ethnographic Encounters from
Monticello to Guinea-Bissau

ERIC GABLE

Indiana University Press

Bloomington and Indianapolis

This book is a publication of

Indiana University Press
601 North Morton Street
Bloomington, IN 47404-3797 USA

iupress.indiana.edu

Telephone orders	800-842-6796
Fax orders	812-855-7931
Orders by e-mail	iuporder@indiana.edu

Manufactured in the United States of America

Library of Congress Cataloging-in-Publication Data

Gable, Eric.
  Anthropology and egalitarianism : ethnographic encounters from
Monticello to Guinea-Bissau / Eric Gable.
    p. cm.
  Includes bibliographical references and index.
  ISBN 978-0-253-35576-8 (cloth : alk. paper) — ISBN 978-0-253-22275-6
(pbk. : alk. paper) 1. Ethnology—Philosophy. 2. Ethnology—Fieldwork. 3.
Equality—Philosophy. I. Title.
  GN345.G33 2010
  305.8001—dc22

                          2010020766

  2 3 4 5 16 15 14 13 12 11

For Larsen, Grace, Ned, and Martin

All ethnography is part philosophy, and
a good deal of the rest is confession.

—CLIFFORD GEERTZ

Contents

Preface and Acknowledgments

Some books take a long time to write, and this one began twenty years ago as a lecture accompanying a slide show that I gave in a class on the anthropology of Africa that Deborah Kaspin was teaching at the University of Virginia. In showing several juxtaposed images of people in the village in Guinea-Bissau inhabited by members of an ethnic group called Manjaco among whom I had been engaged in what anthropologists call ethnography, I wanted to illustrate to my audience how what we learn or don't learn about other people in other places depends on how our desires and prejudices frame our subject. I showed, for example, two images of the Manjaco king, one in a suit, the other in a toga, and asked them to respond to those images. Almost all the students found the king in the toga more compelling, so powerful, so self-possessed. The king in the suit made them cringe. I then confessed that I had felt the same way, and I tried to demonstrate how all anthropological knowledge and how the discipline of anthropology itself is enduringly haunted by that problem of perception by also showing a series of images of rituals. Images of rituals made up the bulk of the hundreds of slides I had taken, yet rituals, in the scheme of things, were only a small slice of life in the village as I experienced it. Rituals were also what intrigued my audience. They were the kinds of images my audience expected from a sojourn in Africa. They made Africa appear at once primitive and exotic. They also were instantiations of that vague something we all had a name for—culture.

In 1988 it was easy to make fun of such expectations and of the kinds of framing that shaped both the expectations and the images themselves. In 1988 anthropologists were busy flagellating themselves for their own complicity in a pernicious form of Othering that drew an all-too-predictable and comforting boundary between "us" and "them" by stressing cultural difference. Anthropology in the late 1980s was a guilty discipline, eager to confess its guilt and run away from the scene of the crime. Culture was becoming an embarassing term, almost as bad as, indeed analogous to, race. So, in showing these slides and in emphasizing the similarity between my perspective and the perspective of my audience, I wanted to rub our collective noses in the stench of that crime. But I also wanted to do something else. I wanted to recover a certain essential creativity inherent in the ethnographic encounter. Photographs are real; they exclude and distort while remaining somehow true. Cultural differences are not mere figments. They are the stuff of what makes us human. And grappling with difference through the distortions of our own desires and prejudices is what we must do if we are to remain true to an essential commitment to human equality.

This book emerges out of that lecture (described in more detail in chapter 6), which subsequently became a central component of my Introduction to Cultural Anthropology course, and out of that commitment, which I believe remains central to anthropology. What I discovered looking at my photographs and listening to my audience's comments on them is hardly original. Indeed, I would argue that my version of anthropology is typical, quintessential. Other anthropologists might disagree. Because we are a discipline that emerges out of highly personal encounters, we develop a certain genealogy for ourselves that connects us with our disciplinary peers and forebears.

So in writing this book, I constantly imagined an audience composed of those anthropologists, chief among them Clifford Geertz, whose own voice and perspective captivated me when I was an undergraduate and starting to read anthropology for the first time on my own. Geertz drew sharp distinctions between Balinese or Javanese and Moroccans to make a case for the existence of "local knowledge," or "ethos," or "culture," in part to assert that those contrasts are more profound than, say, the more pervasive kinds of contrast that anthropology is given to making between the "contemporary moment" and the past, between the colonial and the postcolonial. As anthropology has become increasingly a guilty discipline, it also gives up on the creativity of contrast. That is a shame because exploring contrast is anthropology's enduring contribution to human studies broadly conceived. Geertz always exemplified what he argued. Anthropology was best as an essay, he asserted, and so he wrote beautiful essays. Ethnography was personal and philosophical, and so in his best essays he was present in the large ideas he was using encounters in out-of-the way places to illustrate. Geertz was also casual about those ideas, as if they were obvious and everywhere. Reading Geertz, you did not have to hack through a tangled thicket of citations. Big ideas did not require that kind of journey. I came to love Geertz as one loves any favorite author, and I came to imagine him as an ideal reader. The book is therefore in the manner of an essay, and its central conceit is that in anthropology the personal is always connected to the philosophical by way of the intimacies of the ethnographic encounter. It also passes quickly over what scholars refer to as "the literature," providing only the most obvious and simple maps of that forest of works we produce in our arguments and conversations with one another.

There have also been other audiences more real than imaginary. My wife, Rachel, has been my first and final audience; she has been a constant and sympathetic reader while also offering incisive criticisms of form and content. Joanna Davidson, one of the more educated and astute anthropologists of a younger generation that I know, read the manuscript and gave me exactly the encouragement I needed, as did my colleague Bruce O'Brien, who read it from an educated outsider's perspective. I am also very fortunate to have had two perfect readers of the manuscript—Paul Stoller and Liam Murphy—via Indiana University Press. Both are writers who strive to make anthropology accessible while maintaining the highest intellectual standards. I have admired Stoller's work—for its consistent clarity and insights—not to mention for Stoller's willingness to experiment and to expose himself ever since I was a graduate student. After I incorporated their advice, Rebecca Tolen read the manuscript and helped me to polish it further. I only hope that the book I have edited, following their advice, lives up to their expectations for it.

I have also benefited from years of using bits of the book in my classes at the University of Mary Washington, a fairly small liberal arts institution in Virginia, more suburban, white and middle-class than not. Those students have been a real audience; they also have therefore become a textual or imaginary audience. As such they have a certain perspective and subject position. I write for them—to convince them, to change them, but also in sympathy with their prejudices and desires.

Above all I owe a great debt to Deborah Kaspin. Over the years we have had dozens of productive conversations about the nature of anthropology. Out of those conversations I learned from her one of the crucial themes I use in this book—the idea that culture as a theory emerges as a series of contrasts to other theories of what it means to be human. Didi chose me as her replacement when she took a sabbatical at Yale in 1994. I taught her courses and began to think of cultural anthropology through the mnemonic of "contrast." Had I not taught that year at Yale then I would probably not have a job in anthropology now. Had I not learned from Didi, I would certainly not have had the inspiration for the book as it is currently framed.

As with any book long in gestation I have used some of the material that appears here in different forms elsewhere. In chapters 5 and 6 I use material that originally appeared in "Appropriate Bodies: Self Through the Other in Manjaco and Portuguese Representation, 1946–1973," *Visual Anthropology Review* 14(1) (1998): 3–19. In chapter 6 I also use material covered in "The Funeral and Modernity in Manjaco," *Cultural Anthropology* 21(3) (2006): 385–415. In chapter 7 I borrow from "Beyond Belief: Play, Scepticism, and Religion in an African Village," *Social Anthropology: The Journal of the European Association of Social Anthropologists* 10(1) (2002): 41–57.

Photographs are my own except where noted.

ANTHROPOLOGY &
EGALITARIANISM

Introduction

Culture by Contrast and Theory in Anthropology

One of the most influential anthropologists in recent memory, Clifford Geertz, said that cultural anthropology is the study of people living in "out of the way places." For Geertz, it was because anthropologists studied people far away from the taken-for-granted of their own world that anthropology had something crucial to contribute to our collective understanding of humanity. In an earlier, more innocent era, anthropologists wrote books about "the savage mind," about the "sexual lives of savages" or "primitive government" or "primitive religion." They used these terms—primitive or savage—not to be pejorative, but to provide alternative visions about what it means to be human for people in societies (such as ours) who consider themselves to be civilized. Civilized people, then and today, like savages. They wish they were still like them. They wish they were still as close to nature, to each other, and to God as are savages. But civilized people also hate savages—or at least look down on them—for their slavish superstitions, for their filthiness, for their unruliness. Savages are us, by way of contrast.

For several centuries—at least since Thomas Hobbes and later Jean-Jacques Rousseau, not to mention explorers and missionaries in the Age of Discovery—people of Europe and in nation-states made by Europeans have discovered in the contrast between themselves and the savage a way of illustrating the power of society to shape human behavior and belief. For philosophers such as Hobbes and Rousseau, savages were their warped mirror. Hobbes used savages to assert that humans in a state of nature would be fearful of and violent toward one another. Life would be nasty, brutish, and short as a result. Society, he argued, required some kind of centralized authority with the power to enforce rules, or order, so that otherwise selfish and shortsighted humans could survive and thrive.

Rousseau, by contrast, used what Europeans in the Americas were learning about savages to claim that humans in a state of nature, or close to it, were

altruistic and cooperative. Civilization warped the naturally salutary proclivities of humans, corrupting them, making them greedy and self-regarding.
Rousseau looked into the warped mirror of primitive people and saw a noble
savage. Hobbes saw a savage beast. From so-called primitive people they each
extrapolated a theory of human nature and an argument for or against particular kinds of social orders.

Other influential Europeans, from the Enlightenment up through the nineteenth century and into the twentieth—from Marx to Durkheim and Freud—
used savages and primitive societies in similar ways. When they looked into
that mirror, they saw either what they had escaped from, emerged out of, left
behind, or lost. But above all they saw the power of social forces to mold and
shape human beings in a variety of ways, because whatever their attitudes
toward savages, whether they felt a certain longing for a lost way of life or a
sense of superiority made all the more profound by the savage's abjection, they
recognized a common humanity. If savages differed, it was because of differing
social circumstances.

Indeed, the modern idea of "culture" as Americans tend to use that term—
that there are plural cultures much as there are plural personalities—is an
extension and transformation of this long Western meditation on the savage,
that person who is so different, yet nevertheless the same. Indeed, because
Americans value pluralism and tend to tolerate difference, we hardly use the
word "savage" anymore. It is too nakedly pejorative. So instead Americans talk
about different cultures. We use the word culture constantly. Nowadays when
Americans talk about how the Internet has "changed our culture," or that "the
culture" of this corporation is not in sync with "the culture" of that one, or
that this grocery store chain outperforms that one because it is selling a "whole
culture" rather than merely food items, Americans are using a concept that
emerges out of the modern West's collective encounters with and conversations
about the savage. We are all, in this sense, anthropologists now.

In this book, I explore how people in the West and in America became anthropologists in order to retrieve the reasons why anthropology is so important
as a mode of understanding what we think it means to be human. In doing so
I will also show how professional anthropology as a discipline of study differs
from what I will call vernacular anthropology—the forms of commonsense
understandings of what culture is and does that circulate as taken-for-granted
concepts in our collective discourse about what it means to be human. I will
describe anthropology's articulation of the concept of culture as it compares
to and contrasts with other ways of talking about human difference, race for
example. As Deborah Kaspin has noted, the vernacular theories of culture

people in Western societies deploy have always entailed contrast. We arrive, she says, at the idea of "culture—by contrast." It is from her that I borrow that phrase, and it is from her inspiration that I will highlight two contrasts Americans routinely make. One is the contrast between nature and culture, and the other is the contrast we draw between superior or advanced cultures and inferior or primitive ones. These contrasts Americans make between biology and culture and between better and worse cultures are what constitute a vernacular understanding of human difference. It is our vernacular anthropology. Kaspin argues that professional anthropology emerges from the vernacular by way of further contrast. Professional cultural anthropology is not vernacular anthropology, although it has a similar pedigree.

In the vernacular understanding, Americans use the word "culture" as a matter of habit. Most Americans assume, without thinking too deeply about it, that culture is a powerful force. We recognize that so much of what we think or do is "because of our culture" and we're constantly saying so. We assume that because of the way we are raised, because of what we are taught by parents, teachers, peers, because of what we read or see in the media, we believe and act in certain ways. Yet many Americans, probably most Americans, believe that nature is a more powerful force than culture. Culture, so many Americans assume, might get us off track—teach us to do things that harm us, like smoking, or buying or eating things we don't need, or having sex with the wrong kind of people. In this vernacular understanding, there are healthy cultures and sick ones, cultures of life, cultures of fear, cultures of death. There are cultures that promote and nurture freedom, cultures that restrict and stultify.

In the vernacular (and here I am drawing on many years of listening to Americans talk about the power of culture to shape perceptions and ways of living), some people worry that cultural forces might turn us into "faggots" or porn addicts, or they might make otherwise sane people into suicide bombers; then again, other people assert that culture, if properly channeled, might make us learn to love one another and work together for the common good. In the vernacular, people are always talking about good and bad cultures, and by and large they assume that there is something called nature that makes certain ways of life more natural and therefore better than other ways of life.

In contrast to the vernacular, cultural anthropologists are leery of attributing anything, from a preference in food to a preference in mates or sexual positions, to an innate nature. By contrast too, cultural anthropologists are loath to elevate one society above others as morally superior or unequivocally more advanced. Professional cultural anthropologists tend to be "cultural relativists," and we tend to be cultural constructivists rather than biological essentialists.

As such we are out of step with most of the people with whom we share the cultural space of the American landscape. How can we believe that we have the authority to say these things, to be so critical of the vernacular?

First of all we need difference to discuss differences. From the time anthropology became a profession in the early twentieth century, its practitioners have claimed a certain authority to speak about cultural difference because anthropologists claimed to have directly experienced such differences. Anthropological research is based on being there—living in some out-of-the-way place, participating in the daily lives of some other people. This kind of research is called *fieldwork*, a word that harks back to our origins as a discipline in an era when our subjects of study were imagined to be in some distant and primitive place—out there in nature, out there in "the field"—and where we encountered our subjects in their world as it was. Anthropology was a kind of natural history, a kind of animal ethology. Humans were anthropology's animals. We studied them *in situ*. And while it is true that today anthropologists do not necessarily travel as far away as did their predecessors—they study those who work in obstetrics wards in hospitals in America, for example, or the founders of the private company that mapped out the human genome—or, if they do travel to distant lands, it is as likely that anthropologists end up studying, say, an Indian advertising agency in Mumbai or a rocket-launching station in Suriname, anthropologists still make their claims to authority to speak about the human condition by meditating on the question of difference. Until fairly recently, people of the European-influenced nation-states assumed there were profound differences in the world. Now, in the age of globalization, we are not so certain. Even though most anthropologists today may make embarrassed fun of the image of the lone anthropologist coming out from his mosquito net to converse with and sup with savages, they tend to recognize the fact that if all societies all over the world are basically the same, or all are becoming the same, then it is hard to make claims about the power of cultural forces to mold and shape who we are. One of the issues this book will address is whether we can talk about significant cultural differences in an era when forms of communication and movements of people from one place to another blur social and cultural boundaries once taken for granted.

Not only do we need difference to discuss culture's power, but we also need theory—a language through which to explain and understand human difference. Each chapter in this book will be an excursion ordered by the themes I have mentioned, and each will serve to illustrate what cultural anthropology is after, which above all is a certain kind of disciplining—a trained skepticism about the sources of one's own certainties.

A general rule of thumb most anthropologists follow is that theory can never be divorced from data. Nor indeed can it be divorced from the gatherer of that data, the anthropologist. The anthropologist is the instrument of observation. Quite a bit depends on how he or she responds to, gets along with, enjoys, or dislikes those "natives" she encounters, not to mention the reverse, because the subjects of study are also responding to the anthropologist in highly personal ways. The best ethnography (the written work anthropologists produce as a result of research) entails emotional engagement. But that makes ethnography a subjective product, not an objective one. When you read an ethnography, you are learning as much about the anthropologist's culture as you are about the culture of his or her subjects. A good anthropologist knows this—knows that the work of anthropology is also a work of self-disclosure and self-discovery. As Clifford Geertz puts it, ethnography is always part philosophy and part confession.

I will be brief about the philosophy. First, the touchstone for all cultural anthropologists is that anthropology is the study of human beings as a special kind of social animal. Other animals form societies. But the societies they form are more or less generic to the species. Think of a wolf pack or a pack of wild dogs. A wolf pack here is the same as a wolf pack there. There are no wolf pack monarchies or wolf pack communes. Watch how quickly even your dog, who lives most of its life in your company, will establish relationships with other dogs. Humans are social animals like dogs, like dolphins, and of course like primates. But only human beings form societies that are culturally distinct. Nothing humans ever do is natural in the sense we often construe for the term. How we urinate, defecate, copulate, and die—all these seemingly biological things we do are all, as we shall see, fundamentally cultural. Dogs are social animals. They are not cultural animals. They do not grieve in culturally peculiar ways for lost loved ones. They are cannibals. They might even eat their own kin. They commit what we call incest. The upshot is that a German shepherd from Germany and an American German shepherd are the same for all intents and purposes. But try the same exercise with humans. A German and an American are not necessarily the same, do not think in the same ways.

A second philosophical assumption we make is that anthropology is a discipline that should account for the incredible diversity of human actions while also taking it as a given that humans the world over are basically the same biologically. We know that individuals vary. Humans vary quite a bit, as a glance at a crowd waiting for a bus in most any city anywhere will quickly confirm. We are a polymorphic species. There are Michael Jordans and Mozarts (or their equivalents) in every society. Every society is made up of people of marvelous talent, and also of people who are somehow deficient or flawed in comparison to their peers, but aggregates of individuals do not vary in their aggregate biologies. So if we want to understand the differences between groups of people, we cannot resort to biology; we must resort to theories of culture and society, theories of cultural and social difference.

When we speak of society in anthropology we follow the lead of classic sociology. Indeed, one of the roots of modern cultural anthropology is the social anthropology of England, a discipline that came into being in the early twentieth century as so-called primitive societies were subsumed into European colonies, pacified, and thus made available for extended research. British social anthropologists were concerned with the classic sociological question of order—that question that lay at the center of Hobbes's political philosophy. They wanted to discover how order came into being and was maintained in its simplest forms. If Hobbes assumed that order required centralized authority, they asked, by contrast what kind of order and authority, what kinds of rules and forms of enforcement exist in societies where there was no law and no sovereign? In a general sense, they wanted to discover how a congeries of people, no matter what its political structure, could act as a group and how its members could identify themselves as members of a group. In studying this issue in primitive societies they saw themselves as sociologists of the primitive. They hoped that by looking at such societies they could supply more generally applicable answers to the kinds of questions philosophers such as Hobbes had asked. A further question that came to inform their work—the work of anthropologists such as E. E. Evans-Pritchard and Bronislaw Malinowski—and a question that continues to drive much of current anthropology, is how a particular social structure affects the subjectivity of the people who inhabit that society. It is assumed that people who live in structurally similar societies imagine the world in similar ways. A person in a hierarchical society thinks and feels differently than a person in an egalitarian society. Order at the social level affects the way thought is ordered and systematized at the personal level.

As for culture, it is often the case that when we speak of culture in anthropology, we use the word as a stand-in for society. We talk about this culture or that when we mean this group of people or that group, that is, this society or that society. But more importantly, we use the word "culture" to refer to ideas and their embodiments in artifacts and activities. In doing so, we borrow from a long tradition that goes back to late nineteenth-century German philosophy, a tradition that was transplanted to the United States in the early twentieth century and reached its apogee in the 1940s through the 1970s with the work of scholars such as Margaret Mead, Ruth Benedict, and later Geertz and Marshall Sahlins and a host of others. Germanic views of culture tended to be literally organic. A people, a "Volk," shared a certain common experience, or "history," and developed a common character as a result. Yet German theorists of culture also recognized the arbitrariness of history. Culture was "shreds and patches"—a custom borrowed from here, a habit you acquired there—but by and large shreds and patches that people were intent on knitting or quilting together. Culture emerged as a people or a Volk incessantly endeavored to find and form a pattern out of historical events and accidents.

This ambivalence in Germanic ideas of culture was carried over into American anthropology in the person of Franz Boas. As the anthropologist Adam Kuper notes, Boas "wavered between describing 'culture' as an accidental accretion of traits" and as an "integrated spiritual totality animated by the genius of a people." The latter view was more congenial to prevailing sentiments in America of the early twentieth century, the "melting pot," if often xenophobic and politically isolationist. Americans in that era were eager to see themselves as a new and distinct people, not as colonial shadows of metropoles, not as mere settlers, not as interlopers, but as something if not autochthonous, then at least *sui generis*. The optimists among them also hoped and expected that an emerging Americanness would overcome the cultural particularities of the foreignness of immigrants. Inexorably, the immigrant from Sicily or the Stetl would learn WASP ways, just as the WASP would come to like spaghetti or a good mother-in-law joke. Such a view, in which defining "American" was an invigorating intellectual activity, made shreds-and-patches theories of culture a thing of the past and the idea of culture as "personality writ large," as Ruth Benedict famously put it, a compelling truth.

Today American cultural anthropology blends the preoccupations of the early American anthropologists with the concerns of the British social anthropologists. We talk about society and culture and assume that what people think and feel is engendered by how they live as social beings. And we assume that in order to grasp this interrelationship one has to spend time immersing oneself in their way of life as it occurs, letting events guide the research or fieldwork.

Anthropological fieldwork is a form of scholarship that some anthropologists liken to a science and others to the humanities, in which we observe human behavior and interpret human discussion about behavior. Such scholarship requires funding, so it entails convincing some institution associated with scholarship that the research is worthwhile—that it will serve some practical purpose or that it will add something significant to our collective body of knowledge. I have done fieldwork in three places among three groups of people—Lauje of Sulawesi, Indonesia; Manjaco of Guinea-Bissau, West Africa; and Americans working in and visiting American heritage sites (Colonial Williamsburg, one of the biggest open-air history museums in the world, and Monticello, the home of Thomas Jefferson). A central concern in my field-work was how people experience inequality and wrestle with its implications. Because the United States is an egalitarian society, Americans are constantly interested in the conundrum of inequality. So looking at how this conundrum is thought through among people in other societies or whether they think of it as a conundrum at all is a significant question to Americans, and it allows us to delve into the philosophical underpinnings of American society.

Indigenous conceptions of inequality—especially as revealed in native versions of their history—was a central theme in my dissertation research as I looked at the beliefs and practices associated with the Manjaco local king and chiefs as those institutions were dramatically affected by colonialism and a violent revolutionary struggle for independence. Before doing research among Manjaco I had helped (my then-wife) Jennifer Nourse explore similar issues among the Lauje—ethnically and religiously marginalized citizens in a (typically) peripheral region of one of Indonesia's peripheral islands, citizens who continued to pay allegiance to a king whose kingdom had long since dissolved into the nation-state and citizens who continued to practice certain forms of religion-inspired curing that put them at odds with Muslim religious ortho-doxies and the modernizing imperatives of the Indonesian state. After those fieldwork encounters, I studied Monticello, and then, with Richard Handler, Colonial Williamsburg, observing museum administrators and guides who use a "community of memory," recreated out of clapboard and brick, to talk about the roots of racial and class inequalities in a society supposedly founded upon the ideals of a universal egalitarianism.

Research in all three cases was also guided by a basic theoretical premise of cultural anthropology having to do with what we call *holism*. When we use the word "culture," we are generally referring to a system of meanings, a system of ideas present in a myriad of human actions, from the most mundane to the most exalted. In short, we assume that culture reveals a consistent plan and pattern, or as Robert Darnton put it, that a society's taste in food and fashion and its taste in politics will cohere—will form a single patterned whole. This patterned whole is revealed to us in action (in performances of various kinds, from the consciously theatrical to the seemingly spontaneous) and in various expressions—in talk both off the cuff and carefully planned, and in text from fiction to myth and to science. This system of meaning in all its manifesta-tions includes, in short, what we might call unconscious attitudes—how we comport ourselves as we stand in line at the cafeteria, for example—attitudes Geertz refers to as "ethos." And this system also includes self-consciously formulated models of how the world is, and models for how the world should be—laws and science, moral treatises about fairness and justice, for example— or what Geertz and others, following the lead of the sociologist Max Weber, call "worldview."

Now, clearly not everything we do and think in a particular society can be accounted for as part of a single recurring system of meaning. Not every society is guided by one worldview in tandem with a single ethos. Moreover, clearly not everything we do or even say or think is meaningful in these senses. But culture, as ethos and worldview, act and thought, is more coherent than one might at first imagine. This assumption guided me in my fieldwork and shapes the arguments in this book.

Ethnography is part philosophy. It entails certain theoretical assumptions— that human beings are social beings who inhabit worlds that are meaningful because they have constructed them—and also explores certain issues of enduring significance: power, equality, difference, and so forth. But it also is part confession. The confession part entails something personal or revealing about how the anthropologist got along with the natives. Since anthropologists began doing intensive fieldwork, living closely with their subjects, they have confessed or revealed some of their feelings about their interlocutors. Such confessions also reveal the foibles of the researcher. Thus, for example, one of our most intrepid early anthropologists, E. E. Evans-Pritchard, would tell us why he liked the rough-hewn egalitarianism of the Nuer of the Sudan through a vignette in which a Nuer refuses to answer some simple questions about kinship. He noted too that, by contrast, he found Azande less compelling. Nuer were pastoralists; Azande were a stratified kingdom. Both peoples had been recently pacified by the British—machine-gunned into submission. As for the Nuer, "When I entered a cattle camp it was not only as a stranger but as an enemy, and they seldom tried to conceal their disgust at my presence, refusing to answer my greetings and even turning away when I addressed them." If Nuer were subversively defiant, then Azande were unctuous in their compliance. They answered pretty much any question Evans-Pritchard asked them, but they kept him at a distance as well. "Among Azande," he wrote, "I was compelled to live outside the community; among Nuer I was compelled to be a member of it. Azande treated me as a superior; Nuer as an equal."

In talking in such a revealing and self-deprecating way about his encounters with Azande and Nuer, Evans-Pritchard added a layer of nuance to his ethnographic analyses of these societies. How he felt about them and how they felt about him also expressed something essential about ethos—his and theirs. The fiercely egalitarian Nuer came into focus because of Evans-Pritchard's feelings toward them. Likewise with the hierarchical Azande. Again Evans-Pritchard liked or at least admired Azande aristocrats because they remained aloof, while he found the commoners pitiful but unpleasant because they seemed so slavishly eager to please. That you dislike your natives and can admit as much tells the reader something too. Yet by and large we expect to like our natives. We want to like them, and we want them to like us. That they do, that we do, is a sign of our mutual humanity. But it is a dirty little secret that we don't always like them, and it is a source of embarrassment that they often find us off-putting.

While I did fieldwork in three places, I only fell in love with one people— Lauje—and I also found myself often profoundly discomforted by people I encountered among Manjaco. There are a number of reasons why I might have liked living with Lauje so much more than I liked being with Manjaco or spending all those mornings and afternoons strolling the streets and touring the buildings of Colonial Williamsburg, the reconstructed capital of colonial-era Virginia. I went to the Lauje region first, and the landscape immediately captured my heart: steep rain-shrouded mountains, cloaked in clouds, piled right up against a shallow sea. Our field site required that we follow and ford, and continue fording, a swift, bright river that cut up into the mountains. At every bend in the river we'd run into a blur of butterflies or occasionally a cluster of children bathing, who, like the butterflies, would scatter at our approach, clutching their brightly colored cloth wraps.

My wife and I built a bamboo house on stilts on the edge of a ridgeline—a house that glowed like a lantern with the rising sun, and shook and swayed like a sailboat in the frequent lashing storms. After two years with the Lauje—in the mountains but also in a coastal trading town with its vibrant market, its hidden royal court, and its bored bureaucrats, religious zealots, Chinese merchants, and general air of riotous and corrupt decay—I left for Guinea-Bissau and close to two years in the flat, bayou-like terrain of the Manjaco.

I arrived in the rainy season. The air was thick with mosquitoes and heavy with the smell of bat guano. Worse, perhaps, the village I chose to inhabit was a strangely empty place. In a community that had numbered about six hundred people in the 1950s, there were now only about three hundred. Most had migrated—to Senegal, to France, to Lisbon—escaping a country that had been wracked by revolution and suffered a stultifying poverty. When I left the Manjaco I went home to study my own society through a sustained look at Monticello and Williamsburg—a kind of penance based on a challenge one of my Manjaco interlocutors had made while I tried to convince him to let me witness the rituals of the local aristocracy.

If Manjaco and Lauje were the kinds of "out of the way places" Clifford Geertz defines as standard for anthropology, they were, above all, places of material poverty. Monticello by contrast was a place of extreme and extremely beautiful wealth and privilege. For close to four years I'd lived either in that bamboo hut on stilts on top of a steep ridgeline in the mountains of Sulawesi among a group of people only a few missionaries had ever heard of, or I'd lived in a West African village among Manjaco wet-rice farmers a long dirt road ride away from nowhere in one of the poorest countries in the world, ranking even now 175th out of 178 on the United Nation's Human Development Index. The Manjaco village I chose to live in was the site of a local royal court. I was there to study political power and authority, and I was keenly interested in the ways my hosts talked about differences in wealth and privilege. Not that there were many differences, at least in wealth. The king lived in a mud hut not much bigger than those of twenty-some commoner families who lived in the village as well; the meals he used to share with me were the same large bowls of rice flavored with a little palm oil or topped with a few small fish or a sauce of snails or greens that his subjects ate.

Many Manjaco disliked obviously rich people. They assumed that if you had much more than others you must have done something really bad—hurt someone, sold someone out, killed someone—to get it. They also looked askance at people who seemed to do nothing but sit around. Merchants, bureaucrats, scholars, they were all suspect. And even the oldest of them worked hard in the fields and forests. Old men climbed palms to tap wine. Old women continued to go to the swampy meanders to catch fish or gather snails for sauce. They were embarrassed to eat or drink what others produced without contributing to the common bowl.

Americans have very different attitudes toward labor and leisure and toward differences in wealth and prestige than do Manjaco. We are more concerned, as was Thomas Jefferson, with the freedom to pursue happiness than with the constraints of social equity. But we also have a certain ambivalence about wealth and privilege. We do not like it when other people think they are better than we are. When I began work at Monticello, I wanted to see how Americans used such a place of manifest privilege to think about the nature of privilege itself—its morality.

Monticello troubled me, even as I was transfixed by its beauty. Here was a plantation, a fairly large plantation, yet there were only barely visible signs of the presence of slaves. Mulberry Row was a pathway that ran under an avenue of trees. Along this row had been several slave quarters, a blacksmith's shop, and a "nailery"—a place where young slave boys pounded out nails from long thin bars of iron. The nailery had been quite a success. In Jefferson's day, the plantation usually lost money. But the nailery provided some welcome cash, and Jefferson paid the boys extra for their work. If you visited Monticello as a tourist, you learned all this from plaques along Mulberry Row where the structures had once been. There was still the ruin of a chimney at the site of the blacksmith's shop. You could also read about the row and the 130 or so slaves who lived at Monticello in a brochure, or in signage in an archeological exhibit under the house, or at a nicely compact museum at the visitors' center.

Below Mulberry Row was a beautiful garden and orchard, and beyond that, like an ocean, were the rolling hills of the Virginia Piedmont receding like waves into the flat horizon. At the center of the garden stood a newly reconstructed pavilion. It was a beautiful conceit, a wonderfully planned out trifle of a building. Jefferson's bagatelle. Tall and narrow but majestically proportioned for its size, it harkened to a temple, with Palladian windows doing double duty as doors. In it were two Windsor chairs and room enough for a couple of people to sit and enjoy the view—of the garden, of the gracefully receding rows of hills. That is about all the room there was. Monticello had decided to build the pavilion at great cost. Jefferson had left architectural drawings, and the small structure was quite beautiful. Jefferson himself had written about the pleasures of sitting in that space; he'd written about the joys of working in the garden.

Meanwhile, the foundation that ran Monticello had decided not to build slave quarters. They worried about whether such structures could be constructed accurately. No plans existed, although there were sketches of plans, again in Jefferson's hand. Would they look tacky, obviously new, and detract from the aura of the main building? After all, this building, Monticello's then-director—a man very much dedicated to making slaves' lives a crucial part of the story the place told—reminded me, was "eighty to ninety percent original," and perhaps "less was more" regarding the slave quarters. To build them might "ruin the view," as the site's architect put it, for most visitors eager to see an original and authentic house and decor. And because of this fidelity to authenticity, Monticello jettisoned any plans to rebuild the slave quarters.

When I began observing Monticello, I wondered whether or not visitors would reflect on the contrast that I imagined should be salient on Mulberry Row: the drudgery of teenaged boys put to work pounding out nail after nail six days a week (but getting paid for it!) so that Jefferson could toil in the garden for perhaps half an hour in the cool of the evening. How would visitors reconcile these twinned traces of the past?

I thought the same thing when I began to visit Williamsburg, an entire colonial-era town that had been meticulously restored and reconstructed by the Rockefeller family, and, again, a strangely beautiful yet empty place. When Williamsburg was the capital of colonial Virginia, half of its population were slaves. Had you visited the town in 1770, you would have seen slaves everywhere. But if you visited Colonial Williamsburg, the restored and reconstructed version of that era, you would see no slaves and few African Americans, unless you strolled the streets before the buildings opened their doors to the tourists. Then you would see African Americans cleaning or sweeping. Or if you stayed in the town's fancy hotel, the liveried African American staff would quietly cater to your needs and desires. You might ride a carriage, and again an African American in livery, but perhaps wearing an anachronistic pair of glasses, would guide the carriage past houses where picket fences enclose well-tended gardens. As you rode in your carriage guided by a black man in livery, you would pass a landscape that was familiar and inviting. Boxwoods and a profusion of flowers—jonquils, tulips, Carolina jessamine. The paint colors of the buildings harkening at once to a slightly subtropical England and to upper-middle-class American suburban neighborhoods throughout the east coast and south. Williamsburg had become a model for such communities. Its bucolic charms were an American ideal.

Williamsburg and Monticello made me sad and angry, even as I enjoyed sitting on a garden bench as the breeze filled the air with the scent of flowers. But more of Williamsburg and Monticello later. I will return to these places in several of the chapters that follow. Each chapter will use what I have learned at these places and what I have learned from Lauje and Manjaco to deal, either explicitly or implicitly, with the themes of culture by contrast and of the culture of egalitarianism. In chapter 2 I draw on material from Monticello to meditate on how a typically American kind of egalitarianism is embodied in the way we visit such historical sites and what this tells us about the anthropological enterprise. In chapter 3 I use Monticello's most famous occupant—Thomas Jefferson—to illustrate how the concept of culture was "invented" in contrast to the idea of race in the cauldron of that American pursuit of equality. In chapter 4 I show how colonialism depended on the contrast its authors drew between civilization and the primitive—how colonialism depended on an inequality that could at least in theory be ameliorated by the colonialist project, but in fact never was. In chapter 5 I argue that anthropology became a discipline by contrasting its culturally relativistic approach to understanding primitive societies with the approach of the colonialists, yet it could not escape all of Western ethnocentrism. In chapters 6 and 7 I focus on what are perhaps the most productive topics anthropology has found to illustrate the power of culture to eclipse biology and make for human differences—religion and sexuality. In the last chapter, I return to the Lauje and Manjaco to remind us that people from "out of the way places" have much to teach us about humanity's relationship to ecology. In each of these chapters what I learned at home in places like Monticello will be as important as what I learned abroad in the more exotic worlds of Lauje and Manjaco.

But in the first chapter I want to stick only to Lauje and Manjaco in order to offer a sketch of what it means to think of a society holistically—to take seriously that notion that a people's taste in politics and their taste in food might be somehow related, might cohere as elements of a system of meaning. As we compare a Lauje taste in food and politics with a parallel Manjaco taste, I will also situate those contrasting kinds of ethos in my own responses to them. I liked Lauje more and was made profoundly uncomfortable by Manjaco, and those feelings had more to do with culture (mine and theirs) than it did with the physical features of a place. Why I liked Lauje so much and felt such a longing to be liked by them, and why I liked Manjaco so much less and often found myself wishing I were somewhere else, might say quite a bit about at least one anthropologist's attitudes toward the savage, and by extension the nature of culture as a meditation on contrast, as an encounter with an other that is also a glimpse into a mirror—an encounter that reveals a great deal about ourselves.

1

Supping with Savages

One of the first things our Lauje hosts told my wife and me as they helped us settle into our house on stilts in their ridgeline village about four hours' hard hike upriver from the coast was that they lived at the center of the world. They promised to show us the "navel of the earth," a moss-covered conical stone covered with etched scratches they claimed contained the inscriptions that engendered the cosmos. After a short but scary hike straight down a mud-slick trail, we reached the navel of the earth or "the inscribed rock," which stood in the middle of the narrow riverbed in the steep valley just below our house. The boulder looked only slightly different than the other river-worn rocks that surrounded it. The markings that covered it could have been made by erosion or chiseling; it was hard to tell. Yet its closeness—we could almost see it from the veranda of our bamboo hut—and our hosts' eagerness to show it to us made the air seem to vibrate with mysterious possibility.

Because Lauje lived at the center of the world, they were not surprised that Jennifer and I might want to visit. To them our sojourn was a return of sorts. We were avatars of a long-lost ancestor, the To Modoko, or "voracious child," who not only had an insatiable appetite for food and other material goods, but the strength of will to produce prodigiously. This "younger sibling" had left the Lauje mountains long ago, but his progenitors had returned to the region as Bugis and Mandar, as Dutch, as Indonesians, to rule over them and to inhabit the "stone houses" of Tinombo—the entrepot on the coast.

In telling us such stories, Lauje did not explicitly begrudge us our wealth nor blame us for their poverty, although they did portray poverty as a superior kind of virtue. If the inhabitants of the stone houses down below had more, they also bought and sold everything, even food, and therefore violated cosmological injunctions that what "land and water" gave to humans should be given to others in turn. Lauje in the mountains asserted to us that they, by contrast, always gave food to anyone who asked or who visited and that it was precisely that fidelity to the spirit Owners of Land and Water (Togu Ogo, Togu

Petu) that distinguished them from lowland relatives who had succumbed to commodification's corrupting enticements and seen their soil harden and dry up as a result.

Because hill Lauje "gave food and never sold it," people from distant hilltops would stop at our place on their way down the slick muddy trail and give us "*wuga*," pieces of taro root the length and thickness of your forearm. When we would visit our neighbors' verandas they would invariably offer to share a meal, sometimes of rice or cornmeal and dried fish, often some boiled bananas or taro or cassava that we would all take from a common plate and dip into a little pile of salt and mashed hot peppers. After we ate, we would pass around a glass of sometimes silted water, the surface of the glass usually clouded with the slimy residue of the taro or rice or cassava.

This routine generosity provoked in us a certain guilt-tinged desire to reciprocate. We felt the pain of our wealth and their poverty each time they shared with us their poor meal of taro dipped in salt. We felt the pleasure of belonging each time we ate a meal in common. So we eagerly supplied medicine—for malaria, for worms, for giardia and dysentery—when we had it and were asked for help. We also shared with frequent visitors our supply of cigarettes and tobacco, and our coffee laced with powdered milk and sugar. And we too cooked for others when they stopped on their way down or up the trail to spend some time sitting on our veranda. I did the cooking, as I had generally done back home. The Lauje we came to know took this domestic arrangement for granted. That I cooked and my wife did not seemed to be as much an unremarkable fact of life as was our generosity. We were accepted and we wanted their acceptance.

After a while we learned the nuances of such generosity. You cannot always give to everyone, nor should you always take. Our friends would occasionally gossip about other Lauje—people who always seemed to show up around mealtime and who were slow to leave even as the sun set and the path to their home became more treacherous in the impending dark. They had a name for those kinds of people—"*mepijit*," or "pinworms." They were as irritating as that minute white parasite that lived at the end of one's anus, or so our friends supposed. Pinworms were Lauje who made it a habit of eating at other people's houses even when they had a home of their own to go to.

By contrast, good Lauje were "shy" about seeking out and accepting generosity. If they came to your house and the door was shut, they waited politely at the foot of the ladder, coughing quietly one or two times to signal their presence. It was up to you to open the door and acknowledge them, while it was also up to them to spare you the shame of refusing to do so. Our friends, as we soon found out when we were with them, kept silent in their house when someone they did not want to meet at that moment was lurking outside.

We too used this ploy. Often, exhausted from too much socializing, we'd keep our door closed and bury ourselves in our books, looking up from the page in slightly nervous silence at the sound of discreet coughing outside. Likewise, when on rare occasions we opened a can of pork to supplement our meager diet, we kept our door shut and quietly enjoyed the fatty meat. Lauje were Muslims; we didn't want to withhold a meal they should not eat. Nor was there really enough of it to go around.

For Lauje, sharing food, not selling it, entailed a certain etiquette while encapsulating a moral code. It was at once an ethos and a worldview—an ethos we found easy enough to practice ourselves and a worldview we found fascinating, salutary. When Lauje talked about not selling food but giving it to neighbors and more distant passersby, they also drew a distinction between themselves as moral beings and their erstwhile coastal relatives, the Lauje of the trading town of Tinombo. These Lauje generally were the poor laborers and peasant farmers who lived among the richer Chinese, Bugis, and other Indonesians in that coastal enclave—a center of regional trade and also a center of government, religion, and education. The Lauje of the hills spoke disparagingly of coastal people who sold their crops at market, and they curled their lips at a whole society based on the buying and selling of the basic necessities.

Of Gifts and Commodities

The moral vision ("we give, they sell") that Lauje expressed every time they shared a meal was an element of a worldview we expected, indeed craved. And this had a lot to do with our own cultural backgrounds rather than anything intrinsic to Lauje practices and beliefs. In anthropology, and in Western philosophical discussions of society more generally, it is often taken for granted that so-called primitive societies will be guided by an economy of "the gift" as opposed to an economy of "commodities." For homegrown critics of our own society, commodities and commodification are often seen as symptoms or even causes of much that is wrong with our way of life. To buy and sell is to sever social ties, to privilege autonomy as opposed to interdependence, to learn to believe that satisfaction comes from the consumption of things rather than interactions with people; the cure to many of our ills is to resist materialism and self-centered individualism (buy cheap and sell dear) in favor of a more spiritually charged communalism. This view, this critique, is as old as Christianity (Do unto others as you would have them do unto you) and as

Figure 1.1. Lauje village

young as communism (from each according to his abilities, to each according to his needs), and it is as pervasive as the utopian visions of the future that guide us every time we write a check for the victims of a hurricane or earthquake. You are encouraged to "give to the children" and your heart goes out to them. In your own family, if your family is a good family whose members care for one another, you give to one another—you give on holidays and on birthdays—because you love one another. Yet you go to Wal-Mart rather than the neighborhood store because it is cheaper, and you neglect to tell your real estate agent about the leaky roof because you figure "let the buyer beware." You live in a dog-eat-dog world and you may grumble and growl at the person who speeds by you in her Mercedes SUV yakking on her cell phone while you sit stuck in traffic because you're obeying the sign that says "right lane closed ahead." But you put up with it because you have a family or friends or fellow church members who treat you like family—who would give you the shirt off their back if you needed it. Often you are generous even when you don't have to be. You are standing in line at the buffet and there is only one piece of cake left, your favorite cake, and you don't take it even though it's first-come-first-served but instead ask the older woman right behind you in line if she'd like

Figure 1.2. Manjaco village

to take it, and when she demurs, you pick up the slice and you both smile at each other, feeling good about yourselves.

We recognize that it is often hard to be good, to be generous. Go to a playground and listen to parents telling their toddlers to "share." Watch them smile in embarrassment when their small child tries to pull the toy away from another small child's grasp. We want our children to learn to be generous, but we also think that generosity is a hard skill to master—something you need to be taught, something you easily forget, because in a sense it is more "natural" to be selfish. After all isn't evolution about survival of the fittest, and isn't the fittest the last one left alive on the lifeboat? So people around us who are good and generous are often praised as special. "She was so kind," they might say at that older woman's funeral, recalling her bright smile and demurral as if kindness were a scarce virtue.

Lauje, by contrast, took everyday kindness as a matter of course. People shared food because that was what Lauje did. Children were not told to be generous because everyone assumed that they would be. So in one sense, Lauje were living our dream of a better world, acting the way we wished we always acted. In what they did and said, they were ventriloquizing our utopian philosophers.

Primitive people often act as ventriloquists in this way. We tend to tell our history as a story of transformation in which, for example, societies of the gift preceded societies of commodities, so savages have often stood in for our ancestors in our recountings of the world. Utopian futures, by the same token, often hark nostalgically to utopian pasts. If we can demonstrate, for example, that people in most societies throughout time and all over the world tend to give rather than buy and sell, then we can imagine our society as an aberration and want to do something about it. This is what the influential French sociologist Marcel Mauss argued in his 1924 "Essay on the Gift," a book which continues to excite social scientists, philosophers, and historians today. Mauss reviewed what was known about the economies of "archaic" societies such as ancient India and primitive societies such as those in New Guinea and Polynesia and the northwest coast of Canada to discover general principles of gift giving. What he found was that in gift societies a moral code of mutuality develops as people feel obligated to give and to receive. After Mauss, and after anthropologists did extensive fieldwork in societies all over the world, it came to be an accepted fact that gift exchange was a pervasive feature of life among so-called primitive peoples. Thus I was not surprised to find practices similar to Lauje among Manjaco.

Because I lived in a Manjaco household, eating and sharing domestic duties with a large extended family, I quickly learned the finer points of such routine sharing. Above all there was the common food bowl—sometimes (and always on ceremonial occasions) a dried gourd cut in half, usually a bowl of enameled metal, and more and more frequently a bowl of brightly colored plastic. A group ate out of a single bowl and sometimes a single spoon or a couple of spoons. Manjaco are wet-rice farmers, so the core of the meal was rice. The rice filled the bowl and on top of the rice was a sauce of palm oil mixed with curdled cow's milk or a sauce of peanuts, or vegetables with hot peppers, or fish or snails or clams from the wet-rice fields or tidal meanders, sometimes with palm oil, sometimes without. Very rarely there would be chicken or some other meat. The women caught the fish, gathered the vegetables, or made the palm oil sauce. Those who ate together were divided by age and gender or they were joined by common occupation or activity. Who ate with whom and when was a map of a social group.

Out of social solidarity, when you ate with others, you had to calibrate your appetite so as not to eat too much. One of the first meals I ate in the village where I was to stay, before my wife arrived to join me at my research site, was a festive meal I shared with a group of young men and women who had just helped my household harvest its rice. We ate with one spoon from a large enamel bowl thick with palm oil and small, minnow-like fish. Each of us took a turn with the spoon. As the bowl full of food diminished, the spoon stayed in the bowl longer and longer, and the conversation went on longer as we waited for someone else to pick up the spoon and scoop out one of the last spoonfuls of rice and fish. Eventually the eating stopped altogether, though there was still food in the bowl. As I was to learn later, that would be as it always was, because to eat to the very end made it seem like there was not enough to go around. Worse, to eat near the end of the meal might mean that you had taken a bite that someone else was about to take. That inadvertent tussle with the spoon was to be avoided. Each person needed to calibrate his or her appetite to the appetites of others—family, peers, and most of all those who might be dependent on you.

After Jennifer left several months later, the wives of the married men in my household fixed a meal for the men. We ate from the common bowl, making sure that more than enough would be left over for "our wives" to eat to feed "our children" when they retrieved the bowl and brought it back to the women's hut. But before the wife took the food away, she'd always ask, "Aren't you hungry? You've hardly eaten," or something to that effect. Among Manjaco, men ate first because, so they claimed, they were superior to women and children; they were superior because they could control their appetites. By contrast, at least according to my male interlocutors, women could not control themselves. The men of the household told me that when the women cooked, they also ate, and that sometimes the best morsels disappeared long before the food bowl made it to the husband's table. Once after my host's wife asked for some matches to light the cooking fire (I smoked and I always had a box or two handy), and I gave her a box, her husband scolded me: "Next time give her one or two matches. If you give her a whole box, she'll keep it and ask you for more again tomorrow anyway." Women could not be trusted. They were inferior to men because they lacked self-control and were not as socially generous.

I am fairly certain that Manjaco women did not believe this about themselves as individuals. They too talked about their generosity, about "going hungry" so that children might eat. But the women of my household were also especially irritated when my wife arrived and I took over the task of cooking for the two of us at our own hearth. They made fun of me. They asked rhetorically: Had I married a lazy wife, a useless wife? When she eventually tried to cook and failed to make a proper fire, they made fun of her too.

That genders had their proper places in Manjaco while in Lauje gender roles were looser was one reason I liked one place and people more than the other, but not the main reason. The main reason had to do with something more complex about the nature of the gift and giving itself. Both Manjaco and Lauje shared food and criticized those who didn't, but their targets for critique and the moral philosophies that underlay their actions were different.

Gifts to Spirits

When Lauje told us that they gave food and didn't sell it, they also warned us that it was an obligation to receive such largesse lest we offend the "spirit of hearth and fire"—the domestic refraction of a congeries of spirits that included Umpute (the spirits of the placenta and birth fluids), and Togu Ogo, Togu Petu (Owner of Water, Owner of Land). Each of these spirits was portrayed as having sacrificed itself for human beings to live. Hearth and fire exhausted their essence so that food might be cooked. Owner of Water and Land gave of itself and suffered as a result so that humans could grow crops. Umpute, or the twin siblings of humans, died at birth so that a person could be born. Each of these spirits (and in the dominant Lauje view each spirit was essentially a different manifestation of a single spiritual essence) was owed a debt by humans for its sacrifice. Humans "paid tribute" to the spirits when they were ill. Illness was a form of repayment—suffering for suffering—yet illness remained within a certain bounds because spirits were "poison and cure." They caused illness, but they also left human beings alone, making them well again—as long, that is, as humans recognized the spirits' sacrifices by holding periodic celebrations involving the shared consumption of foods.

Eating a daily meal in common was a mundane version of such a celebration. If you, as a guest or visitor, came to a house when a meal was being cooked, you had to partake of the meal lest "hearth and fire" be insulted at your refusal to recognize their sacrifice. As Lauje explained it to us, "Even if you are not hungry, take a bit of rice or a bit of taro and touch it to your throat." That, they counseled us, would be enough to satisfy the spirits and ward off the effects of the sin of *ampunan*—a sudden slip along a treacherous trail, or a drowning in a flash flood while fording a steep-banked stream—that horrible abomination that occurs when you fail to accept the largesse of "hearth and fire." As long as we fulfilled that minimal obligation we were safe from sanctions that the spirits, not Lauje, enforced. So Lauje enjoined us always to accept the offer of a meal or at least make the proper gesture of thanks.

From our perspective, we might say that a shared meal in Lauje was a religious act, or at least an act that encapsulated a cosmology. This cosmology also encompassed the relationship Lauje had to their erstwhile king, or Olongian. Before the Dutch conquered this region in the early 1900s and before the

Indonesian government inherited it from the Dutch, Olongians had presided over a kingdom that comprised the scattered hilltop communities along the Tinombo River. The king's court was in a village close to the river's mouth on the coast. Although by the time we arrived the kingdom had been politically defunct for close to eighty years, the king still hosted a community-wide curing ceremony in which Lauje recognized the awful powers of "The Center of the Sea" to spread epidemic illness—cholera and smallpox—up from the coast and into the mountains, or to withhold rain for the mountains that came from the sea. During the ceremony the king hosted a feast for the spirits of the sea, the people of the scattered communities providing the food and sharing in the meal.

In the couple of years before we arrived, local representatives of the Indonesian government had declared the ceremony illegal, bowing to pressure from modernizing and fundamentalist Muslims in Tinombo who asserted that offerings to spirits of the sea could not be tolerated in a community that was ostensibly Islamic. Lauje in the coastal communities reacted by threatening not to vote for the Indonesian government's slate of candidates in the upcoming election, and the ceremony was again performed with the government's official blessing.

Meanwhile, Lauje in the mountains looked down toward the coast and blamed their kin there for a recent inexorable ecological decline. Once thickly forested hills were now choked with spiky grass. Once fertile fields were now stripped of their crops by vermin; pigs rooted among the tubers, tore down corn, and trampled rice. It rained too much in one year, causing mudslides, stripping away the soil. In another year it rained too little, stunting and wilting anything they planted. To hill Lauje this was evidence of a cosmology gone wrong, they kept telling us, because their lowland cousins had failed to maintain ritual obligations to the spirits. Their telling of this story encompassed the history of colonialism and the postcolonial rise of state-protected fundamentalist Islam. Lowlanders, especially the aristocratic ritual specialists and increasingly those who no longer honored local spirits but only Allah, had begun selling rice and corn, and by extension had sold the essence of the land itself. As a result the lands began to harden and the forest to recede.

In blaming their kinsmen for failing to maintain cosmological balance, I should add, Lauje did not overlook what seemed so obvious to me: the years of interventions from elements of global political economy that led directly to this state of affairs. Global warming and El Niño, for example. But more directly affecting the Lauje were Indonesian laws decreeing that shifting cultivators stay put, remaining on one ridge rather than another, or, similarly, laws and practices that made Lauje into good Muslims, so that pigs which had once been a prized food were now polluting and untouchable pests. Indeed, when Lauje made such connections between global and local forces, they assimilated them into a cosmological idiom: the governments of the world, and the world religions, were Togu Ogo, Togu Petu's agents.

Because the villains in the Lauje story of destruction and decline were safely distant, it was easy to live with them. It was pleasant and exciting to be encouraged to participate in an enchanted mutuality in which the world's degradations could be blamed on a failure to keep up a relationship of recognition human beings had with nature in nature's various spiritual refractions. It was also easy to project into their enchanted sensibility an implicit critique of capitalism's corrosions, and to liken their allegiance to the Lord of Water, Lord of Land as local resistance to state-sponsored Islam. Modern Muslims at the time accused Lauje of polytheism, or, worse, of worshipping the devil, when they made offerings to "Lord of Land and Water." The more forward thinking, if less religiously fundamentalist, members of the government found such practices wasteful and backward. But the Indonesian government also recognized the potential importance of local customary practice, and Islam too had a place in its worldview for "custom." Lauje therefore had room to maneuver. It was also a pleasure to become their occasional allies against the state and against Islamic fundamentalism, as when we were enlisted as experts in culture to argue for the centrality of the curing ceremonies centered around the Olongian and local folkways and customs. It made us giddy to be on their side. It thrilled us to be invited, if touristically, into a place they claimed was at the world's center.

Perched on their mountain, Lauje seemed to see the whole world from a vantage point we also shared. I loved the long, uneventful hours spent sitting in their small huts on stilts, endlessly smoking cigarettes we'd roll from tobacco we each kept in a bag on the floor in front of our crossed legs so that anyone could reach for it. Someone would arrive unannounced. Still slick with sweat from a steep hike, he'd sit in silence close to the ladder and look out the open doorway at distant ridgelines as if the last place he wanted to be was squatting in the corner of someone else's small house. He'd slowly roll his cigarette, or stub the ashes against his calloused toe, or spit through the gaps in the floorboards while invariably pretending nonchalance when the food was brought out—that meager meal of taro with salt, or rice with a sliver or two of dried fish. I recall the host's quiet, high-pitched pleading, "Eat, Eat; don't be shy!" And then the slow uncoiling as the guest finally sidled over to the food to accept the first hesitant mouthful.

Gifts that Poison

When I met Manjaco I was struck by how different they were from those Lauje whose "shyness" was signaled in the silent space between the slow cigarette and the meager meal reluctantly eaten. If Lauje stressed that their very lives depended on the quiet obligation to receive, then Manjaco seemed to assert loudly their right to take.

This was especially marked at rituals honoring various tutelary spirits that protected various publics—households, groups of families who farmed a particular patch of wet-rice fields bounded by a shared dike, villages, clusters of villages. The Manjaco landscape was full of such shrines, and during the relatively leisurely months of the dry season, Manjaco were constantly attending some ceremony or other. Such ceremonies required that they bring a carefully calibrated offering—at least this many liters of palm wine and a clay pot of at least this size of cooked rice mixed with a sauce—which was then shared among the participants in a communal meal. Before the wine was drunk and the food eaten by the assembly, the elders spoke to the spirits, often berating them to do more or reminding them that the food, the largesse they enjoyed, only was possible if the spirits continued to do their job. One phrase the elders used struck me as particularly evocative. "You work for the company," they would tell the spirit, and "he who works is paid, he who doesn't work is not paid." For Manjaco, guardian spirits were like prized and powerful employees, or at best allies in a mutual endeavor. They got their "share" of the offering, but only if they earned it by providing a tangible benefit to Manjaco—their employers!

Manjaco attitudes toward spirits and Lauje attitudes, in short, were dramatically different. If Lauje stressed the obligations people owed to nature's refractions for the sacrifices they in their various guises had made to people, then Manjaco focused on a more contractual mutuality. This extended into the way Manjaco thought of participating in such ceremonies. Everyone who brought food and wine to a ceremonial meal signaled by their participation that they trusted one another. Manjaco claimed that in traditional times people might use a shared meal to secretly poison an enemy. Though they assured me that such poisonings were a thing of the past, they also claimed that some people were secret cannibals who enlisted others in their nefarious efforts to obtain human meat by getting them to taste it mixed into a shared meal. To eat together, then, was to display a certain social solidarity against the backdrop of potential betrayal. That smiling host offering you a choice morsel might be up to no good. But if you ate with him, you showed that you trusted him. If Lauje ate together because they were mutually obligated to the spirit refractions of nature, then Manjaco shared a ceremonial meal to signal a potentially fragile social solidarity.

At such ceremonial meals, what fascinated me most of all (and indeed shocked me after those years among shy Lauje) were the quick and loud claims elders made to their "share" of the wine once they had finished their antago- nistic orations to the spirits. Elders always drank first. Once they'd drunk their share there was occasionally little left for the younger men who'd done most of the wine tapping. On one such occasion an elder, eager for more wine than the gourdful he'd already gulped, pressed me to claim my "share" as a sort of honorary elder. Shouting at me in drunken jocularity, he cajoled, "Take your share, and give your share to me if you don't want it." To be an elder was to have the right to make such claims—to the first gourdful of wine, to the first bite of the pot of rice mixed with sauce, and to the last crusty but delicious bits that clung to the bottom of the clay bowl. Elders seemed to enjoy lording it over others.

To take a share in this way was to remind everyone else who was an "owner" of things and, in a sense, of people. And the young men who waited and smol- dered while the elders drank their fill felt, as they told me, the sting of their subservience.

To talk of shares and to be quick to assert one's right to claim one's proper share also implied that others might take more than their share. This was how Manjaco talked of their king and the various others whom they claimed had "eaten" more than their due during the colonial era. After the war for independence in Guinea-Bissau, the postcolonial government ordered that all "traditional" authorities—tribal chiefs and kings—abdicate because they had been allied with the Portuguese government. Nevertheless, in 1986 when I began fieldwork, the dethroned king still lived and still tended the royal shrines as a "divine king" should, but he resided in a village whose inhabit- ants shunned and scorned their erstwhile leader. Manjaco—who were hardly patriots, who had for the most part stayed out of the revolutionary struggle, and who were as likely to resist as follow the dictates of the new nation's leaders— assured me that they "laughed" in celebration when they learned that their king would be forced to step down. To them he was a corrupt despot who had abused the authority the Portuguese colonial presence made possible. And so in 1986, long after the revolution, long after the new state had ceased to blame old rulers for colonial-era complicities, the Manjaco I met continued to deride their king. One way to explain the king's fate is to blame colonialism itself for his political demise. In recalling the circumstances of colonial rule in the decades that led up to and throughout the revolution, Manjaco stressed that era's corrosive corruptions.

As they recounted it, as Manjaco aristocrats competed for local political "titles" and the valuable wet-rice fields associated with them, they allied themselves with Portuguese administrators, made under-the-table deals, bribed and were bribed, and enriched themselves at the expense of their subjects. By the late 1950s, most of the "titles" (symbolized by the ceremonial gourd-bowl associated with the rice field's shrine) and the "titled fields" that were the collective property of the Manjaco realm were under the control of usurpers—members of aristocratic houses who "sat where their fathers sat" and who "refused to pass on the gourd-bowl" in defiance of royal prerogatives.

The king was one of many corrupt officials, but they were especially bitter about him. During the revolution the Portuguese stationed in Bassarel needed to be fed, and, according to some villagers, the quartermaster left it to the king to organize the villages to supply meat. The king, for his part, took advantage of the Portuguese presence. Before and during the revolution it was the king's right to receive a foreleg of at least one of the livestock sacrificed at every funeral. Before the revolution the king distributed what he could not eat to the young men of the village. During the revolution, so the villagers recalled, the king sold all he could to the garrison. But what the king himself was able to provide was only a small portion of what the garrison needed, so the Portuguese also paid for livestock the king expropriated from the villagers at an official price that was horribly unfair to the owners. As the garrison grew, the Portuguese's ever-greater appetite became an imposition upon the people. Late in the war, too, the villagers were ordered to move into specially constructed huts closer to the garrison. Ostensibly the move was meant to "civilize" the natives. The huts had zinc roofs, windows, four rooms, each with a certain volume meant to encourage a more sanitary lifestyle. Both those who were forced to move away from cool and scattered households to tight and hot quarters, and those who were burdened with providing meat, blamed the king. Although "everyone" ostensibly was to move, some stayed put and escaped punishment. Although all households were to provide livestock in rotation, some seemed to provide it less frequently than others. The king used his powers to play favorites or to punish his personal enemies.

This was how the king was remembered. It was because they wanted the king to suffer for committing these fairly banal sins that the Manjaco "laughed" when the postrevolutionary government ordered him to abdicate. But they also talked of all kings in disparaging ways. For Manjaco the collective portrait of royalty was a rogues gallery. And in this rogues gallery the final king was merely one more instantiation of a warped pattern. When people complained of the last king, they did not spontaneously hold him up to some ideal standard or compare him with a past king who had acted properly. When, indeed, I heard Manjaco speak of kings in the past, it was usually to disparage them. The king who preceded him was, if anything, even more reviled. This king, named Mango, was known for his avarice. He had used Portuguese decrees about corvée labor to force villagers to farm peanut fields he owned rather than to work on projects that served the public good. As one story goes, King Mango refused to eat fish or chicken, but craved only goat meat or pork. Each day he sent his sons off to confiscate livestock from the villagers. Should they complain, he called in the colonial police—the *cipaios* or sepoys—to beat them. The villagers nicknamed Mango "Eats the she-goat, not the he-goat," an ironic inversion of the hunter's praise name "Kills the stag, leaves the doe; we'll eat, we'll eat." If the hunter took his prey, but by killing only males ensured there would always be prey for others, then Mango by contrast was a selfish destroyer effectively cannibalizing his kingdom.

Manjaco, like Lauje, claimed that rulers were somehow at fault for large social and environmental degradations. Unlike Lauje, though, it was not because kings and others had failed to fulfill cosmological obligations that their subjects inhabited a world out of whack. Rather it was because they had betrayed fellow human beings. Manjaco, like Lauje, inhabited recently damaged or degraded lands. They pointed out once productive wet-rice fields now overgrown by scrub forest or given over to salt marsh. They told me that the "land"—which referred at once to nature and to the community occupying it—had "broken." Drought, they emphasized, caused this, but they blamed ecological collapse on human agency. They noted that because of corruption among the kings and chiefs many fields which had once been the property of the kingdom had been usurped by selfish men who later left the country for the city to pursue jobs as petty bureaucrats or to flee a vendetta, leaving those prized rice fields and letting their dikes fall into disrepair. Or they blamed themselves, stressing that Manjaco youth selfishly seeking better-paying work elsewhere meant that the stay-at-homes could no longer manage to maintain the labor-intensive system of dikes that kept the wet-rice fields intact and functioning. But they also blamed people like me for "breaking the land." A group of young men once told me that the drought was the result of the work of European and American "scientists" who had used technologies to suck the rains from Africa and deposit it on fields in their countries. Or as an older man once remarked, the drought began when an "*uasinyor*," or engineer from an American oil company, had dug a deep well in the forest just outside the village. In the world of moral mutuality that Manjaco imagined, they assimilated even drought into an interpersonal idiom: European and American scientists stealing rain from African fields.

Such a worldview made fieldwork among Manjaco far less pleasant than it had been in the Lauje mountains. Rather than welcoming me as a returned avatar of a lost ancestor, Manjaco routinely confronted me as a contemporary agent of colonial and postcolonial inequities. They wondered aloud why I had come to live "in the bush" with them, rather than staying home in the land of gleaming cities and modern conveniences. What was I after? What was I trying to take from them? Every day was an argument as I tried to collect the raw materials of ethnography. Could I tape record this ceremony or take notes at that meeting? Why should they let me? What would they get out of the book I'd write and get rich on? What would their share be?

A Taste in Food and in Politics

Two kings, two shared meals, two encounters—all in the end adding up to two ethoses, two cultures, yet always perceived by way of a third: my own. Anthropologists, like other people, become aware of cultures by way of contrast. I began this brief excursion into the worlds of Manjaco and Lauje to illustrate a point about anthropological ethnography: that it is part philosophy and part confession. The philosophy part, restated, is that what people do and think in a society is patterned, so that as often as not "a taste in food and a taste in politics" convey the same underlying messages. Manjaco attitudes about kings and their attitudes about food are of a piece. Likewise with Lauje. This philosophy—that people in particular societies do, say, and think things that form a systematic set of messages—is central to anthropology. When we speak of culture or the cultural it is usually in reference to those kinds of patterned messages contained in a plethora of forms.

This idea that culture is a system of meanings was stated early and illustrated persuasively by (among others) Ruth Benedict in two bestselling books—*Patterns of Culture* and *Chrysanthemum and the Sword*. In the latter, a comparison of Japanese culture to American that was published at the end of World War Two, she showed how much one could learn about "values" and "culture" by comparing how Japanese and Americans taught their children to eat. In America we expect our children not to necessarily like or crave what is good for them. So a meal can become a battle as we try to cajole a child to eat his or her peas or broccoli, and as the child struggles, sometimes with incredible ingenuity, not to eat what their parents are saying is good for them. Broccoli disappears underneath a napkin, or bits of this and that are surreptitiously fed to the household dog waiting expectantly under the table. According to Benedict, this struggle over what to eat teaches children to think of themselves as separate from society, autonomous, individual. By contrast, she stressed, Japanese children are never forced to eat or forced to abstain from eating. As a result, the boundary between the desires of the self and the wishes of society are not as clearly drawn. And, according to Benedict, this contrast in attitudes toward eating was also revealed more generally in ideas about "good" and "bad" and even in politics and international affairs. A taste in food and a taste in politics were of a piece. That holism is the philosophical position that characterizes anthropology. That position in turn defines how anthropologists approach fieldwork. In the field, you follow what makes you curious. But you tend to take the mundane and link it up to the exalted.

The confession part, restated, is that anthropologists, like anyone else, will find it easier to like some tastes and easier to be put off by others. Evans-Pritchard, for example, liked his rough and ready Nuer; he did not like the more deferential Azande. Manjaco troubled me, left me feeling guilty and angry and put upon. I felt a bit cold toward them. Lauje made me excited and warm. I felt good about myself when I was in their company. But it is dangerous to let one's tastes do the thinking and judging. You have to learn to get beyond snap judgments based on taste. Yet because you are a member of a culture, you inherit a certain "taste." Taste is not a universal. It implies a certain set of attitudes. Yet you cannot easily divest yourself of those attitudes.

Take taste at even its simplest—what counts as food and what doesn't, what tastes good and what is somehow, despite your best efforts, disgusting. Some things you just can't swallow—they make you, no matter how open-minded you are, sick. Cultural difference cannot be merely intellectualized, because culture is literally embodied; it gets under your skin, into your emotions. Food preferences are more than mere preferences. One society's food is another's (almost) poison. Or to take a less drastic example, one society's food is filling while another's leaves you hungry. No amount of bread will satisfy an Indonesian. They want rice and lots of it. Food is nutritious, but what counts as a nutritious meal varies from society to society.

Because taste at its most basic is so hard to unlearn, sharing food during fieldwork can be a real chore. One of the first meals I ate with Manjaco was a shared meal of rice covered with palm oil and curdled milk. The curdled milk was cold and smelled like baby's vomit. Palm oil is red and has a vaguely spicy taste, but when it cools, it coagulates. The textures of both the oil and the soured, thickened milk it was mixed with were nothing I was used to. When we ate (there were about a dozen of us—all young men and women, all sweaty from a hard day of shared work harvesting rice in the fields of an elder), we shared a single aluminum spoon. When I picked up the spoon to take a bite I noticed the lip tracks on it—minute red and white stripes, the tracks you'd get if you dipped a spoon into a bowl of creamy ice cream and sucked at the spoon as you pulled it out of your mouth. The spoon looked and felt dirty. I noticed more than I would have otherwise the dirty and stained work clothes of my companions. The food was hard to stomach. I ate my share, pretending to like it. I could not help thinking of hygiene.

Several months later I shared another, far more momentous, meal. I was attending an initiation ritual for blacksmiths. Among Manjaco, as in much of West Africa, blacksmiths are special, sacred, and their work is hedged by secrecy, imbued with a magical and at times sinister aura. Blacksmiths deal in occult transformations. They make metal and shape it. They also can curse and cause illness. The food we were eating was meant to signal things about their occult status, and one of the bowls contained the chopped up pieces of a dog they had sacrificed on the blacksmith's altar. When they passed that bowl around, I took a chunk of it and ate the pungent meat with more or less feigned gusto. I had eaten dog before (in Jakarta, at a Chinese restaurant where I also sampled snake, lizard, monkey, and other exotic meats). I was proud of my gustatory tolerance. I felt like an adventurer. The dog at the Jakarta restaurant, like the dog in the Manjaco village, did not really taste good to me, even though the flavor itself was fine, more or less familiar, but the thought of dogs—barking, jumping, playing catch, being pets—made the taste more or less irrelevant. Again, I felt that feeling of mild repugnance, yet I could pretend otherwise, even to the point of tricking my own taste buds.

As I ate, my companions looked at me in befuddlement. "You like dog?" one old man, one of the priestly officiants at the ceremony, asked. I replied, "Yes," thinking how clever I was, how much I must be demonstrating my solidarity with them, how much of an insider I was becoming. He looked down at the floor in front of him. "We don't like dog here. It is too much like a person. It is like eating a person."

Blacksmiths, I would later learn, undergo an initiation that requires them to do repulsive things. One such repulsive act—like cannibalism, close enough to make the point of the potentially sinister quality of their soon-to-be-mastered occult powers—was to eat a morsel of dog. I had inadvertently demonstrated how Other, how potentially savage and sinister I was. Yet for blacksmiths to share in such a revolting meal was also to make them into a special and powerful society. It tied them together as a moral community.

In both Manjaco and Lauje, a widely ramified system of moral mutuality is encapsulated in the fact that food is shared. Eating together brings people into communion, makes for a community. In both places people encouraged me to become a member of their community. This is what people in the West expect, given our collective understanding of what primitive societies are like. And our expectations are generally on target. Go to any village anywhere in any of those out-of-the-way places that used to be anthropology's primary research locations, and, if you'd read Rousseau's *Essay on Inequality* or Mauss's *The Gift* beforehand, you'd be prepared for their generosity. The shared meal, the constant favors, that thrilling and troubling sense that you owe something in return—that you, the erstwhile guest, are being made through their largesse into a member of the household, the family, the village.

Most anthropologists who leave the comforts of home to spend time in distant and dirty villages have read Mauss or people like him. Like Mauss, we crave (at least touristically) the intertwining that gift exchange entails. We tend to romanticize the village and criticize the place we've left to go there. We make dichotomizing comparisons—between gift and commodity, between the person who knows he is the sum of his social relationships and the individual who suffers—yes suffers!—the illusion that everyone is an island. For us it is the commodity, not the gift, that poisons. This is the essence of what we hope to experience in our foray into the out-of-the-way. We are especially pleased when the natives we visit share that perspective.

Both Lauje and Manjaco fulfill our dreams of the primitive, but I would suggest that the Lauje do so in a way that is less disruptive of our own cultural complacency. Lauje were easier to sympathize with—to act with as an ally against an authoritarian state, against a fundamentalist Islam—but most of all because they made their criticisms through the indirect discourse of a cosmology off kilter. For them nature was the victim of a collective disrespect. To make things right again all we would have to do was recognize the sacrifices nature in its various guises made for us. We—that is, my wife and I, and by extension our fellow inhabitants of "stone houses" in America—were no more or less guilty of transgression than they potentially were. This made it was easy to feel for them because our sins were not singled out as special, nor were we forced to make individual amends for them. Recognize Lord of Land and Water (and we gladly did), make offerings to the Center of the Sea (and we did), give thanks to Hearth and Fire (and we did) and you are off the hook and on the side of the good not the bad.

By contrast, Manjaco asserted a far more troubling moral mutuality. In their world it often seemed as though everyone was culpable and publicly being taken to task for doing others harm. Their criticisms always had a particular person or persons as a target of blame, a particular villain, a particular victim. It was the king's fault; it was because my brother or cousin or kinsman had gone off to seek his fortune in France or Portugal that I stay at home and suffer. And it was because of you and your "scientists" that we in Africa are sitting "in the bush" in poverty while you live in rich and pleasant cities. Why, they constantly asked, would I want to leave the good life to spend time in the bush with them? What was I taking from them that made my excursion worth it? Always on the defensive, I felt less than sympathetic toward them. Their cynicism was easier for me to dismiss as a symptom of social decay than to take seriously—to listen to, to understand on its own terms.

But this would be a mistake. Introducing Manjaco and Lauje through the fieldwork encounter has shown how hard a truly transformative anthropology can be. Nowadays it is quite easy for people in the West to express sympathy for those we used to call savages. We lament their passing into the past much as we lament the way our lifestyle is destroying nature even as we continue to drive our cars and hope that the next item we purchase will make us as happy or as sexy or as smart or as much a part of a family as the advertisement seems to promise. And just as we lament their passing, so do we also celebrate cultural diversity as manifested in exotic foods and folkways and in the kinds of cultural knick-knacks we can use to decorate our domestic spaces. When we recognize such cultural diversity—when we are as comfortable eating Thai, say, as Italian—we pat ourselves on the back for our cosmopolitanism. In the Western vernacular, cosmopolitanism—in contrast, say, to localism—is not only the recognition of difference but the celebration of difference. In this vernacular, no one was more cosmopolitan than the anthropologist, who visited the savage slot and believed that by preaching a kind of cultural relativism back home, he or she enacted and exemplified this cosmopolitan ideal. We have supped with them. We have eaten what others may find repulsive—coagulated palm oil mixed with curdled milk eaten from a shared spoon slick with the lip marks from the last person who ate with it. We have shared a drink of wine from the same gourd, blowing away the bodies of dead bees as we slurped our sip. We have drunk and eaten with them and it tasted good.

That we eat what they eat and actually enjoy it, or at least are polite enough to pretend to show how tolerant and flexible we can be, demonstrates our common humanity. In that way the fieldwork encounter is a cosmopolitan encounter. But actually sharing a meal, and by extension much more than that, should be a cosmopolitan encounter not just because it confirms venerable truths (or truisms?) about cultural relativism and the need for tolerance, even acceptance.

Rather it is because their assertions of moral mutuality force us to scrutinize constantly our own positions as citizens of a world we all should share.

Some kinds of scrutiny are more painful than others. Lauje have much to say that is critical about the world's problems. They remind us of the violence we collectively do to nature. But Lauje's criticisms are also comforting because they leave open a space for us to occupy as their allies against a system for which we are only tangentially responsible. Manjaco, by contrast, force us to ask what right we have to do what we do. For them, cosmopolitan belonging is not about mutual celebrations of multiple cultures, but the recognition of peripheries and why they persist. They live in the bush. We do not. They are cosmopolitan because they recognize the repercussions of that fact. By the same token, we are provincial if we fail to own up to our responsibility for their condition.

2

Standing in a Line

I started to study Monticello, Thomas Jefferson's hobbyhorse and home, because of an argument I had with a Manjaco aristocrat. His name was Louis,
and though many people—especially the younger men in the village who
were beginning to take on positions of responsibility as household heads and
so forth—complained of his haughty manner and belligerent style, he was the
de facto leader of the aristocrats in the royal village of Bassarel, where I lived
and carried out ethnographic research. One of the questions that guided my
research was to find out how the aristocrats exercised and maintained their
political power. They were far richer than most Manjaco. So I became preoccupied with finding out how much they had and from where they got their wealth.
Aristocrats usually had family members who had worked for the Portuguese
in the colonial era as clerks and other petty officials. Small salaries added up
over the years, allowing the children of well-placed aristocrats to acquire a
higher education and an even better job in the national government, or to in-
vest family capital in small business ventures such as bush-taxi and transport
services or small taverns or general stores. Colonial-era patterns continued
into the age of national independence. But more important than occupation
for giving them access to wealth, aristocrats controlled large valuable wet-rice
fields (which were linked to local political titles) that they could divide into
parcels and rent out to commoner families. Louis was among the richer of
the aristocrats in Bassarel. He owned all three of the village cantinas, renting
them to petty merchants. He also controlled the second largest of the erstwhile
"titled" fields in Bassarel.

Because I wanted to learn about aristocratic privilege and power, I wanted to
talk with Louis, but Louis did not wish to talk to me because he did not know
what I would do with the information I wanted. He and the other aristocrats
were the subjects of often backbiting acrimony. Many, in fact most, were using
land that according to local custom was not theirs. They had inherited from
their fathers fields that were the property of the Manjaco kingdom—fields

which traditionally had been allocated by the king to chiefs for use only in their lifetimes. According to many of their neighbors, men like Louis were, in effect, usurpers or the sons or grandsons of usurpers. Moreover, most of them were also technically in violation of a national land rights law (written with Manjaco specifically in mind) that forbade individual households to "own" wet-rice fields larger than a few hectares. Louis thought of me as a representative of that government (after all, I had gotten government permission to do my research) and therefore a kind of spy or at least a potential snitch.

The king, by contrast, was eager for attention and more than happy to answer any question I might have. He was a pariah who spent his days more or less alone under the eaves of the veranda of his hut. The national government had stripped him of his official title, and, like all previous kings, he had been born and raised elsewhere, so he had no extended kin in the village to act as allies. Indeed, most of the villagers were glad to see the king suffer. During the revolution, according to many, he had made money making shady deals with the Portuguese garrison that had been set up in Bassarel to protect it from the guerrillas. Because the king had a tarnished reputation to refurbish, he was glad to talk with me to get his version of the facts onto paper. Commoners also had their axes to grind, so I learned more or less what I needed to without Louis's help. But I still liked him and I think he too enjoyed our frequent jousting matches. We developed a relationship based on antagonistic banter.

Finding ourselves in the cantina one day, he shouted at me, "White, you're rich. Buy me a glass." I countered that I could see the money he had sticking out of his shirt pocket. He had just returned from visiting his sons in Senegal and, wearing a straw hat, glasses he did not really need, and a short-sleeved shirt of translucent cotton, he looked like a gangster out for a stroll on the boardwalk in Havana circa 1953. He reached into his pocket as if to buy me a drink. But I did not want to be bested in a competitive display of generosity, so I countered, "You're the elder. Let me pay."

One afternoon I visited Louis alone at his house to try to explain to him my work and why I wanted to hear what the aristocrats talked about when they reviewed their business at an annual ceremony. We drank several gourds full of palm wine as we chatted, so our conversation was tinged with the affection of shared wine. When I finally asked him outright if I could participate while the aristocrats held their ceremony, Louis pointed to some shirts hanging on a line to dry in the courtyard. "Ask me for one of those and I will give it to you." He then gestured toward the chickens scrabbling in the sand near our chairs: "Ask me for that and my wife will cook it for you." But then he asked rhetorically, "In America, if I went to the White House and asked to sit with the president, would they let me?" I answered "No," and he explained that the same rule applied in the village. "What you ask for I cannot give you because it is not mine. What you ask 'the law' [that is, the state] cannot give you because it is not theirs."

With those few words I felt that Louis put me in my place. He had exposed the fraught core of modern anthropological fieldwork: the moral dilemmas we face as we pursue knowledge in the name of the common good. Anthropology depends on openness, on access. It assumes as a kind of right that the pursuit of knowledge is a laudable exercise. But anthropologists also know that some forms of knowledge are dangerous, are proprietary, cannot be freely divulged or circulated. Indeed, because we live in a society that is highly stratified—insiders, outsiders, those in the know, those who haven't got a clue—we expect and assume that even in our own backyard we will never get to the bottom of certain things. So, in a sense, we go elsewhere to ask the kinds of questions we might not get much in the way of answers for at home. Louis reminded me of that, so I promised myself that when I got back to America I would take up his challenge—to study the White House. For reasons that will become clear, Monticello was the closest thing to the White House I could find. But first an excursion into what we might call the cultural landscape of knowledge.

Think for a moment of what knowledge means to us in a society such as ours. We all recognize that there are some kinds of knowledge that are like property. People own property. They can sell it if they wish or keep it for their own use. So too with some forms of knowledge. To get, say, a formula for a certain kind of manufacturing process, you must fork over some cash. This kind of knowledge is protected, guarded. That is what copyrights and patents are for. But much knowledge in our society is also thought of as a kind of free good—a common property we all can share in, use, and profit from. Indeed, certain domains of knowledge must be free to all or at least accessible to all for our society to continue to claim that it is an open society, that it is a fair society, a just and good society. Democracy in a sense depends on the open flow of certain emblematic forms of knowledge. Markets work best (so we're told) if they are transparent, as their advocates seem constantly to say—if, that is, everyone can have access to the same information. This is why investors go to jail if they trade on knowledge that they keep others from having. "Insider trading" is a violation of the moral foundations of the market. Likewise, politics works best (so we'd like to believe) if politicians were more honest and if citizens more knowledgeable, less swayed by mere opinion, prejudice, fear.

Perhaps the most emblematic form of knowledge is what we call science. Science is paid for in a variety of ways, but one crucial way is through the public allocation of resources. What scientists discover about "our world" becomes a common property, especially through public schooling. What people learn in school depends on the common sharing of knowledge, not to mention a general consensus about what constitutes knowledge. That we have public schools and that scientists share knowledge and make it as publicly available as possible indicates how much we value and expect this kind of free exchange.

I say these fairly obvious things about knowledge because they are a taken-for-granted backdrop to all kinds of research, including anthropological research. An anthropologist goes to the field to acquire knowledge that will contribute to the common good in some not always explicitly defined but always assumed way. We go to places, though, where we know already that the landscape of knowledge is profoundly different from our own.

Thus it was in Lauje. There a number of people were recognized as having special secret knowledge which gave them power. They were "shamans," "curers," "healers," "spirit mediums"—such words are more or less equivalents of the terms Lauje used for men and women who had special access—through prayer, magical spell, or special capacity—to influence invisible forces to make people ill or well. Because we wanted to understand Lauje "religious" beliefs and practices, we talked much with such people. I put the word "religious" in quotes because that term means something very different for us than it does for Lauje. Lauje were Muslim. Muslims believe that truth is contained in the pages of a written work called the Qur'an—words via Muhammad from God or Allah. The Qur'an is written in Arabic. Commentaries about it, plus other texts crucial to putting Allah's word into social practice, can be written in local languages, in Indonesian for example. Therefore Islam can be taught, as all it requires is that you learn to read. Everyone, in theory, has access. Yet Lauje are illiterate. Some can recite verses from the Qur'an in Arabic. They have learned the sounds and have on occasion been taught glosses of what these words mean. They also, like Muslims in general in Indonesia, recognize that there is a distinction between "religion" or *agama* and "custom" or *adat*. To make a complex story a little too simple, in Indonesia in general and in Lauje in particular, old, traditional spirits and the ceremonies and other practices associated with such spirits were as often as not relegated to the category of *adat*. Yet in many instances, because Lauje are only haphazardly schooled in Islamic knowledge, they assimilate into Islamic religion local spirits and practices. Because of this blurring of practices, we called "religion" what Lauje did and believed about spirits, whether about Allah and Nabi Adam or about the Lord of the Sea or the Mountaintop. This knowledge (or if you'd rather, these beliefs) was intriguing to us. We wanted to make sense of it, wanted above all to make sense of Lauje using it to make sense of their world as they currently confronted that world.

Often, when we asked general questions about, say, Lord of Land and Water, or Placental Sibling, the curer or shaman we approached would require us to make a vow of secrecy before divulging any information. Then we would meet at the shaman's hut to talk, usually late at night once most everyone else had gone to bed. The euphemism for such conversations was "to meet as four eyes"— meaning two people only: student and teacher. Before an encounter among "four eyes" could occur in earnest, we would often have to make some kind of payment, usually a token payment, always a highly symbolic payment, to seal the bargain, to ratify the exchange of powerful information. The information we got that they considered to be the secret stuff—the gold, if you will, that made the excursion to a distant mountain village worthwhile—was useless to us as knowledge. A spell perhaps, a handful of words—to stop a bullet in mid-flight, to keep the flu at bay. What instead was useful to us was the knowledge we gained about the form the exchange of such secret powers took. Knowledge in Lauje was by its very nature secret and scarce if powerful, if effective. This told us a lot about Lauje society and it told us a great deal about the ways that official or recognized forms of Islam were entangled with older, often dispar-aged beliefs, as Lauje used what they had learned (from a variety of sources) to cure the ill, to protect themselves from harm, or to harm their enemies before they could cause them harm.

Among Manjaco too, knowledge of the kind I was interested in circulated in restricted ways. Manjaco are divided into what we often translate as lineages or clans. A more direct translation of the term Manjaco use for a kinship group that holds or shares property in common is "house," because Manjaco kinship groups are groups of families who build huts around a single courtyard and share chores as well as cattle and the rights to use rice fields. When Manjaco referred to "house" business, they would say that "every house has its coven"—a word they also used to talk about the secret society of witches that Manjaco believed existed in their midst. "Every house has its coven" because every house has sinister secrets that put it at odds with other houses. To learn about how something as basic as how a village operated as a community, I found myself up to my elbows in the murk of covens and conspiracy theories about the secret powers of neighbors.

For both Lauje and Manjaco, knowledge was also potentially dangerous. Among Lauje, when you studied with your guru, he or she might teach you a little too much. You would know when you had gone too far because you would see through things as if you had X-ray vision. Your teacher would stand behind a tree and you would see him as clearly as if he were right in front of you. Having acquired that penetrating power, you had also become one of the evil ones. Called "Pongko," such people, from then on, had to kill and cannibalize in order to live. They preyed on their neighbors and family, offering to heal in order to cast their killing spells.

Likewise with Manjaco. The young, for example, were not allowed to listen too closely to the conversations in the household "covens" lest they be tempted by the household tutelary spirits to make bargains they could only repay with their own lives or with the lives of family members. Hidden powers were everywhere in Manjaco. You needed "a strong head" to resist their enticements.

The landscapes of knowledge in Manjaco and Lauje are fragmented and divided landscapes. They parallel, and one might even say they produce social distinctions and divisions. Elders keep certain forms of knowledge to themselves. Men know some things. Women know other things. The king or the aristocrats keep what they know secret from the commoners. Curers are effective because they only pass on what they know in the secrecy of "four eyes." Remembering now that long-ago conversation with Louis, I marvel at my ignorance and arrogance then. I am Louis's age now. Then, I was a kid. And in Louis's society far more than ours, the elders cannot and will not think of those far junior to them in age as equals. Not, mind you, that they were given deference by those younger than them. After two years with Lauje, where a raised voice was rare, it sometimes seemed to me that Manjaco youth were always yelling, always shouting at their elders, and vice versa. Many people, young and old, male or female, were adept at the cutting quip delivered in public: verbal antagonism as an art form.

Knowledge, Manjaco and Lauje know, is power. When Lauje or Manjaco gave me some kinds of knowledge, they were making the kind of gift that entails obligation. When I promised to keep something secret, I kept my promise. But that I thought (without really giving it much thought) that I should be free to let my curiosity guide me in the pursuit of knowledge revealed that I was acting on the kinds of models my culture generates, not theirs. We are free (so we assume) because we can freely pursue knowledge.

Knowledge and the Museum

Louis was right in so many ways. He would never be able to visit my White House. Neither could I, except as a tourist. I could not interview the president or spend time relaxing with him as he chatted with his friends and cronies. But

I could do so in Manjaco and in Lauje, albeit with much less exalted political figures. Indeed, one of anthropology's ironies is that we expect to be able to learn far more about distant others than we would ever be able to learn about the lives of people in our own society.

To be an anthropologist you take it for granted that you can travel. Anthropologists are, one of us said, professional tourists. Think for a moment of the presuppositions that undergird tourism. The world is our playground or our campus. We go anywhere we choose for pleasure or enlightenment. Tourism is a luxury we take for granted, a symptom of our purported freedom. But it is a practice that goes on against the backdrop of a certain constraint in our own society. We are not as free at home although we assume we should be.

Because of Louis's challenge, I decided to study an institution in America that is premised on the assumption that the free and open dissemination of knowledge is an ultimate good. I wanted to look at what Americans would recognize as a kind of shrine to core American values. I happened to be in Charlottesville, Virginia, and a perfect place to carry out such a study—Monticello—was close by. Monticello was a very lucky choice.

Monticello was the residence of Thomas Jefferson, one of the nation's exemplary founders. The motto of the foundation that runs the heritage site is to "preserve and maintain Monticello . . . as a national shrine and to perpetuate the memory of Thomas Jefferson and those principles for which he contended." "Those principles," guides at Monticello will tell you, included the idea of religious freedom, the notion that education should be a public good, with the best schools open to all who qualified. These principles are embodied above all in his authorship of the Declaration of Independence. Thus Jefferson, by authoring the Declaration and the Virginia Statutes for Religious Freedom and by founding the University of Virginia, is associated in a more general sense with root American political values—individual freedom, equality of opportunity, the pursuit of happiness. But Monticello was also a plantation and Thomas Jefferson was a slaveholder.

Monticello was a good place for me to study because it exemplified a contradiction in American values. How can egalitarian principles be reconciled with the absolute inequalities of slavery? How can egalitarian principles based on an idea of equality of opportunity and a premise of individual freedom be reconciled with the fact of a landed aristocracy?

Thomas Jefferson is a complex and contradictory figure. His life could be interpreted as a kind of lesson about the nature of egalitarianism. Most Americans subscribe to a certain kind of egalitarianism that allows for difference and distinction. We expect some people to be richer and some to be poorer, but we hope that such distinctions reflect intrinsic differences in ability or effort. If all individuals are equally free and individuals are also different, then freedom will inevitably yield inequality. Jefferson was a rich man. He inherited his wealth; he did not earn it. He was also a very smart man, widely recognized for his nimble and profound intelligence. Jefferson's preoccupation with intellectual and aesthetic pleasure—his love of gadgets, art, literature, music, gardens, architecture, archeology, science, food—can be portrayed as signs of a certain intrinsic merit. His love of knowledge and the good things in life have been portrayed as both a sign of and a reward for his success at living according to the civic virtues he authored. Yet because Thomas Jefferson was a slaveowner, this celebratory narrative has always potentially been threatened. Jefferson's freedom to pursue happiness for himself and his family could be linked to immiseration of others. Or Jefferson could be dismissed as a hypocrite whose exalted words did not match his deeds.

At Monticello, enduringly perplexing questions about the nature of egalitarianism are always at or just below the surface of routine encounters between guides and tourists, even when what is being discussed has nothing to do with political ideas and grand philosophical themes. The more than half a million visitors a year who take a twenty-five-minute tour of the house and spend perhaps an hour exploring the grounds are more likely to learn details of Jefferson's aesthetic interests than of his political principles. When they first enter the house they are confronted with the traces of Jefferson's wide-ranging curiosities—the mammoth jawbone, the Indian artifacts collected for him by Lewis and Clark, the convex mirror that reflects images upside down. While in this room, they are treated to brief vignettes about mechanical wonders such as the Great Clock, whose weights, one for each day, disappear into a hole cut into the floor. They are allowed a glimpse of the narrow stairways that lead to the "invisible" upper floors and the mysterious dome or "sky" room that none of the general public would ever see. But mainly there are books, paintings, musical instruments, furniture, wallpaper, and, outside, flowers from around the world. Visitors receive a quintessential "house and garden" tour, with Jefferson—who guides would almost immediately tell you "stood six feet two and had red hair and freckles," his height, as it were, reflecting his stature—playing invisible host.

Monticello was an appropriate choice for my study, because I was looking for a kind of shrine and I found one that my natives—that is, Americans—recognized as a shrine. It was a fortunate choice because it was a shrine to the author of American egalitarianism. It was a fascinating place to study because it was so fraught with tension around the vexed issue of slavery and privilege.

And it was a fortuitous choice for another reason as well, having to do with its status as a "museum."

Anthropologists often play a rhetorical game with our readers, our students, and our publics. It is a game of making the strange familiar and the familiar strange. Because we want readers to recognize that what they believe or do is not natural or obvious or even necessarily what any sane person in a similar situation would do, we offer an alternative. Manjaco believe there are witches who wish them harm. If a person told most Americans that he or she was being attacked by witches, they would think that person needed to see a psychiatrist. Yet many Americans believe that aliens have paid us periodic visits. By describing the social context of Manjaco witchcraft beliefs, I illustrate by depicting the strange that human rationality (what counts as believable or what counts as obviously false or crazy) depends on culture and not on an individual's direct appraisal of the world as it is. To show the power of culture to affect perception, we use the strange and make it familiar. Or we show, from a slightly different perspective, that what might seem normal or natural is in fact very weird. Once you see it as weird or strange, we take the next step and show that it is cultural. Monticello is a very strange place. It is a place that would be entirely alien to Manjaco or Lauje.

Yet there are thousands of Monticellos all over America. Indeed, places like Monticello—houses no one lives in that are meticulously restored to look more or less like they did when they were inhabited long ago, houses thousands of people pay money to visit for an hour or so. Such houses are a quintessential feature of the landscape of modern societies. We go to them to learn about what we imagine (without stopping to think why) to be our past. We conflate ourselves with a place that in turn is thought somehow to be a piece of a nation. A nation, we take it for granted, has a past, just as a person has a memory; people who live in that nation today not only need to learn about that past but should, if they are good citizens, want to learn about that past. They must, in short, conflate their memory with the memory of the nation they inhabit. Yet a visit to Monticello should be a voluntary act. You go because you are free to go where you like. But you also go to Monticello because you know somehow that you ought to go.

As with Monticello, so with other sites. Our landscape is strewn with buildings or monuments on display for our edification. We have built massively expensive edifices to contain a myriad of objects: paintings, sculptures, airplanes, the facades of movie theatres, scraps of blood-stained paper, seashells, dinosaur bones painstakingly sutured together; stuffed elephants and gorillas, mice and migratory birds in lifelike poses in vitrines; real animals—jellyfish, sharks, sea anemones—in giant sea water tanks; pieces of ourselves—a liver in a jar, the embalmed fetus of a two-headed human. To even begin to list the objects we enshrine, to even begin to add up the costs of this careful work of preservation and display, not to mention to add up the hours spent gazing at such objects and listening to experts tell you the significance of what you are looking at, is perhaps to start to get a sense of how strange this activity is. But also how strangely familiar; you look to learn. You go to a museum or Monticello to learn. These contain pieces of knowledge—often very expensive pieces of knowledge—that have become a public property.

Museums and places like Monticello are fairly recent entities even though we take them for granted because they are so ubiquitous. It is hard to find, even among the smallest wide-spot-on-the-road kinds of towns, a place that doesn't have a museum or a historic house. Museums that are open to the public and are therefore public property are a modern phenomenon. That is a singularly strange fact about them. Tony Bennett marks the "birth of the museum" as coincident with the beginnings of modern democratic nation-states. We can travel back in time to the eighteenth century or earlier and find people who collected valuable artifacts and displayed them. But they displayed them for friends and peers. Such "cabinets of curiosities" (as museums' immediate ancestors were sometimes called) were hidden from the public. It was not until the middle to late nineteenth century that museums opened their doors to the public as part of a larger project, an often self-conscious and explicit project to make citizens—to turn the masses into a patriotic and cultured body politic, to make them worthy of the nation and to make them feel a sentimental attachment to the nation's aspirations.

Museums seem so attached to the nation-state in their origins that a visit to one might count as a ritual of citizenship marking a certain identity within the ambit of citizenship. Middle-class people go to museums. Historically significant edifices often stand as icons for places. New York: the Met, the Statue of Liberty, the Empire State Building. Paris: the Louvre, the Eiffel Tower. Washington, D.C.: all those monuments in marble but above all else the wide rectangle of open space known as "the Mall," flanked by free museums such as the Smithsonian Institution, which someone famously called the "nation's attic." It costs money to enter most museums, but they are about as cheap as a ticket to a movie. Museums are cheap or free because they have a contract with the citizenry to be available to them. We are all equal in that we all can get into a museum if we want to. Go to the Smithsonian and watch the streams of children climbing the high steps to the massive doorways. They are from all over the country. We make schoolchildren go to museums or historical houses or battlefields on field trips; it is a way to enhance their educations and it is also an act that reflects the hope that even the poorest among us can, if they are properly exposed, become, like us, worthy of the nation-state and beneficiaries in what the nation has to offer. To visit museums is to be a citizen.

Just as going to a museum is an obligation of citizenship, so too does not visiting museums, or not visiting them in the proper state of mind as expressed by one's comportment, reflect something about one's status in the modern nation-state. From the time museums first opened to the public, those who run them have worried about the kinds of visitors who would make too much noise or touch things they weren't supposed to. Such people (imaginary and real), Tony Bennett notes, were characterized as a kind of rabble, and their comportment was talked about as a symptom of their incapacity for true citizenship. In modern nation-states all it takes to belong to the nation is an accident of birth. As long as you are born somewhere within the borders of the nation, you belong to it and it belongs to you. Nation-states are profoundly egalitarian in that way. But most of us also tend to assume that some people are more worthy of an active belonging than others—that some people should shape the nation and guide its course while others should remain safely on the sidelines. Our country, for example, makes it hard, not easy, to vote. The polling booth is open to anyone, but you have to register before you get there and you have to go on a Tuesday when you probably are at work. You must make an effort to get there, and the assumption (or hope) is that only citizens with some degree of commitment and knowledge will vote.

The same goes for museums. They are open to everyone, but not just anyone is really worthy of crossing the threshold to commune with what they contain. This, according to the world-renowned sociologist Pierre Bourdieu, is the main message museums deliver to their publics. Museums make "distinctions" among people according to class and status, but they do so in a way that makes class or status seem to emerge out of a kind of intrinsic aesthetic ability. Museums contain cultural objects that range from the esoteric to the plebian. People who visit art museums and understand the most arcane forms of art contained there often look down their noses at those who have to read the brochure to make sense of what they are seeing or those who opt out of going at all. Likewise, some kinds of cultural objects appeal to a range of tastes and are more inclusive, so much so that the cultured may rarely visit them. History museums lie in the middle of this continuum. Because they are ostensibly about a collective past as a kind of collective identity, the fact that a range of people participate in their project by going and showing proper respect is treated as an endorsement of a shared identity.

Historical houses such as Monticello are especially interesting because they straddle the divide between art museums and history museums proper. People visit them because these places are at once associated with the past and as often as not are identified with famous or significant persons from the past, and because they are aesthetically appealing. The artifacts they contain are important because of their association with a history that is deemed worth remembering. The artifacts are also worth looking at because they are beautiful. Their value to the visitor is double. Yet aesthetics often trumps history as a chief attraction. This is especially true for houses that were once associated with the very rich. Thus many of the dozens of slave-era plantations such as Monticello, which were bought in the first decades of the twentieth century by philanthropic organizations for the edification and enjoyment of the public, are little more than three-dimensional versions of an "Architectural Digest" excursion. They are appealing because of their rich decor, ostentatious buildings, and beautiful, well-tended gardens. The people who visit such houses are mostly middle-class and white, but even among the vast category of people who think of themselves as middle-class there are distinctions of "class" in the aesthetic sense. Some middle-class people live in suburban houses that mimic or echo in their design these more ostentatious historically authentic edifices they visit as tourists. While they visit, they appropriate at the gift shop, for their own lives, versions of pieces of the past on display. In doing so, visitors recreate through consumption patterns a form of identity that is more than merely about a shared past. It is also a shared aesthetic. Others try to separate themselves from the common visitor. They shy away from the masses. They pride themselves in having specific, even esoteric interests. They spend time in the garden, for example, while paying only perfunctory attention to the guide on the tour inside the house. Still others like to quietly poke fun at the ostentation they see around them. They smirk or sneer when the guide talks about the gaudy furniture. In short, a visit to a place like Monticello is an opportunity to at once assert an identity as a citizen and to make claims for a certain class or status based on matters of taste.

In America we often imagine that we are all the same. We are equal. But we are also each allowed, indeed encouraged, to be different. In American egalitarianism the ideal is "to each according to his tastes," rather than "to each according to his needs." Yet it is also recognized that there are those with taste and those clearly without taste.

Monticello as Ritual Space

When I began work at Monticello, I told its director that I wanted to study rituals of egalitarianism and citizenship at the site. Anthropologists often use the word ritual without bothering to explain what we mean. I don't think the director knew what I meant because he later was surprised and frustrated by what I wrote about Monticello. He would call it "gossip in the guide's kitchen," because much of what I wrote involved interpreting what the guides said to one another about visitors as the guides chatted amongst themselves on lunch break. A lot of what they said was unflattering. They found many of the visitors to be insufferable. To the guides, some were boorish rubes, others were impossible snobs. They had mean (but funny) things to say about these visitors that were in a sense ritualized, clichéd, and, to me, illustrative of all the problems inherent in typical encounters at places like Monticello. These conversations, and the encounters they harkened to, were the rituals of citizenship I was after. To the director, by contrast, ritual conjured up an image of celebration—ritual as religion in its most uplifting of senses. And ritual had to be something formal, something obviously marked or labeled as such. He talked to me, for example, about the Independence Day celebration Monticello did every year during which a federal judge presided over an official swearing in of dozens of new American citizens, all residents of the county that surrounded Monticello. What I meant was something akin to the idea that ritual is part and parcel of religion, but something also very different. A study of ritual can be a critique just as easily as it can be a celebration. Rituals express religion. They also make you believe a certain version of a truth, because they are not merely an expression; they are also a reality that you experience. The idea of ritual as a reality that makes you believe a certain way is at the heart of anthropological theory.

For example, take the act of genuflection at a Catholic Mass. You kneel bowing your head slightly and you cross yourself; you make the sign of the cross across your chest. That simple act is the essence of a ritual because in that moment you are embodying a complex set of religious ideas. You feel them in your body: the bowed head, the fingers sweeping across your chest. You might be able to articulate what the ideas are that you are expressing in that simple act, but more importantly those ideas are impressing themselves upon you. You cross yourself and the ideas of Christianity are inscribed on your body.

For an anthropologist, a ritual is an act that is an embodiment of an idea. Note that a ritual can in a sense be read or interpreted, much as a theatrical performance can be interpreted. You could go to a Catholic Mass and read it as a text, written in action, which tells a version of the story of the Christian faith. Watch communion there, then go to a Protestant church and watch communion, and the act will tell a somewhat different story. When I told Monticello's director that I wanted to witness firsthand rituals of citizenship, I meant that I wanted to watch the various more or less public and more or less routinized or habitual ways that visitors and workers at Monticello acted.

I will return to the day-to-day rituals of citizenship at Monticello, all that "gossip in the guide's kitchen," but first I turn to an even more prosaic act—standing in a line, and all that it entails. When I was studying Monticello in 1988, almost all of its half-million visitors took a tour of the house, and most strolled in the gardens and grounds. A much smaller number took special tours of the garden or of Mulberry Row, which used to be the site of some of Monticello's slave quarters as well as a blacksmith's shop and nailery. An even smaller number of visitors—VIPs; Monticello called them "persons of stature"—got special treatment. They received a tour of the main part of the house that was more capacious and informative than the standard tour. Their tour of the house included the rooms on the upper floor—rooms that were not all that interesting in and of themselves, but rooms that had a certain cache, especially the "dome" or "sky room" that gave Monticello its distinctive architectural profile, and that was used on occasion in Jefferson's day for dance parties. "Persons of stature" rarely stood in line. On busy days most of the other visitors stood in line quite a while. A few of them chose not to bother with lines at all but opted to stroll the grounds on their own without benefit of a tour.

On a summer day when it is hottest and also busiest, waiting in line to enter the house might take up to an hour and a half. When you pay for your ticket in the shelter down at the parking lot, you are told how long the line will take. Monticello does not want you to be disappointed when you get off the shuttle bus at the top of the hill and see the long line. Most people will get on the bus, keep whatever complaints they have to themselves, then stand in line in the heat and eventually go through the house. When they emerge, most will say that they really enjoyed the experience. Some will be given a survey. On the questionnaire, almost everyone will express satisfaction: the tour was "excellent," the guide was "informative" and "courteous"—these being the choices the questionnaire supplies. But some are not pleased at all: they wanted "more smiles from the guides" and found them to be "haughty" or "not friendly," or "courteous but too rote, not spontaneous." One guest, who wears a baseball cap and comes from a small town in Pennsylvania, writes (and these are all quotes from an actual survey at Monticello) that he was waiting in line and noticed that a "private tour" walked by: "That's shit. It shouldn't happen in this country. We fought wars for that."

Now imagine all of this from the perspective of the guides and the administrators at Monticello. Public shrines such as Monticello needed, so they constantly told themselves, to cater to two kinds of publics. They needed to cater to "persons of stature" because from among these would come the "heavy hitters" who made large donations to Monticello's endowment. In turn, they needed the masses of visitors because these visitors were, as one of the foundation's presidents put it, the "lifeblood" of the place. Thousands of people paid millions of dollars in small increments. Without their patronage Monticello would not be able to support itself.

From the perspective of the administrators at Monticello, special people demanded special privileges. Yet from their perspective such privileges also had to be kept hidden. Persons of stature got tours of the dome room. They never stood in line. But every effort was made to keep those facts hidden from what one president of the place used to refer to as the "passing parade."

One way to hide the special tours was to use the geography and architecture of the site. Special tours were brought up to the house via a covered walkway on the side, while the mass of visitors waited patiently in line at a gate through a brick wall about fifty yards from the front of the house. The guides became quite skilled at speeding up tours through the house so as to allow for the surreptitious entrance of a special group without seeming, from the perspective of those waiting patiently in line in the hot sun, to disrupt the steady march of visitors toward the front portico and into the house. Only occasionally, and because of a snafu, would a special tour actually pass in front of this line of normal visitors. Likewise, because many normal visitors did have a hankering to see the upper floors, it became standard procedure for the guides to always remark on every tour that the upper floors were off limits to the public because of "fire regulations"—the stairs were too narrow and steep to allow for safe entrance and exit.

Guides did their job of keeping sheep and goats separate with remarkable skill in large part because they subscribed to the values that lay behind such a system of surreptitious crowd control. Many of the guides counted themselves as a kind of elite, and they wished to be recognized as such. They dressed in the tweedy materials of the landed gentry and some even lived on contemporary versions of country estates. Yet most were not rich. A few were even in what used to be called in Jefferson's day "straitened" circumstances. They were divorcees or widows. Many more were the spouses of professionals—physicians, lawyers, professors—and for the most part the guides thought of themselves as cultured, educated, and intelligent, if also poorly paid. Each one identified in small ways with Thomas Jefferson. They acted like hostesses and hosts, and they felt they were giving something of themselves and their knowledge to each and every person who crossed that threshold into what they almost took to be their house. They ran the gamut of political persuasions. Some were friendly with most of their peers; some couldn't stand each other. But they all ate their lunches together in the kitchen in Monticello's basement—lunches that hardly ever consisted of sandwiches, but were usually something in a Tupperware dish that could be heated in the microwave, and sometimes included a homemade dessert that could be shared. It fascinated me to listen to them talk about their visitors as they took their breaks in the kitchen in Monticello's basement.

There they vented their venom about visitors. They made fun of them. Or they shared stories of the unfair treatment they had suffered because of a visitor. The stories took on a kind of generic quality. Like mini-myths, they seemed to circulate and repeat themselves, weaving common themes. The persons of stature were the subjects of stories of shame and chagrin. A remark that became almost a litany was how awful it felt to give a tour of a group of VIPs and to notice, as one talked, that some member of the exalted audience "wasn't even listening" or was looking at something on the wall totally unrelated to what the guide was telling the group about. It was as if such VIPs were trying to make the guide feel insignificant.

Guides also liked to poke holes in the pretensions of the many persons of stature they had to entertain. A common joke among them was that "you have to be six feet two to get a tour of the upper floors." Because it was a physical fact about Thomas Jefferson that was one of the first things they told visitors when they crossed the threshold into the house ("Thomas Jefferson was six feet two and had red hair"), guides thus made fun of the haphazard way that Monticello's powers that be decided who deserved special treatment and who did not. Basically a VIP was someone who somebody else, making an appointment on their behalf, said was a VIP. Yet the guides also, for the most part, assumed that some people indeed deserved special treatment. As one guide summed it all up during a lunch chat:

They sometimes call us the day before to arrange a tour. . . . Someone, they didn't announce themselves, explained that they needed to arrange a special tour for an "important celebrity" who didn't want to "be exposed" to the public and would be at Monticello tomorrow. . . . I was eating my lunch and didn't want to be bothered. . . . I told them to call back and talk to the head guide. . . . I made it all sound so mundane. . . . It turned out to be Mary Tyler Moore and not some shmoe like Dom DeLuise [who had been given a tour a few months before]. She is one of my favorites, so I almost said, "No problem. You come tomorrow and say you have an appointment with me!"

Thus guides accepted the notion of a person of stature, while asserting that not everyone who makes such a claim deserves to be recognized as one. They wanted a kind of mutual recognition—VIPs who looked at them and listened to them when they shared their privileged knowledge with people of privilege. But that such epiphanies only happened occasionally made many encounters with "persons of stature" disappointing or painful.

If persons of stature were the topics of frustrated remarks and occasionally of funny stories, the passing parade bore the brunt of the jokes, jokes that usually involved their stupidity or their pathetic attempts at making themselves stand out. So every guide knew the story (I heard it told so many times) about the guy in the baseball cap fresh off the tour bus on a hot summer day who, after being told that everything in the house is original, remarked out loud, "I didn't know they invented air conditioning in Jefferson's day!" Such a pitiful attempt at humor! So too there was the visitor who, after the guide points out the convex mirror Jefferson had hanging in his entry hall (along with mastodon bones, Indian artifacts, and other elements of an eighteenth-century cabinet of curiosities), asks, "If you turn it upside down will the reflections be right side up?" Or yet another rube who asks where he might see the "statues of religious freedom" he's heard so much about.

Such stories received knowing nods and sniggers of solidarity in the guides' kitchen. It would not be too far-fetched to say that some guides liked and expected to look down on most of their visitors, and that every dumb remark the visitors made tended to confirm a general suspicion among those guides that most Americans were not all that worthy of crossing Jefferson's exalted threshold. No one in America is more fun to make fun of than the ignoramus. We put down the rube and raise ourselves up (or so we think) by contrast.

Conspiracy Theories

The preoccupations of some of those rubes in the passing parade made them especially annoying to Monticello's guides, unworthy of anything but condescension. In 1988, when I was listening to the guides and watching them work, a growing number of the visiting public were openly questioning the foundation about a rumored liaison Thomas Jefferson had had with a slave by the name of Sally Hemings. According to some, the recently widowed Thomas Jefferson had taken the very young Sally Hemings to Paris to care for his two daughters and had begun a surreptitious affair that lasted decades, during which Hemings gave birth to several children, all of whom were technically slaves, but all of whom were given the best jobs slaves could have and were then eventually freed by Jefferson. Sally Hemings was the biological half-sister of Jefferson's wife, Martha, her mother having been the slave mistress of Martha's father. "Dusky Sally" was said to resemble Martha, as sisters would. The story had a long shelf life. It had dogged Jefferson while he was still alive, even after the "vengeful" journalist who circulated it wound up dead, drowned in knee-deep water in Richmond, Virginia. It resonated with similar stories that circulated as constantly reappearing rumors around every famous plantation owner. Obviously many such stories were true. Almost all were hard to verify.

The system of slavery conspired to keep such stories surreptitious. By definition there could be no acknowledged sexual relationship between a slave and a master. But when I was studying Monticello, this story of "Sally and Tom" had recently been the topic of a bestselling novel, *Sally Hemings,* by Barbara Chase-Riboud and a popular biography, *Thomas Jefferson: An Intimate History,* by Fawn Brodie. And it was to be the subject of various films that were about to go into production, although the more established Jeffersonian scholars had dismissed the story as a rumor.

Because the story was "in the news" so to speak, various visitors would occasionally ask about the liaison. To hear the guides talk about their troubles with such visitors, hardly a day went by when they were not asked by someone about Jefferson's "slave mistress" or Jefferson's "other [meaning unacknowledged] children." Often, the visitor would phrase the question in an accusatory or mocking tone—the kind of tone I associate with reporters at White House press conferences when the event turns stonewalling into a kind of theater. And, not surprisingly, the guides' general response—the response their superiors encouraged them to make—sounded a lot like stonewalling. The guides discounted the story as a kind of rumor by invoking the authority of "professional historians." Sometimes the form of the question was benign and direct—"Could you tell us about Sally Hemings?" But when the question was aggressive if transparently sly—"But what about Jefferson's other children?"—this made it impossible, according to the guides, to do anything but react defensively. As one guide told me, "a little while ago a visitor asked a guide [who had just finished her tour],

'What did you tell them about Thomas Jefferson screwing colored girls?' Now how are you going to answer a question like that?"

The constant questions about Sally Hemings made the guides feel uncomfortable or even angry. Some asserted that such constant pestering revealed a barely hidden desire among the public to besmirch Jefferson's reputation—to "knock him off his pedestal," as they often put it. To many of the guides, the public's belief in the Hemings story revealed not only their ignorance of facts but, worse, their generally plebian tastes. Such visitors were contemptible or at least pathetic because they combined an excessive interest in the seamy side of the "private" and personal with a woeful ignorance of the civic and political. So when the guides interacted with such visitors, some took it upon themselves to act as they imagined a man of Jefferson's stature would in a similar situation. Thus in one exchange a guide responded to the inevitable query about Jefferson's slave mistress with: "Jefferson believed strongly in the right of personal privacy. . . . How do you think he would have reacted to your question?"

If an interest in discussing Sally Hemings' sexual liaison with Jefferson was a sign of poor manners, some guides also believed that such questions also reflected a more general, if misplaced, fascination with secrecy. Secret knowledge certainly was an important topic for many visitors to Monticello. They often talked as if the upper floors of the house (especially the dome room), which were off-limits to the general public, were themselves secret, containing special objects. Visitors would get off the bus and want immediately to be directed to the "hidden" passages that, to hear these visitors tell it, honeycomb the house and grounds. These secret passageways and rooms were often associated in the popular imagination with Sally Hemings. So guides complained that when a visitor occasionally pestered them to show the "secret room" just above Jefferson's bed, it was because the visitor assumed that that secret room was where Sally Hemings remained hidden and waiting for him until the rest of the household had gone to sleep. Some visitors wanted the guides to show them the ingenious system of pulleys that allowed Jefferson to hoist his bed up into this secret cubbyhole. Others asked to see the air tunnels they thought led not to the "privies" or toilets but to secret and distant locations for "Sally and Tom" to continue their love tryst. Usually the guides countered such outlandish requests with a courteous if often icy resort to a "just-the-facts" accounting. But one guide made this telling remark to me as we discussed this common fascination with a "secret subterranean landscape" at Monticello:

After one tour a woman came up to me and demanded to know why we didn't mention anything about the secret passageway to Michie's Tavern.

*I would like just once to wink or to give some sign . . . to pretend just once
that the secret does exist, that the foundation is part of some vast secret
conspiracy to keep the truth from the people [but] because of some flash
of communion with this particular visitor I'm going to lift the veil and
reveal it all.*

There were many plausible reasons for visitors to ask sneaky, provocative,
or antagonistic questions about Sally Hemings. Some probably got a certain
bigoted pleasure from discussing the subject in public, and others no doubt
wanted their suspicions confirmed that in things American there is always a
conspiracy afoot. At least that was how this guide saw it. Visitors in pursuit of
the secret of Sally Hemings were asserting the existence of a body of knowledge kept purposely out of the public domain (knowledge that, if they knew it,
would give them an insider's status). It was likely, the guide surmised further,
that when the guides routinely dismissed the Sally Hemings story as fiction,
they simply confirmed this suspicion.

Rituals of Equality

Ten years later, in 1998, a study was done on the DNA of Jefferson's and Hemings' descendants, and it turned out that the evidence made it as certain as such
things can be that there was a sexual liaison. As a result, professional historians
began to portray Hemings differently, and Monticello's guides began speaking
about the liaison as a fact rather than a rumor. The public's conspiracy theory
was not that far off after all. But what that liaison can teach us—especially about
race—is a story I will take up in the next chapter. For now I want to return to
the simple act of standing in a line and what it entails.

Standing in line is such a simple and natural act. You have done it since you
were a little kid, and you still do it all the time. You stand in line for a ticket
to the show and if you get there a little later than you wanted to and the line is
really long, you might kick yourself or wring your hands and hope it is not sold
out by the time you get to the window. When it is, you shrug; first-come-first-
served. That's the way it is as long as everyone has to do it. But if someone cuts
in line or if someone saves a spot for a bunch of friends, you get annoyed.

There's something so democratic about a line. We're all equal in the line.
But there's also something troubling about that equality. An older neighbor
of mine, a fine old member of the southern gentry, was telling me about a
trip she once took to Washington, D.C., to see the White House. "Everybody
should see the White House once in their lives, don't you think?" she asked.

"Everybody should see the president's and first lady's bedroom. So there we were trudging two by two, two by two, and it took so long I couldn't stand it anymore—all those people trudging two by two—so I left." To line up is to express social solidarity. We're all in the same boat; first-come-first-served, and all that. But to stand in a line is also to become part of the herd. It threatens our individuality, our uniqueness; it turns us, perhaps, into nobodies. And we don't want that either.

A line at Monticello is like a line anywhere in the United States. But it is also, perhaps, a line with more significance. A line at the grocery story is a taken-for-granted routine—a way to efficiently serve a mass of customers "equally." But at Monticello, as we have seen, standing in line is an act fraught with the paradox of American egalitarianism that we should all be treated the same, yet we should also each be different, individual, or special. Monticello is a place that was inhabited by one of the founders of American egalitarianism. It is now a place Americans visit because they feel a hard-to-define compulsion to do so. It is a visit my neighbor might say "everybody should do"—a kind of pilgrimage to America as a civic religion. When we make that pilgrimage, we are perhaps a little more sensitive than we routinely are about the ambiguities and contradictions that are part of the social landscape of our egalitarianism. The man whizzing by in the Mercedes: Who does he think he is? Jefferson at lofty Monticello: Who did he think he was?

Standing in a line at Monticello is but one of a series of more or less interrelated acts that emerge out of and potentially speak to such egalitarian ambiguities. It is an act that seems at once spontaneous and structured by the necessities of efficiency. It is also a ritual. Likewise, when guides and visitors converse, they also rehearse and re-enact the same ambiguities. As we saw when we looked at Lauje and Manjaco eating habits and their tastes in politics, the little things are wrapped up in the larger things. Culture produces and is reproduced in this congeries of acts, which, for their part, are modeled on and model basic values that become part of common discourse. As we look at these models in action anthropologically, we can see them generate a variety of consequences, unintended or not, that are cultural in the largest of senses.

One of Jefferson's famous sound bites was "trust the people." It's an idea that emerges out of an optimistic version of the egalitarianism Jefferson championed. The people were to be trusted because they were equally endowed with the kind of knowledge and mental capacities that allowed them to choose what was right for them, what would best satisfy their interests. Jefferson's populist faith carried him to the presidency on America's first democratizing wave. Ever since, American public institutions, like Monticello, have had to pay lip service at least to the notion that all voices should have an equal say. But this kind of pluralism is messy. Indeed, it generates mistrust as much as trust, because, ironically, the very fact that visitors were obsessed with Sally Hemings, or, alternatively, suffered what to the guides was a delusion that Monticello was purposely lying to them, revealed to the gatekeepers at Monticello how unworthy they were of anything but the most cursory conversation. Monticello may have seen it as its duty to educate these people. It could not imagine learning from them. So, at least when I was studying this shrine to American values, two parallel social terrains were commemorated: a visible terrain of shared spaces without controversy or conflict, and an invisible terrain of paranoia and mistrust. This, one might say, is the way knowledge is imagined in a stratified egalitarian society such as ours. Insiders, outsiders. People trying to keep you out and you know it. People trying to get in when they don't deserve to get in.

3

Jefferson's Ardor

Every discipline has its own mythology—those stories we tell about ourselves and our origins. For anthropologists, the myth inevitably harkens to one of our illustrious ancestors, Bronislaw Malinowski, who because of the accident of World War One, spent years in the Trobriand Islands, where he was technically a foreign detainee under the watchful eye of the English but was in fact living with and studying his "natives." Before Malinowski, anthropologists mounted expeditions in which groups of scientists with differing kinds of expertise traveled through native territory, making maps, gathering artifacts, transcribing myths, collecting vernacular terms. There was a certain inevitable distancing in such research. The natives—like the artifacts, the maps, the word lists—were more like objects than subjects. Malinowski's chance confinement in the Trobriands made for a very different kind of research. As he later wrote in the book that quickly became one of the canonical works of anthropology, *Argonauts of the Western Pacific,* "The ethnographer's magic" entailed living "without other white men right among the natives." The goal of such fieldwork was to transform "a strange, sometimes unpleasant, sometimes intensely interesting adventure" into a systematic analysis of a society. To do this the anthropologist had not only to learn the local vernacular and eschew scheduled interviews in favor of spontaneous conversations, but also to take advantage of serendipitous events: "it must be emphasized that whenever anything dramatic or important occurs it is essential to investigate it at the very moment of happening."

Since Malinowski, we have always recognized that good anthropology owes a lot to serendipity. You go to the field with a particular set of questions in mind. You plot out, via various applications for funding, what the contours of your research will be. When you get there, it is not as you expected, or you are confronted with a dramatic event that calls out to you to be interpreted, understood, explained. Before my wife and I went to live with the Lauje, we had already decided that our research would focus on local religious beliefs and practices and how they were related to the Lauje position in a global system of capitalist exchange. We already knew that Lauje could not, according to religious injunctions, sell foodstuffs, but that they participated in the cash economy by selling shallots and garlic. However, we did not know anything about the community-wide curing ceremony known as *momasoro*, with its focus on a Lauje king whose office had not been officially recognized by the Dutch in the colonial era or later by the Indonesians. In fact, that rite had been banned by local government authorities because they said it was a violation of Islamic principles. Knowing nothing about the *momasoro*, which was at once a political and a religious ceremony, we did not anticipate how much of our work would concern the fraught relationship between local religious practices and state-sanctioned Islam. But because this relationship was a chief preoccupation among Lauje, and because this preoccupation was so clearly distilled in the *momasoro*, that is what we focused on as well. Fieldwork depends on serendipity. You know what you want to study before you go. When you get there, you must always be prepared that something else may become more significant.

When I went to Monticello, I was interested in the way public history sites not only represent our nation's past—they are embodiments of our egalitarian heritage—but how a visit to such a site is also an enactment of egalitarian values in the present. Monticello, as museum and tourist destination, was a Geertzian model of and model for reality. The unexpected serendipity had to do with the controversy surrounding Sally Hemings' and Thomas Jefferson's sexual liaison and specifically with a dramatic attack on Monticello by a group of African Americans who used this controversy as a platform to talk about racial inequality. Race was not at all on my mind when I went to Monticello. Once I had spent a few months there it was almost all I could think about. The equality question had become, because of the serendipity of events, the race question.

The race question bothered those who work at Monticello because the museum, like most American heritage sites, wanted to be broadly inclusive. Yet in the early 1990s, like almost all plantation sites, most visitors were white and a very few were black. Part of the reason for this has to do with what a site like Monticello feels like to visitors. Do visitors "identify" with the place and the people who are represented there? Do they feel comfortable, or do they have a certain diffuse sense of ownership or belonging? Such questions are all in one way or another questions of identity, to use a simple word that contains much complexity. When most Americans see a portrait of Thomas Jefferson, or when they hear that he was a tall man with red hair and freckles, they also imagine, without really thinking about it, that Thomas Jefferson was "white." Likewise, when most Americans learn that Sally Hemings was a slave and the half sister of Jefferson's wife, and when they hear that she had long flowing hair, they also imagine that she was "black," albeit a "light-skinned black" or "a black who might pass for white" or a black who might have looked a lot like Mariah Carey or Halle Berry.

Indeed, no matter how white Sally Hemings might have looked, we cannot imagine her as anything other than black because of the history of how these racial categories came into being in the United States and how they continue to be deployed as core identity concepts in America today. This history began in the slave era and extended into the era of segregation and up to the present. In the slave era the child of a female slave was a slave no matter who the father was. Meanwhile, though countless men who were free or white had sexual relations with women who were slaves, and while such unions were considered to be illegal or transgressive, "miscegenation" produced offspring. In America the offspring of miscegeneous unions were occasionally recognized as a separate set of categories—mulattoes, people of "mixed blood," half-breeds, and so forth. But they were also, via the magic of social conventions and legal codes—the one-drop (of blood) rule for example—assimilated into the larger category of black, or Negro, or, eventually, African American.

Even today, the one-drop rule tends to work in one direction only. It is a direction that also implies hierarchy. White is somehow better than black. As comedienne Sarah Silverman put it in a skit about her "half-black" boyfriend, if he were more of an optimist he'd call himself "half-white." Americans are far more likely to think of Tiger Woods as black rather than white or Asian, although there is mounting pressure nowadays to open up a new category, multiracial, for people like Tiger Woods to choose if they wish.

But multiracial is a new idea in America. The older idea, the still dominant idea, is that there are two more or less distinct races in America. You are white or you are black. Thus Barack Obama—the child of a Kenyan man and a white woman whose parents were from Kansas—is America's first black president, not America's first multiracial president. To be black means you have a black parent. If you are white that means that you cannot have a black parent or even a black ancestor, or at least cannot have one you remember or are willing to admit to having. Plenty of people who are white have black ancestors and do not know it. Many of Sally Hemings' descendants, for example, were considered to be white and thought of themselves as such. But if they were white, they did not know or remember or claim a connection to a black progenitor. In the era of slavery, in the segregation era, and by and large today, if you have a black ancestor, even if many of your ancestors are white, you too are black.

So in our way of imagining race, Sally Hemings is black and Thomas Jefferson is white, and people who work at Monticello assume this racial dichotomy. Consider for a moment a conversation I had with a former director of the Thomas Jefferson Memorial Foundation. He was enumerating all the ways that Monticello—a place, as he put it, where slavery had once been "the 's' word," where slaves were referred to as "servants," and the issue of slavery and race was not discussed—was now making slavery and the lives of Monticello's slaves an integral part of the story the foundation told. He asked if I'd visited the gift shop lately. They were now selling a postcard (the first in a series commemorating the slaves) with the daguerreotype of Isaac Jefferson, the slave blacksmith. Isaac's image was also prominently featured on a new brochure dedicated to the slaves who lived and worked on Mulberry Row. To sum up why these new efforts had been a success, he told me about a conversation he'd recently had with a school teacher "from Oklahoma" who remarked that now that there were slaves on the mountaintop, her black students were interested in history, when before they hadn't been.

White museum administrators feel they are doing the right thing when they find and display black history for black audiences. To give them Isaac to identify with is, by extension, to give them a place in history from which they were once excluded. But this also implies that white people's identities are already taken care of at Monticello. If black schoolchildren need a postcard of Isaac to take home with them as a memento of their visit, white children already have Thomas Jefferson. And no matter how dignified, how hardworking, how noble is Isaac, he will always be a second-class citizen in comparison to Jefferson.

In an egalitarian society such as ours, the identity problem is a race problem, because identity implies similarity and difference, equality and inequality. Race as identity means that "I," white person, identify with Thomas Jefferson, not with the slaves who also occupied the site. Worse than this, "I," white person, expect that "you," black person, will identify with the slaves. They are your ancestors. Thomas Jefferson is my ancestor.

Thomas Jefferson is the reason most white people go to Monticello. White people may be interested in Sally Hemings or sympathetic toward her; they may be curious or otherwise well disposed to the hundreds of slaves such as Isaac the blacksmith who lived and worked at Monticello, but they go to Monticello because it was the home of Thomas Jefferson. When white people go to Monticello they often feel a certain kinship to Jefferson by virtue of his race. They may also recognize, simultaneously, that they are not at all like Jefferson—that they are poorer or less intelligent—but they also feel a certain connection of identity to him that they are not as likely to feel with Sally Hemings or any of the other slaves at Monticello.

Race, to Americans, is a category of biological similarity. Just as we share blood with family members, so too are we of the same substances—blood, genes, bodies—as those with who we share a racial identity. Race is kinship writ large. Because race is kinship, some white Americans might even identify fairly closely with Jefferson. They might be able to stand on the threshold and imagine that just as Jefferson became president, so too will they someday become president. It is far less likely, for the same reasons, that those who think of themselves as black will do the same thing (or at least it was less likely until Barack Obama won the White House). Rather than admire Jefferson and secretly wish to fill his shoes, they might feel anger toward him and look over his shoulders toward Mulberry Row, where people "like them" toiled and lived so that Jefferson might enjoy his copious library, his gourmet meals and French wines, his violin, his horses, and his fragrant garden.

It is that kind of segregating identification that places like Monticello encourage, both explicitly and implicitly by accident. Guides who are taught to "connect" visitors to the site also segregate as they invite "you" to imagine yourself as an inhabitant of the colonial past. When I was studying the Wythe house at Colonial Williamsburg, for example, guides would stand at the threshold of the parlor or dining room and tell their visitors about the slaves in the back rooms. "They" launder, cook, and clean while "you" are invited by your guide to sip sherry or drink tea with your imaginary hosts.

Monticello needs paying customers. They need donors and people who will buy things in the gift shop. It is far easier to make a donor want to give to Monticello if you treat that donor as if he or she were a peer to Jefferson, his virtual equal. So you invite donors to elaborate banquets where the best wines and many courses of perfectly cooked foods are served on china and crystal that evoke Jefferson at his epicurean best. For even the common visitor, versions of those same goblets and china are for sale at the gift shop or through a catalogue. Those who manage the gift shop, or who write the copy for the catalogue, assume (more or less rightly) that to want to buy these expensive replicas of Monticello's furnishings and décor you have to like what Jefferson liked, want to be (at least a little bit) like Jefferson, and like or admire Jefferson. It is profitable if visitors and donors identify with him. His whiteness sells; his position as master of a slave plantation made the upscale décor possible. So, by the same token, it comes as no surprise to those who run Monticello that

African Americans do not flock to a site that reminds them of the ongoing injuries of racism. Such sites are painful for African Americans to visit. They do not find ancestral versions of themselves in prominent positions at such places. They do not want to buy the goblets and china.

Yet to those who manage places like Monticello—to those who believe that all Americans, in order to be Americans, must share common understandings of their collective past, disparities in who visits and who does not require rectification. While I was working at Monticello, the foundation did a survey to find out how many African Americans were visiting the site, then made several efforts to make Monticello more appealing to African Americans. The caretakers of Monticello wanted to make black Americans identify with the site, and they did so by offering them historical personages with whom they could identify. They tried to make Mulberry Row and the people who lived and worked there more central to the stories they told, and find African Americans who might feel a special kinship to the site. In 1992, they hosted a reunion of the Woodson family, whose members claimed to be descendants of slaves who had lived at Monticello.

A few months before the reunion, Monticello's director called it a lucky coincidence—"a milestone in Monticello's dealing with this part of history":

I think a wonderful thing is going to happen next spring. That is, we believe we're going to have a reunion here of the descendants of some Monticello slaves. . . . We participated in Black History Week this year and [our research historian] gave a wonderful talk . . . to a packed house. . . . And she led them on a walk along Mulberry Row and explained to them what took place when, and how much we do know about these people—a lot. And this guy [who plans the Woodson reunion] was in the audience and has become a friend. And he mentioned the possibility of a reunion and I said, "Gosh that's a wonderful idea." So he's coming next week, and we're having lunch. And we're going to plan this homecoming and we're going to do everything that we can to see that it happens.

The homecoming the director envisaged was to have been a quiet and private one. The Woodsons would get a private tour of Monticello, the kind of tour the foundation routinely gives to "persons of stature"—corporate and governmental VIPs, celebrities, and also the hundreds of Jefferson's legitimate descendants who hold their annual reunion at the family cemetery on Jefferson's birthday.

But the Woodsons seemed to have sandbagged Monticello because they made sure that the reunion would be televised by NBC national news. The discreet attempt at inclusion would become a public re-enactment of exclusion. So on NBC, it was announced that the Woodson family came to Monticello "to claim what they say is their plantation." They claimed to be the descendents of Tom Woodson, the putative first and unrecorded child of Sally Hemings and Thomas Jefferson.

In so doing they echoed what the political activist Jesse Jackson had said about Monticello on a visit that occurred shortly before. Jackson accused Monticello of "throwing sand on the fires of history" because it failed to give credence to the love affair between Hemings and Jefferson or mention the offspring they created together. To Jackson (and to many other African American intellectuals), Monticello's squeamishness about talking about the possibility of this liaison was symbolic of the inability of white America to accept black America as a part of the same overarching national family. Racial difference, Jackson and others argued, was the wedge that divides Americans, and it is the assumption that racial difference exists that allows us to act inequitably in a society premised on egalitarian principles. Like Jackson, the Woodsons asserted that Monticello had not been forthcoming in addressing their claims. Exposing secret miscegenation could be seen as central to telling a story of kinship denied.

After the NBC broadcast, which played up the reunion as an antagonistic encounter, with the Hemings story resonating as a kind of exposé of typical establishment stonewalling, every Monticello employee I talked to noted that the foundation had taken a public relations beating. Monticello did not expect the Woodsons to produce (with the collusion of the media) such derogatory sound bites. Why then did the televised version of this event become an antagonistic encounter rather than the "homecoming" of new friends that the director anticipated in his interview with me?

Initially I thought it was because the foundation was not aware of the Woodsons' genealogical claims. (Note that in the excerpt above the Woodsons are characterized as "the descendants of some Monticello slaves"). But in an interview I had with him after the visit, the director insisted that he knew all along about their putative ancestry. In that second interview I was especially intrigued by his befuddlement with the public's continued preoccupation with the Sally Hemings story. He stressed that the foundation wanted to accommodate their reunion because "Jefferson would never duck any tough questions like race. But he's a man for the ages . . . and we don't want to be too provincial in this stewardship." To the director, Jefferson's status as slaveholder counted as a provincial issue when compared to his authorship of the Declaration of Independence, an achievement "for the ages." Because Jefferson stood for so much, and accomplished so much of global significance, the director could not understand why people continued be "so fixated"—as he put it—on race, much less the (possible) liaison with Sally Hemings.

Yet "race"—or rather the idea that biological differences between groups of humans account for differences in thought patterns, personality, attitudes, and the like—is an issue of global significance, and it could be argued that race should be the chief topic Monticello addresses. And this is because the concept of race is like the concept of culture, or the idea that different social practices between groups of people account for differences in thought patterns and personality, attitudes, and so on. Race and culture are similar ideas that share a similar history. They are both ideas that emerge out of Jefferson's era and out of attempts by people such as Jefferson to account for human difference in the context of egalitarianism.

That is what the serendipity of the Woodsons' claim made me see. Jefferson was as much the author of absolute racial difference as he was the author of the idea of universal human equality. The incandescent phrases of the Declaration of Independence ("We hold these truths to be self-evident, that all men are created equal, that they are endowed by their Creator with certain unalienable Rights") assert the latter; the meticulously objective paragraphs of a far more obscure text, but one just as important historically as the Declaration, *Notes on the State of Virginia,* assert the former. To understand what America is culturally, it is more than worthwhile to read closely and critically Jefferson's *Notes*; for it is in that text that we glimpse both the birth of the idea of culture and cultural equality, and the very different, indeed opposed, idea of race and racial hierarchy.

Jefferson, Race, and Culture

Thomas Jefferson wrote *Notes* in the 1780s. Its purpose was to offer a portrait, using the scientific tools of the day, of Virginia's geographical, economic, and human resources. In his characterizations of Virginia's slaves, Jefferson asserted the biological inferiority of people of African descent. In his characterization of Virginia's "aborigines," Jefferson asserted the essential equality of Indians and Europeans, and he used a theory of cultural relativism to do so. As we shall see, there are troubling and revealing inconsistencies in his assertions. The same kind of evidence that he used to claim an essential African inferiority he also used to claim that Indians are inherently the same as Europeans. Historians have long noted such inconsistencies. They stress that Jefferson was a slaveholder, yet he tended to assume that humans were equal. So he needed to believe that somehow slaves were not the same as other humans, to prove to himself and others that they were inherently inferior. Jefferson was an American, and Indians, for complex reasons, had become iconic of America. So Jefferson needed to emphasize their equality with Europeans in order to claim the equality of the new nation in relation to the old European states.

Jefferson's assertions of Indian equality were part of an argument he had been carrying on with the Compte de Buffon, a French naturalist who asserted that the American continent was in a state of degeneration and that as a result America was naturally inferior to Europe. In the eighteenth century, theories of degeneration were used for much the same purposes as theories of evolution were later used to explain differences among biological species and among cultures or civilizations. If evolution often seems to work in tandem with an idea of progress—that primitive forms are on the whole inferior to advanced forms—then degeneration depends either on the idea that the world is slowly falling apart, becoming less perfect than it was in the distant past, or that parts of the world are less salubrious, less congenial to the development of life and civilization. Evolutionary theories of progress reached their peak of popularity in the late nineteenth century and they are still very much with us. They work well with a capitalist ethos, in which competition is enshrined as a way to make markets "more efficient"—that is, more beneficial. Evolutionary theories of social progress, along with the ethos of capitalism, tend to imply that new is better than old, that young is an advance on old, and that the future will be brighter and better than the past. By contrast, theories of degeneration are more compatible with ideologies of aristocratic privilege—with explicitly stratified or hierarchical societies rather than egalitarian ones. Degeneration theories invariably assert that age confers virtue, that change is often destructive rather than constructive, and that pedigree takes precedence but needs to be protected.

To argue that America was more degenerate than Europe, and that it was therefore inferior, Buffon used two sources of evidence. He compared American and European mammals and claimed that American mammals of the same general type were smaller and weaker than European versions. And Buffon compared Indians to Europeans and again claimed that Indians were smaller and weaker. As the historian Bernard Sheehan noted, "Buffon's attack left little of the Indian's reputation unscathed," especially the Indian's "sexuality and the human qualities that flowed from it, which held a central place in Buffon's interpretation as it did in Jefferson's response."

Jefferson made quick work of Buffon's thesis regarding animals. Recall the mammoth bones so prominently displayed in Monticello's entry hall. But he made his most intellectually nuanced arguments in defense of the Indian's reputation, above all his "ardor." According to Buffon, the typical "savage is feeble and has small organs of generation; he has neither [body] hair nor beard, and no ardor whatsoever for his female." Because he was lacking in "ardor," or a kind of biogenic desire and capacity, he also tended to be "cowardly" and have "no vivacity, no activity of mind." For Buffon, the course of the causal arrow was clear. Indians "lack ardor for their females, and consequently have no love for their fellow men: not knowing this most tender of all affections, their other feelings are also cold and languid; they love their children but little; the most intimate of all ties, the family connection, binds them therefore but loosely together . . . hence they have no communion, no commonwealth, no state of society."

For Buffon, sexual energy lay at the foundation of all life. Because Indians had no sexual energy—no ardor—they were indifferent to women. They did not love them. Because they did not love women, pursue them, covet them, or wish to protect them, they also could not make a society of any lasting importance. Buffon's theory of ardor was a common one of the time, one that Jefferson subscribed to as well. According to such a theory, civilizations were dependent on the channeling of male ardor. Women, in being modest, created in men the kind of sublimated or deflected desire that led to love, to bravery, to salutary competition, to creativity, to ingenuity, in short to, in effect, all the attitudes upon which civilization depended.

Jefferson agreed with Buffon that the highest achievements of humans depend on channeling ardor, but he disagreed with Buffon about how to interpret (what we would call today) "the ethnographic facts" about the Indians. According to Jefferson, Buffon had misunderstood Indian customary practices. From the distorting distance of Europe, Indian practices often seemed to confirm what Buffon claimed. Indians, so it was widely reported, shared their wives with European visitors. They gave away property and such crude valuables as they had. Their generosity could be construed as a kind of fecklessness, as incapacity to love, cherish, or protect. Jefferson took every one of the negative stereotypes of Indians and turned them on their head. Their generosity was a virtue, not a symptom of a more pervasive weakness of character. The Indian of North America, Jefferson countered, "is neither more defective in ardor, nor more impotent with his female, than the white reduced to the same diet and exercise."

This was typical of Jefferson's argument against Buffon. If Indians, according to Buffon, had no body hair, which was a symptom of their weak ardor, then to Jefferson, Indians plucked their hair because they had a different, if equally refined, standard of beauty than did Europeans. "With them it is disgraceful to have hair on the body. They say it likens them to hogs. They therefore pluck the hair as fast as it appears." If Indians treated their women as drudges, well, that was hardly different from what was common practice among Europeans.

In making such arguments Jefferson anticipated the basic tenets of modern cultural anthropology. Your own prejudice makes you fail to notice what is inherently good in others whose practices seem to diverge from yours. Your upbringing and habits make you inherently intolerant. Today anthropologists would call this ethnocentrism. We would argue instead that environment—one's ecological and social milieu—makes you who you are. No environment, social or ecological, is inherently superior to other environments. No society is inherently superior to any other. All are equal or equivalent in two senses. One, their members are all equally human. As individuals and as a collectivity they have more or less the same capacities. In any society there are those who are smarter or stronger or more morally or aesthetically refined than their peers, but no society has even a near monopoly on reason, strength, virtue, artistic capacity. Second, societies are also equivalent in that they all are adaptations to particular circumstances, outcomes of particular histories.

This double notion of societal equivalence (which stresses the diversity of social forms while positing the essential equality of human beings) came to be central to American cultural anthropology at the beginning of the twentieth century, as Franz Boas and his students mounted arguments against what was becoming a dangerously dominant view in the American and European vernaculars—social Darwinism. In the social Darwinist scheme, some societies, whether because of especially salutary environments or because of superior (genetic) stock, were manifestly better by any standard than other societies. The position Boas and his students took is now known as cultural relativism. Cultural relativism dovetails neatly with American egalitarianism. We are (we like to think) all equal, yet all different. Like snowflakes, no two of us are alike. Like snowflakes (we tell our children in kindergarten), we are all equally beautiful in our differences. Modern cultural anthropology is very much a product of American egalitarianism. It is very much wedded to the twin ideas of cultural tolerance based on an awareness of the problem of ethnocentrism. And it is also culturally relativist.

Modern anthropologists constantly caution their publics against assuming an essential superiority. We use cultural relativism to argue against those who automatically assume that when a woman wishes to cut off her clitoris she must be from a defective or inferior culture, or if a man chooses to commit suicide to further a political cause that his culture is somehow sick or depraved. As cultural anthropologists, we can sometimes be extremist in our cultural relativism, but we see ourselves as battling against the unconscious extremism of ethnocentrism.

Jefferson's cultural relativism regarding the Indian would have seemed at least equally if not considerably more extreme in his day, at a time when those in Jefferson's social class drew a sharp distinction between art in an exalted sense and mere entertainment. He argued that even the simplest and most notional forms of artistic expression among Indians—crude cartoon scratches, minimalist music—was on par in spirit at least with the highest artistic achievements of the European courtly tradition. Indians inhabited a simpler society, but they were just as creative, just as smart, just as morally keen.

Indeed, Jefferson stressed that the social simplicity of Indians was to be admired and contrasted to the corruptions of European society. For Buffon and others, that Indians lived in small communities was at once a symptom and a cause of their lack of civilization, their degeneracy. Jefferson argued in response:

> This practice results from the circumstance of their having never submitted themselves to any laws, any coercive powers, any shadow of government. Their only controls are their manners, and their moral sense of right and wrong, which, like the sense of tasting and feeling, in every man makes a part of their nature. An offence against these is punished by contempt, by exclusion from society, or where the case is serious such as murder, by the individuals whom it concerns. Imperfect as this species of coercion may seem, crimes are very rare among them: insomuch that were it made a question, whether no law, as among the savage Americans, or too much law, as among the civilized Europeans, submits man to the greatest evil, one who has seen both conditions of existence would pronounce it to be the last: and that the sheep are happier of themselves than under the care of the wolves. It will be said, that great societies cannot exist without government. The Savages therefore break them into smaller ones.

"Savages" in Jefferson's appraisal were freer, more like the egalitarian ideal, than were Europeans. As such they were a kind of model, an ideal to be emulated by the new society Americans were making on the continent—a society where "government" would often be equated with "tyranny."

Ultimately Jefferson went beyond cultural relativist theory in making a connection between the America he and his peers were making and the societies of "Savage Americans" it was replacing. He claimed a connection of ancestral kinship between Indians and Europeans that was at odds with most of the theorizing about Indian origins in his day. Most of Jefferson's contemporaries assumed that Indians were kindred to Asians and that their ancestors had migrated in the distant past from Asia. The evidence was thought to be overwhelming. But Jefferson took linguistic evidence of dubious value to argue that because there were far more languages in America than in Asia, they were older in origin than Asia, and Jefferson would advance as a "tentative" hypothesis that Indians actually originated in Northern Europe and were related to Celts and Irish. Jefferson's cultural relativism thereby collapsed into a kind of literalism. America's aboriginal inhabitants were more than merely our kindred spirits by analogy. They were the new nation's avatars because their ancestors were also ours.

Cultural Relativism versus Biological Essentialism

In making Indians into American avatars, Jefferson deployed a relentless cultural relativism. The Indians, no matter how things appeared, were our equals (if different) in art, intelligence, and morals. With "the negro," Jefferson would be just as relentlessly consistent in asserting an absolute and unbridgeable inferiority. Again it would be an issue of ardor. If the ideal of ardor was to have a strong passion for one's own women, then Jefferson would assert that the "negro" was "more ardent . . . but that love seems to be more an eager desire than a tender delicate mixture of sentiment and sensation." Excessive desire made Negroes inferior to whites, so inferior in fact that, according to Jefferson, negroes preferred white women over black, much as "the Oran-Utan" preferred Negro women to its "own species."

Excessive desire made it possible for Negroes to have powers that appeared to be like those that Europeans admired, but upon closer appraisal were inferior. "They are at least as brave and more adventurous," but these qualities emerged from "a want of forethought." Negroes in short were foolhardy, not heroic in their bravery. Jefferson also asserted that blacks were quicker to forgive if they were angered or hurt. But this was not because they could claim this as evidence of a higher virtue. Rather, "their griefs and wraths are transient" because such emotions were precipitated "more by sensation than reflection." Most importantly, in "faculties of memory, reason, and imagination," they were "equal to whites in memory; much inferior in reason . . . in imagination dull, tasteless, anomalous." Excessive ardor entailed mental deficiency.

In making this assertion, Jefferson anticipated what is often a critique of racialist arguments for mental difference. If it is indeed the case that one group seems to be less mentally acute than another and if this group is also less educated, less endowed with what we call "cultural capital"—a casual and thorough exposure to the arts and sciences—then it is hardly fair to compare them according to a single standard. You cannot compare, say, children of the upper middle-class in New York City who go to the best of schools with, say, children of Appalachia who hardly go to school at all, and assert that because fewer children of Appalachia play piano or cello or appreciate Cezanne and Picasso, their intrinsic mental capacities are inferior. In Jefferson's day "blacks" or Negroes were slaves. They lived in conditions of near-absolute abjection. So, Jefferson allowed, "It will be right to make great allowances for differences of condition, of education, of conversation, of the sphere in which they moved." But Jefferson was not going to compare the "many millions . . . confined to tillage." Rather he claimed that he was making his case by focusing on those blacks "so situated, that they might have availed themselves of the conversations of their masters," those "who have been liberally educated and had before their eyes samples of the best works from abroad." Of these, Jefferson claimed, "Never yet could I find that a black had uttered a thought above the level of plain narration; never saw even an elementary trait of painting or sculpture."

To reinforce his argument for an absolute biological inferiority of blacks to whites, Jefferson returned to his cherished Indians:

> Who with no advantage of this kind will carve figures on their pipes not destitute of design or merit. They will crayon out an animal, a plant, or a country, so as to prove the existence of a germ in their minds which only wants cultivation. They astonish you with strokes of the most sublime oratory; such as prove their reason and sentiment strong, their imagination glowing and elevated.

For Jefferson, Indians could do no wrong. Even the most manifest differences in accomplishments—between the Sistine Chapel, say, and the iconographic markings (to indicate tepees and tribes) on a buffalo hide—were elided so that the difference between an Indian and "you" was a cultural difference, a simple matter of "cultivation." For Jefferson, by contrast, blacks could do no right. "Misery is often the parent of the most affecting touches of poetry. Among the blacks there is misery enough, God knows, but no poetry."

Even when there were black poets in Jefferson's ambit, he made sure to excoriate them in the most crude and ruthless terms. He cites two—Phyllis Wheatley and Ignatius Sancho. Of Wheatley, he impugns her authorship as he dismisses out of hand the work she ostensibly produced. "The compositions published under her name are below dignity of criticism." Of Ignatius Sancho, he is more capacious in his biliousness. Sancho, Jefferson writes,

Has approached nearer to merit in composition; yet his letters do more honor to the heart than the head. They breathe the purest effusions of friendship and general philanthropy, and show how great a degree of the latter may be compounded by strong religious zeal. He is often happy in the turn of his compliments, and his style is easy and familiar, except when he affects a Shandean fabrication of words. But his imagination is wild and extravagant, escapes incessantly from every restraint of reason and taste, and, in the course of its vagaries, leaves a tract of thought as incoherent and eccentric as is the course of a meteor through the sky. His subjects should often have led him to a process of sober reasoning; yet we find him always substituting sentiment for demonstration. Upon the whole, though we admit him to the first place among those of his own color who have presented themselves to the public judgment, yet when we compare him with the writers of the race among whom he lived and particularly with the espistolary class in which he has taken his stand, we are compelled to enroll him in the bottom of the column.

But Jefferson is not satisfied with merely taking upon himself the role of severe headmaster in some imaginary classroom of cultural merit. As he did with Wheatley, Jefferson also questions Sancho's authorship: "This criticism supposes the letters published under his name are genuine, and to have received amendment from no other hand; points which would not be of easy investigation." Indeed!

Jefferson finds it hard to imagine that even those he considers to be such poor poets as Sancho and Wheatley are who they claim to be. So he implies shadowy authors, secret ghostwriters because, for Jefferson, it is impossible to think—to even consider—that a black might approximate a white in the capacity to reason. Thus Jefferson concludes his crude critique of Sancho with what he must have imagined was a coup de grace: "The improvement of the blacks in body and mind, in the first instance of their mixture with the whites, has been observed by everyone, and proves that their inferiority is not the effect merely of their condition of life." For Jefferson, when "blacks" did succeed, did seem to approximate whites in imagination and reasoning, it was either because they were not really the authors of the works attributed to them or, more insidiously, it was because those who did display a glimmering of intellectual merit were not really black at all. They were mulattoes—products of "mixture with the whites." It is with such spurious reasoning that Jefferson was able to maintain the illusion of absolute racial difference.

When we read Jefferson's *Notes on the State of Virginia* today, we glimpse the history of the origins of two crucial concepts in a nascent social science—race and culture. The two concepts came to be used to interpret the significance of differences in the behaviors of groups of people and to compare groups to one another. *Notes* should appear to a modern reader to be fraught with contradiction. It should show more than anything else how much Jefferson's desire to portray one group of people as different and inferior and another group of people as different but equal shaped the evidence he presented. *Notes* documents bias—Jefferson's ardor, not black ardor, not Indian eloquence. When blacks act like whites, achieve or produce what whites do, Jefferson impugns their authorship or assimilates them into whiteness itself. And it is precisely because he was so willing to embrace Indians as intellectual equals that the race card he plays seems so anomalous. In explaining difference vis-à-vis one group, Jefferson uses arguments that might count today as excessively culturally relativist. Are Indians really less hairy than Europeans because they depilate themselves? In dismissing similarity vis-à-vis another group, he seems obsessively essentialist. In a lifetime of associating with slaves who cooked the finest meals, made the finest furniture, and talked and most likely talked back—all in cultural idioms and accents which were also Jefferson's— could he not find one black person who would have counted as an "author" or "artist" or "orator," with a head as well as a heart?

Jefferson and Whiteness

Despite the logical contradictions evident in a close reading of *Notes,* Americans collectively, especially white Americans, are a lot like Thomas Jefferson, America's author, America's amanuensis, in our paradoxical attitudes toward "Indians" or "Native Americans" and toward "race." Like him, we tend to assume that there are fundamental differences among people because of "race," even when such differences are not readily apparent. Like him, we also assume that some profound differences in the way groups of people act and in what groups of people believe belie a deeper similarity. Manifest difference can be dismissed as merely about culture. Cultural difference can be incorporated into cultural relativism. As we currently practice the politics and poetics of identity, we can embrace otherness or we can push away sameness. Race and culture continue to be our templates.

White Americans like to identify with Indians. Their culture excites us because it is at once exotic and exalted and also, somehow, our birthright too. Sure, our ancestors, or rather people who were white like us, but not as enlightened or open-minded or advanced or progressive or "free" as us, killed Indians, slaughtered them, wiped them out indiscriminately, women, children, dogs. But when we watch the violence in Hollywood films such as *Dances with Wolves* or *Little Big Man,* there is always already a white guy like us who appreciates them, lives among them, is accepted and even loved by them, and who fights with them against the grim-faced blue coats who cannot possibly be of any relation to us. We find it comforting to have a dream-catcher hanging from the rearview mirror of our Jeep Cherokee or Pontiac. In elementary school when we play-act the first Thanksgiving, we are proud and happy to cut out construction paper headdresses and make ourselves into the Indians who welcomed and fed the Pilgrims. So many Americans have (or believe we have) "native blood," it is as if we're all a nation of part or erstwhile Indians. To be a Virginia Dame, one of those blueblood societies that are a WASP quintessence, you have to be a direct descendant of Pocahontas, that Indian maiden who saved Captain John Smith's life and later married John Rolfe and bore him children. White Americans have been "playing Indian," as Philip Deloria so perfectly put it, ever since the Boston Tea Party. Like Thomas Jefferson, many associate Indians with America itself. We fire tomahawk missiles, attack our enemies with Apache, Blackhawk, or Kiowa helicopters, and we may not think it is insulting to anyone to wear war paint and root for the Redskins. On any given Sunday half of those of us who care about football want our Redskins to beat those Cowboys.

A few years ago, the Army Corps of Engineers found the bones of a ten-thousand-year-old human in a washed out riverbank in Washington State. When the bones were widely reported to have "Caucasoid" characteristics, a flurry of articles appeared in the popular press about the European origins of ancient American society. Like Thomas Jefferson, many white Americans want to be Indians or at least to believe that Indians are the best, most noble, most spiritual part of us.

Race is another story. Regarding race we are also a lot like Jefferson. We see race all the time marked in the faces and bodies of the people we brush against in our day-to-day lives, or on the news or in the movies. Everyone we meet is black or white or Asian or Hispanic or . . . Some of us like to believe and wish everyone would believe that race is only skin deep, that under the skin we are all the same. Thus the many white people who responded to Monticello's survey question "What is your race?" with the response "human." Yet most of us are rather quicker to assume that race is more than a matter of cosmetics. Race is deep; it is in our genes. It makes us different in profound ways. And here we echo Jefferson, amplify him, dress up his words in the garb of modern science. Some people are stronger, some are smarter; some are sicker, some more healthy. For many of us, these differences in individual abilities and capabilities are racial differences that no amount of "culture"—no amount of learning, no amount of living in a different place—can erase.

We might say that we owe that idea to Thomas Jefferson and people like him, who needed the idea of race to make the systematic exploitation of slavery palatable. Slavery requires the idea of absolute superiority and inferiority. Without the moral security that an idea of absolute superiority offers, slavery, as Orlando Patterson reminds us, would simply and obviously be a form of parasitism. A parasite consumes its host without giving anything to the host in return. The master consumed the slave in two ways: the master used the labor-power of the slave to enhance his life at the slave's expense, and he used the slave's servility to make himself feel superior. When he felt the need, he could beat the slave because the slave was a morally inferior being who needed a firm hand. Or he could pat the slave on the head because the firm hand could be employed by the soft heart. His paternalism could be benign or ruthless, but in all cases it remained paternalism. Paternalism is impossible to square with egalitarianism.

Jefferson, owner of slaves and author of the idea that "all men are created equal," is also the author of the idea that an African American, no matter how long in America, is still somehow fundamentally inferior because of his diminished capacity to reason and imagine. Jefferson also inscribed into our national consciousness that this defect in mental endowment was because the black race was excessively endowed with "ardor," making people of such a race slaves, as it were, to their bodies. Bodies need minds to manage them, much as horses need riders or children need parents. Jefferson talked of his slaves as his "family." They were that part of the family that would never reach adulthood, that would always require the gentle or firm hand of paternalism.

Because men like Jefferson have been so persuasive, so sure are we that race exists, some of us are able to make persuasive arguments for racial difference and inferiority that mimic Jefferson's arguments and are as riddled with inconsistencies. Recently, for example, the evolutionary psychologist J. Phillipe Rushton replicated Jefferson's triad of black, white, and Indian by transposing it to black, white, and Asian. Rushton continues the long, dare we say Jeffersonian, tradition of linking ardor and intelligence as opposed capacities. For Rushton, Africans are quick to mature sexually, have larger sex organs, are more reproductive, and because of the way they develop both as neonates and as whole cultures, they are both individually and collectively less intelligent. By contrast, Asians develop more slowly, are less sexually productive, have smaller sex organs, and are more intelligent. Whites are in between and therefore "just right." Ardor and intelligence are perfectly married in white ontology and culture. No wonder then that white civilization is superior to other civilizations. No wonder that African Americans perform below par in school and end up so often in prison. That is Rushton's argument in a nutshell. Many Americans, far too many, find it a persuasive argument. It confirms their own suspicions.

Jefferson made Rushton possible. Rushton in turn is a member of an influential group of intellectuals who believe that blacks and whites are separate categories and that blacks are intellectually inferior to whites. They write popular books (among them, for example Herrnstein and Murray's *The Bell Curve*) and influence public policy. And because of Jefferson, even for those of us who find Rushton repulsive—a racist hiding behind pseudo-science—it is almost impossible to imagine a society where people are "color blind," even when that would seem like the just and fair way to be. To not see race we assume that someone must make every effort not to look, not to notice what is as plain as the nose on your face.

This is what we are stuck with today. This is why it seems so perplexingly impossible to integrate our collective past at places like Monticello today, despite our best intentions. There, a virtual segregation—we have our ancestors, you have yours—underwrites resentments and discomforts which reinforce an ongoing self-segregation. Administrators of places like Monticello dream of a day when such virtual segregation might disappear, as the demographics of the visiting population changes—as it becomes, so the euphemism goes, more "diverse." But racism would not be a problem at all if it were simply a matter of your believing that you are better than me because of the racial differences that you believe divide us into separate groups. Racism is only a problem because belief seems to be translated, in a systematic way, into material inequity. To return to the image of Isaac at Monticello: Isaac (who, like other slaves, did not have a last name of his own—a patrimony) lived in a shack on Mulberry Row and was a blacksmith because this is where people like Jefferson believed he should be and where people like Jefferson had the power to keep him. The large differences between racial categories in distributions of wealth, income, and in the access to what Pierre Bourdieu calls "cultural capital" is but the echo and ongoing reiteration of this material and cultural fact. Race is a cultural construct. Because it is a cultural construct it continues to affect how we live in our world, how we make and remake it, and how we experience that world of our own devising.

Lauje, Manjaco, and Race

In riposte to the obviousness of race, anthropologists have, beginning with Franz Boas in the early twentieth century, argued that race is a folk category, not an empirical fact. Race is a folk category like the belief in Umpute among Lauje or in the belief in ancestors among Manjaco. Both Lauje and Manjaco make momentous decisions based on the knowledge that things we know do not exist indeed do exist, do have power. Because they act as if Umpute and ancestors are real, these things effectively become real. That is, they have a *reality effect.* Culture is a conjurer; it is the magic of culture to make a belief come to life.

Thomas Jefferson's wife and Sally Hemings were half sisters. The magic of cultural conventions, and the laws they gave rise to, made one woman white and the other black. In the American vernacular, the dark alchemy of the one-drop rule made a person who might look white into a person who was defined and treated as black. Yet, paradoxically, in the same vernacular, an Indian ancestor, distant and dead to be sure, makes some of us more American rather than less white.

The vernacular legerdemain of the one-drop rule continues to define us today. You cannot be white and know that you have a black ancestor. You can, however, be white and proud to have Cherokee blood. Likewise, at Monticello, the Woodsons and other African Americans, whatever their genetic heritage, are black and are expected to feel a certain kinship to a blacksmith whose image Monticello so proudly reproduces, or to Sally Hemings, while white people, no matter what their origins, are thought to be associated with Thomas Jefferson, even if they are short and dark-haired, swarthy, stupid. Our vernacular makes me kin to Jefferson and the Woodsons my dark Other; our vernacular makes me see separate races where no rigid separations in fact exist.

Vernaculars are the stuff of culture—of folk beliefs. But it is nearly impossible to make "a folk" see that what they know for a fact is merely a bunch of folk tales and superstitions. One way anthropology has tried to do this is via comparison. We reveal the magic of culture by way of contrast. So anthropologists have tried to ascertain whether there are societies where race does not exist.

I would say that race does not exist in Lauje and Manjaco. Though, because I am a white American, steeped in the kinds of routines of seeing and believing that are our collective habit, it was not until I had come back to America, worked at Monticello, and read Jefferson's *Notes on the State of Virginia* that

I finally noticed how profound were the differences in how they saw human difference.

One day I was with a group of young Lauje men, walking—nearly jogging—in single file as Lauje do, along a narrow path in the mountains. We were stripped to the waist and sweaty. The Lauje, with their machetes slung low on their hips, barefooted with thick, wide-splayed toes, moved smoothly and quickly along the muddy trail; in running shoes, I was slipping and barely keeping up. We plunged through some tall grass around a curve to confront a bunch of children playing near a couple of small houses on stilts. As soon as the children saw me, they ran. When I asked my companions why, one answered, "They're afraid of your body hair," touching his smooth chest for emphasis. My body hair: evidence to me that Lauje and I were biologically different. Yet to me their wide-splayed and thickly padded flat feet were not such a sign. I figured the feet flattened that way, and the toes grew strong and independent, like blunt fat fingers, because of all that climbing and descending along rain-slicked paths. Lauje trails never traversed; they always followed the shortest route, straight up a mountain slope or straight down. Walking those trails daily would turn anyone's feet into such perfectly adapted (ugly to be sure) appendages. My toes had practically atrophied from years of wearing shoes. But when my Lauje companion alluded to my hair—they had none, no beards to speak of, and no body hair—I assumed that he was noticing what I would call a biological difference. Yet that was not his perspective. For him my hair was—like the difference between his flat, splayed feet and my narrow, arched ones—a consequence of lifestyle. "Your hair," he explained, "your chest hair, and the hair on your legs—if you didn't wear a shirt and long pants, and you always walked in the thickets and sharp grass like us, it would all wear off and you'd be smooth-skinned just like us."

Lauje tended to treat the differences they discovered between us in much the same way that Jefferson had treated differences between Europeans and Indians. Like Jefferson, they also assumed a fundamental kinship that transcended any obvious differences in appearance or attitude. My wife and I were, after all, the descendants of the "younger sibling"—the voracious child with the huge appetite and the wherewithal to satisfy it. If all humans were essentially kin, all children of ancestors who shared a common origin in the ridges around the "*polu irandu*" or "inscribed rock" in the river valley just beneath our ridgeline home, Lauje also recognized variations in body types and shapes of people. Humans in contrast to other animals were like chickens in contrast to other birds. Chickens, they pointed out, could be one of several colors, yet a black or red or yellow or speckled chicken was still a chicken, while "all other birds" (in the Lauje vernacular ornithology) were of a single color, a single type. Thus the varieties of parrots or doves that cleaved the air of the mountains were each considered to be a separate type, but not the chickens. Thus too humans were multiple in shape, color and form, yet all the same. Lauje had an understanding of biological variation that dovetailed with modern Western biology. Human beings are a polymorphic species; they are not a polytypic species.

Above all, Lauje tended to privilege culture and environment when they talked about differences between groups of people. I had body hair because I wore a shirt and trousers. In privileging cultural differences over biological ones, Lauje were much the same as Manjaco, who, despite years of racializing colonialism, still tended to overlook skin color in favor of cultural difference, a fact I tended to overlook because of my tendency to translate Manjaco words signaling cultural difference into Western terms of race. Thus it was that after an acquaintance of mine, an African American who worked in the country's capital of Bissau, came to visit me to get a taste of village life, it took me several moments to realize that when a Manjaco asked me, "Who was that white guy?" they were asking about my very dark-skinned friend. Manjaco tend to use the terms white and black—words they inherit from the Portuguese—as cultural markers. Manjaco who spend time in the city and who work in white-collar kinds of jobs are "white." They wear "white" clothes and eat "white" food. Whites, whether they have Manjaco grandparents or Portuguese or American grandparents, it is often assumed, do not like to live "in the bush" with "black" Manjaco. And this is because they find the food unpleasant, the accommodations all too rustic. So when they asked after my "white" (African American) friend, they were especially curious why a well-off "white" like him would want to visit a village. What would be the pleasure in such an excursion?

Even though Manjaco privileged cultural differences over biological ones, they did recognize that there was such a thing as race. Race, as they recognized it, was a European vernacular. They were quick to point out to me that Portuguese were "racist." They used the Portuguese word to say so because there was no equivalent in Manjaco. To Manjaco, that Portuguese were "racist" made their way of looking at things especially *atrassado* (backward, stupid)—another word they borrowed from Portuguese, and one the Portuguese had routinely used to characterize Africans. "We are *atrassado* too," a young Manjaco man explained to me as we rode a bus together in Lisbon one summer when I visited Manjaco living and working in that European capital. "Africans are *atrassado* because of colonialism. But Portuguese have no excuse. They could be as advanced as anyone, but many of them choose to be *atrassado,* choose to be ignorant, to be lazy, and to call us lazy and stupid. Yet, who works hardest here in Lisbon? Africans!"

The idea of race is not a human universal. The idea that entire groups of people are superior to others because of inherent biological qualities is an idea we owe to the history of the transatlantic slave trade in the context of the development of egalitarian worldviews. Once there were racist Portuguese; now there are Manjaco who speak fluently the language of race and racism. This is because the concept of race is a compelling concept. This is because the kinds of racializing discourses that Americans such as Thomas Jefferson invented and perfected have become, like capitalism and democracy, universalized discourses—they are a part of the collateral damage of globalization.

Like race, the idea of culture is also becoming a universal discourse. At times culture can stand as an antidote to race and racism when culture is talked about in relativistic terms, when we assume that all people are cultural beings but that no one culture has the best only answers for what constitutes a good life and a good society. But when cultures are ranked or when culture is seen as an unchanging essence, it can also be a kind of cage, as limiting and stigmatizing as race. Indeed, it is the concept of an almost insurmountable cultural difference based on cultural Othering that allowed for colonialism—a topic we turn to next.

4

The Colonialist's Dress Code

If you think about Monticello as Geertz would, it, like *Notes on the State of Virginia*, is a text. But Monticello is a text written in artifacts. Jefferson clearly thought of his home as a model that conveyed a message. When Jefferson was designing and decorating Monticello, he considered the messages it would convey—through its architecture and accoutrements on display—to those who visited him there on his mountaintop. Nothing about Monticello was accidental, or at least much of what was in the building was there for display. Even though he often wrote about the house as a private refuge and a place he could inhabit with his family, he also thought of it as a public place—an office, a library, and above all a museum and monument that told a story to its many visitors. That story, like the story Jefferson told in *Notes on the State of Virginia*, is about the nature of human nature. It is also about the nature of culture.

When you visit Monticello today, you enter through the East Portico. This is how you would have entered in Jefferson's day as well. After you pass under wooden pillars painted to look like sandstone, you see a clock face on the temple-like entryway. In an era when God was often likened to a great clock-maker, this giant timepiece signaled much about Jefferson's aspirations—to understand the world and take its pulse, to discover its patterns and movements, and to show that there were mechanisms and systems that governed such movements. Jefferson kept a close watch on the passage of time; he also maintained a meticulous record of the weather. Science was a hobby as well as a mission.

Entering Monticello, you pass under the clock to enter into a roomful of artifacts, including various objects Lewis and Clark collected from the Indians on their expedition: painted buffalo robes, weaponry, painted shields, moccasins, and a peace pipe. There are also mastodon bones, maps, a model of an Egyptian pyramid, copies of Renaissance paintings, and a concave mirror. This room—Jefferson called it his "Indian hall"—was the most public space in the house. People who came to ask Jefferson for favors sat here while they waited to be called for their interview.

Straight ahead are double glass doors. Beyond them is another public space, albeit a more exclusive domain. Here honored guests—people closer to Jefferson in social station, and there were several such visitors to Monticello every year—spent their evenings with Jefferson and his family. They might have played music or listened to music; Jefferson was adept with the violin. There is also a harpsichord—standard equipment for an aristocratic house-hold. On the wall are paintings—there is a portrait of John Locke, and there are copies of Renaissance art works Jefferson acquired while he was in France.

These two public spaces amount to a commentary on human nature and culture. They divide up in a way that was to become a standard in Western thinking about these questions. The first room is about nature and conveys the idea that some cultures are more natural than others. The Indian is close to the land; of the land, nearly naked in his humanity, the Indian is original. But it is also about the continuity between those Indians and more elevated so-cieties such as Egypt. It argues for the possibility of a global all-encompassing human nature that is an extension of nature itself—mastodon bones, maps of continents. The second room is more exclusively about culture in its elevated sense: culture as civilization, being cultured as being civilized.

Jefferson was well aware of what Europeans of culture and bearing thought of Americans: They could never be civilized; they would always be tainted by the brute nature that surrounded them. To many Europeans of culture and taste, Americans were a new people and therefore callow, less sophisticated, crude. *Notes on the State of Virginia* was one answer to what Jefferson regarded as a common European prejudice about Americans. The second room, with its harpsichord and its copies of European masterworks, was another answer. This room demonstrated that Americans could be civilized, as civilized as any European, because they appreciated what civilization had to offer.

This room, like museums today, was built on the premise that if you as-sociate with the right kinds of objects, then their power—the knowledge they contain, and the beauty that imbues them—will rub off on you. Look at a portrait of John Locke, and you will perhaps learn to be like John Locke, or at least to recognize what an elevated sensibility looks like. Play music on the harpsichord or the violin and not only are you demonstrating your civility, but you are acquiring it. Culture, or civilization, is something any human—if they have basic intelligence—can acquire. This is the nature of culture. Culture, or becoming cultured, is a pedagogical process.

From this room, you could walk straight out into the garden, which Jefferson designed to be encountered along a meandering oval path. Walk on that path and you pass beautiful flowers culled from around the world—South Africa, Asia, Europe—all the known places of Jefferson's day. Bracketing the oval is a stand of august trees also from near and far. Jefferson's garden is at least as beautiful as his house and just as innovative in its creative copying. His house harkens to a Roman temple. It encapsulates the Jeffersonian dream of America as a civilization emerging out of the wilderness. The garden harkens, in its rounded forms, to nature. It blends into the forest groves that surround it. Both speak to Jefferson's worldliness. He is civilized because he is cosmopolitan. His taste is eclectic, but nonetheless exalted. His acquisitiveness is expansive, but what he likes is always the best of what there is. He can take the best that the world has to offer and make a home for it on his mountaintop. Plants, paintings, architectural features, technological devices, hundreds of books, the best of the Western philosophical and scientific traditions in six or so languages— everything from everywhere. In collecting, he demonstrates and displays that he has the best, most sophisticated and refined taste. He likes pasta, vegetables, and fish (not just any meat); he likes wine, not just cider; and he tries to make wines that will rival those he has collected from France. What he plays on his violin and what he reads in his library are the best civilization has to offer.

Jefferson never considered America to be less civilized than Europe even though it was a young country. Nor did he think he would become less American in being civilized. The two rooms argue that one could be both at once. The first room displays a collection of artifacts that assert that America has a natural history. Mastodon bones and maps, but also Indians. You collect and you possess. Others see what you collect and they infer something about your character. Jefferson is American. His portico, as the historian Merrill Peterson emphasized, "faced the wilderness." The room behind the portico contained this wilderness, and Jefferson's appreciation of its beauty and value intimated his stewardship over that land. Just as Americans such as Jefferson occupied a land with its own peculiar flora and fauna, so too could they have a local culture. They would share in the collective possession of a nation, they could have a common sentiment based on a common relationship to the land they inhabited, and they could also participate in a global culture, the culture of a universal civilization. The second room and the garden speak to that.

But the separation of the two rooms also hints at a certain potential segregation. The Indians are over there with the artifacts. They inhabit a separate space from John Locke, even as Jefferson straddles both spaces. Thus Jefferson admired Indians because their culture was an ancestral version of the culture he asserted the new America would exemplify. Jefferson was a sort of cultural relativist, but the question the two rooms ask, perhaps without his realizing it, is whether an Indian could cross the threshold from nature to civilization and still be an Indian. This is a question that links the concept of culture with the concept of history. History is about change and transformation. What happens to cultures, like Indian cultures, when they change through contact with other cultures?

In Jefferson's era the answer was equivocal. Indians were still a presence to be reckoned with. They occupied large parts of the land that Jefferson, through the Louisiana Purchase, had appropriated for the United States. One solution to the problem of their presence was to drive them further away into the wilderness or to fight them and exterminate them; another was to encourage assimilation. Jefferson once emphasized that in a war "they would kill few of us" but "we would kill most of them." He, like others of his time, saw such wars as inevitable if repugnant, so he often argued for the second solution. Both solutions, however, implied that Indian culture could not survive in tandem with the culture of the settlers. Wilderness and civilization were antithetical.

Those who asserted that Indians would have to be driven away or killed to make way for civilization assumed that the Indians would never give up their customs. By contrast, Jefferson had argued in *Notes* that Indians had the capacity for civilization and claimed that they could become American, especially through intermarriage. Indians as a group would die out; Indian individuals would live on, but they would be stripped of their culture. Later Jefferson would become more pessimistic. Indians who tried to become like Europeans inevitably corrupted themselves as a result. They lost one culture and gained at best a caricature of another. They ended up as drunken buffoons, bums.The view that people lost something when they tried to become civilized became the dominant view after Jefferson. It came to be a common assumption that the cultural hybrid, like the racially mixed person, the "half-breed," was worse off because of that mixing.

It was a view that would eventually be enshrined in museums throughout the Western world. If in Jefferson's day there was still the possibility of blurring boundaries between nature and culture and among cultures—Indians or Egypt in the first room—by the later part of the nineteenth century the two kinds of culture were housed and displayed in entirely different spaces. For civilization, there would be art museums and museums of national history. In these museums, history itself, as the forward march of time, would organize the way rooms were arranged and the way artifacts were displayed in those rooms. The nation would be portrayed in such museums as the culmination of a historical process. By contrast, for non-Western cultures, there would be ethnographic museums, which often became part of what would be called natural history museums. Artifacts of the Indians, and of tribal people from places like Polynesia, New Guinea, and Africa, even dioramas depicting tribal people in their natural habitat, were displayed in one wing of the same building that contained stuffed birds and mammals, reptiles and fossils, meteorites, gemstones—nature in all its plenitude. If these cultures in nature had a history, it would usually be associated with the past or with an era that was "timeless"— that is, without progress.

Such museums came to exemplify an attitude that was perhaps already emergent in Jefferson's views toward Indians and culture. His views about being cultured reveal an often-remarked-upon paradox in cultural theory. The paradox is that if you are of a dominant group you assume that you can take or borrow ideas and practices from other groups without losing your identity. Your culture is civilization, and civilization is omnivorous. By taking from everywhere, but only what is the best, you reveal the essence of your culture. You are civilized because you can pick and choose. Art museums contain elements from all civilizations. Because they represent the best the world has to offer, they exemplify your taste, your exalted position in the scheme of world cultures. You are in the present and you face toward the future as you look back on the past you traversed to arrive at this culminating point. Yet if you are a member of the dominant, you also assume that if a member of the dominated group borrows from you, they lose their identity. Or worse, that even when a member of the dominated group takes from you, they inevitably fall short. By borrowing and borrowing inappropriately, they reveal their inferiority.

Clothing as Culture

Throughout the West's history of its encounters with cultural others, this paradox has also revealed itself in the way Westerners use clothing to talk of cultural borrowing. Indeed, it could be argued that clothing is among the most fascinating and revealing metaphors about how Westerners since the Enlightenment have thought about culture. In the West, the naked person is close to nature, is natural. The clothed person is cloaked in the cultural. Just as there are different styles of dress, so too are there different kinds of culture. That there is always a naked body underneath the clothing reveals that nature precedes culture and that nature—human nature—is potentially a universal.

Westerners have often imagined that they could become like the natives or closer to nature by stripping off their clothing. In the original novel about Tarzan by Edgar Rice Burroughs, Tarzan is the child of English aristocrats. Naked in the African forest, he reveals his capacity to learn from all the animals and to dominate them with a kind of firm paternalism. Naked, that is, stripped of the trappings of civilization, he reveals his inner and natural superiority. Yet after meeting Jane, rescuing her, and learning English, he returns to civilization, where he easily fits into the garb of a lord. In the Western imagination, a lord is always a lord, no matter what style of dress he wears.

By contrast, in this same imaginary, if the native tries to dress in a civilized style, he always makes a fool of himself. The English had several words for such natives. In the African colonies they called them "savvy boys." In India and elsewhere, they called them "wogs," supposedly from "Right (or as it would be spoken by someone affecting, in an exaggerated way, the accent of the upper class, "Wright") honorable gentleman." Wogs—those "right honorable gentlemen"—talked like you and dressed like you, but they looked and sounded like clowns when they did. They were too polite, too neat, too concerned with how they looked. They were oily, unctuous; they pronounced their words too perfectly and too elaborately, as if their tongues had to massage every syllable. They exaggerated without meaning to and they therefore announced in every aspect of their comportment that they were not really like us at all. A wog always was and always would be "not white, not quite."

This enduring idea about culture and clothing—that the natives can never quite escape who they really are even when they imitate Westerners "to a T," while Westerners can strip off their culture at will to be like natives if they wish—became especially prevalent in the late nineteenth and early twentieth centuries, in the era of Western imperialism or colonialism. During this era, the nation-states of Europe and the United States took political control over vast spaces of the globe in order, so they claimed, to more rationally manage the production of resources and in order to bring progress to primitive places. Because this idea of cultural difference is associated with colonialist domination, I will call this the colonialist's dress code. I will argue in the next chapter that the colonialist's dress code also has had its influence on anthropology. As we shall see, the anthropologist's dress code shares much with the colonialist's dress code even though the history of anthropology is a story of anthropology's struggle against the underlying ideas that endorsed colonialism as a civilizing mission. But for now I will stick to the colonial era and specifically to a patch of colonial landscape I know well—the area that was made up in part of the future Guinea-Bissau.

Naked Maidens

While Jefferson was writing *Notes* and working to make Monticello into a museum, two Frenchmen—Gaspard-Theodore Mollien and Silvestre Golberry—were visiting that patch of West Africa. Their descriptions reveal the colonialist's dress code. Golberry was an engineer and amateur naturalist. He wanted to explore West Africa in the same scientific spirit as Captain Cook when he sailed through the Pacific. Golberry, like Jefferson, believed that he was helping to make the world a better place for humanity at large. Golberry went to Africa to gather information that would be useful to traders and merchants in France. He wanted to collect information about local kings and chiefs and about what their subjects grew and manufactured. He also wanted to learn about Portuguese and English slave trading. Golberry was a patriot and his mission was to discover how to give the French an advantage in the regional economic system. Golberry was a Frenchman, but he was also a man of science. He also went to Africa to find out as much as he could about the natural world in the Senegambia. Among his many goals was to bring back several skins and skeletons of the hippopotamus for the French natural history museum. Golberry wanted to bring hippo bones back to France because he assumed that the natural history museum was a place that French citizens visited and learned about the ubiquity of reason in nature. Science led to social progress. Social progress led to a materially and spiritually better life for more and more people.

Like Golberry before him, the geographer Gaspard-Theodore Mollien had been ordered by the French government to make a tour of the Senegambia region. Mollien traveled more or less alone, roughing it when he had to, visiting places rarely encountered by Europeans. He also visited the entrepots—the fortified villages that were European trading enclaves along the coast. Bissau at the time was among the oldest. Ostensibly a Portuguese possession, most of its inhabitants were *grumetes*—Christianized natives who worked for pay as crewmen on coastal trading vessels, stevedores, boat builders, artisans, and clerks. Others in the entrepot included *degredados*—criminals who had been conscripted into military service—merchants, their African wives and offspring, and a handful of government functionaries. It was a hodgepodge and hybrid place. The fort was in disrepair, the rusted cannon no longer worked. The cemetery and the only freshwater well were beyond the entrepot gates. The Africans surrounding the entrepot treated its inhabitants as their paying guests. So the local African ruler (a king of the same kind as the nearby Manjaco had) periodically visited Bissau to collect his *daxa,* or tribute. Mollien described him thus with characteristic sarcasm:

> At noon the great monarch . . . made his entry. . . . Never did a Negro more strongly resemble an orangutan: he wore a red coat, short breeches of the same color, fastened at the knees with crystal buckles, his spindle shanks were covered with white stockings, but from habit he walked without shoes. . . . This negro was so uncomfortable in his European costume that he might have been taken for a wicker effigy.

Uncomfortable, perhaps, but such clothing had long been the style of choice for local rulers who received their outfits, along with a sword, umbrella, and other accoutrements, as part of the tribute the Europeans paid for the privilege of clinging to their tiny sliver of Africa and carrying out trade there. To Europeans, however, such "unshod monsters" were a kind of insult. That they dressed like Europeans made the insult sting all the more, and the Europeans' response was to ridicule these rulers. "This negro was so uncomfortable in his European costume he might have been taken for a wicker effigy" or an "orangutan."

Here Mollien was echoing what other Europeans were saying about Africans or people of African descent pretty much everywhere. Recall Jefferson's disparaging comments about the creativity and intelligence of "negroes" in his *Notes on the State of Virginia.* Thus too, David Hume, upon traveling to the Caribbean, could dismiss civilized black Jamaicans as "parroting" European ways. "In Jamaica indeed they talk of one negroe as a man of many parts and learning; but its likely he is admired for very slender accomplishments like a parrot who speaks a few words plainly." Clearly race intersected with the distinctions Europeans wished to make between themselves and their primitive *alters.* Indeed, while it is true that others who are "not white, not quite" have similarly been sneered at, it is blacks and Africans who have been most consistently accused of merely aping Europeans when they appear to act like them. Africans are modernity's monkeys.

Mollien's animus combined the generic with the personal. He had arrived in Bissau after a long and rough overland journey. He was exhausted and in a low mood:

> The state of my clothes which were almost in rags, drew around me an innumerable crowd of negroes who incessantly insulted me and laughed at my appearance. . . . When I presented myself at the gate, the black sentinel inferring the meanness of my condition from the bad state of my clothing, said to me in Portuguese, "Comrade take off your hat." Offended at receiving such an order . . . I pulled the hat further upon my head.

Mollien, like so many others, found the local Africans to be typically if inappropriately disrespectful. As the Portuguese trader Andre Almada had reported some two hundred years before, "because they are very practiced in our language, they treat us very badly, giving us beatings, deceiving us, and taking from us our hats and swords in broad daylight."

If Europeans such as Mollien wanted to disparage those clothed Africans who lorded it over them, they often praised the naked African by way of contrast. Here is Golberry describing the girls he encountered on his visit to Guinea. He is writing at the same time that Jefferson purportedly began his affair with the very young Sally Hemings:

> I have often contemplated with much attention girls of thirteen or fourteen . . . when she is tall or slender, supple and well formed, but particularly when she has only a natural degree of obesity, is a species of beauty unknown in Europe: her large, tender and gentle eyes are full of benevolence, languor, and voluptuousness, they dart forth with inexpressible candor, the rays of health and love, and it is impossible to prevent their impression . . . their teeth are small, even, and of a more agreeable whiteness than the most beautiful pearls. . . . These young negresses when they are well made have a small head . . . straight neck . . . the lines from the neck to the shoulders, back, and breast are extremely graceful; their bosoms, which indeed are often literally overflowing, are well defined, properly separated, and of such freshness, and substance that their extremities, instead of tending toward the pendent position, are rather inclined to an opposite.

The naked maiden would become a constant figure in colonial-era writing. She appears from the earliest traveler's accounts all the way to the end of colonialism in the mid-twentieth century and beyond. Take, for example, this description by Archibald Lyall of his visit in the mid-1930s to a Guinean village ("a sunny little Utopia such as I had never seen") as the guest of a Portuguese administrator, named Osorio:

> At sundown we heard the sound of singing in the forest, and all the village girls appeared in single file along a forest path, singing a triumphal chant and bearing on their heads, like a row of ebony caryatids, basketfuls of fish caught that day. . . . Osorio distributed beads and brightly coloured kerchiefs among his little girl friends and soon we had a crowd around us. There was Musa's sister, Fatu; she was about fifteen, very pretty, vivacious and light-skinned. The village belle, I think, was Cadi, who was about the same age; she had a beautiful figure with small firm breasts and a skin of black satin. . . . All day we idled . . . pottering around the village, watching the life of the people and flirting with such of the village girls who knew a little Creole. Osorio said what a success little Fatu

would be if only one could bring her to London as she stood, always laughing, naked to the waist, with blue and red beads twined in her hair; but of course, even if it were possible, the sunny little negress would simply whither and die in the cold, unhappy city, like a flower plucked from the garden.

For Lyall, it is the innocent maiden that makes the village a "forest paradise." Her innocence and beauty encapsulate the beauty of the landscape and of her culture. To Lyall this culture is exemplified by a kind of naïve lack of material-ism. He describes the villagers prizing "every possible waste-product of our visit . . . empty bottles, empty match-boxes, even used matches were snapped up for use as toys. . . . It was a very pleasant sensation to be able to act the Santa Claus to these simple, unspoilt little creatures by merely distributing the things one would have thrown away anyway. . . . All the next day we left our most highly prized treasures, beads, beer bottles, tins full of cigarettes, laying about unguarded. Anybody could have walked off with them, nobody did."

Here Lyall echoes what Golberry wrote 150 years before. Golberry averred that "[h]ospitality is in Africa a general virtue; and misers are unknown in this country. . . . I did not see a single man afflicted with the passion of accumulating gold, silver and other precious articles," and he admonished his readers:

> You pity the negroes because they are poor . . . but reflect on all the desires which you are tormented, on all the things which are wanting to your happiness, and on all those which they do not require in order to be happy. Let us think about all the crimes and all the vices that are generated by riches. . . . The ancients placed poverty on the level of the gods. Happy negroes! She is your tutelary goddess. You are rich in what you do not covet, as well as everything with all the use of with you are unacquainted.

Golberry's celebration of Africa's moral superiority might scan as hypocriti-cal. His mission, after all, was to discover how best to insert French economic interests into a region that was largely controlled by Portuguese and English trade—how, in short, to pry open the African market and make terms of trade that would favor the French. Thus he was pleased to note that "[i]t should never be forgotten that they are far from possessing our ideas of vanity and pride; that we may gain their goodwill at a trivial expense, and that those things which they do not possess, however trifling may be their value, often form very desirable objects for them." In sum, primitive people are morally superior to us and therefore they can be exploited. As long as they are "unspoilt," as Lyall kept stressing that they were, they remain honest, upright—but they also go for trinkets, toys.

Lyall contrasts his "unspoilt," "sunny little negress" with a traveling companion called "the talk of Bolama"—a notorious prostitute who paints her nails and dyes her hair, all in a futile effort to ward off the effects of the cigarettes she incessantly smokes and the alcohol she drinks as she keeps up with the men. When Lyall wrote his chapter on a "Forest Paradise," he was deploying images from a long history of images about the primitive in relation to the modern that connect him to explorers such as Golberry and to the more exalted discourses of European philosophy associated with what came to be known as the Enlightenment. Enlightenment philosophers stressed that the future could be better than the present by escaping the superstitions and constraints of the past in favor of a social order built on reason. Yet Enlightenment thinkers such as Rousseau also criticized the social order they saw around them as corrupt and corrupting—courtly comportment was described as a kind of prostitution. Better, according to philosophers such as Rousseau, to strip off the layers of a corrupting civilization and return to a human nature most closely approximated by what Rousseau called the noble savage.

Rousseau put the noble savage on a pedestal, so as to more thoroughly denigrate courtly society. For him the denizens of Versailles were all much like Lyall's "talk of Bolama"—that painted and pasty backwater whore. For other thinkers in Rousseau's era and after, the noble savage was balanced with another image of the primitive that stressed tradition's tendency toward irrational or unfair constraint. Again the maiden is an important figure, except in this case she is, to give a typical example, consigned to a harem, veiled, in purdah, or perhaps a victim of suttee—that is, forced to commit suicide at her husband's death. In this scheme, traditional society is seen as less free than modern society. Women suffer, and shadowy men—their husbands, the pasha, the raja, the fat, bearded man in the turban—benefit from their constraint.

In short, for Europeans from the Enlightenment onward, women embodied two sets of images and discourses about the primitive or the traditional in relationship to the civilized or modern. In this twinned scheme, the primitive can be morally superior to the modern, much as the Garden of Eden is better than all the civilizations that come after it, yet the modern as a future possibility is also defined as superior to the past, to tradition. It is a paradox that later lies at the heart of what anthropologists and sociologists and scholars in history, philosophy, and literature call modernity.

Modernity is a term that refers to the form of consciousness of people in modern societies. Modern societies are defined as societies that are knitted together by a capitalist economic system while being divided up into independent nation-states. Members of such societies assume that capitalism—a particular economic system—and nation—a particular form of government—are wedded together, and that both systems are at once manifestations of and motors for progress. They generally believe that progress is good. It is the goal that drives us. But they also know that progress—entailed in the expansion of capitalism and national control—can be painful, can destroy. In this view modernity is contrasted with tradition, with tradition standing for all that resists progress but also all that will be destroyed by progress. That which can be destroyed by progress includes a sense of community, a religious sensibility, and an affinity for nature. Modern people, in short, can believe in the power and essential rightness of progress while also being nostalgic for tradition, for the primitive, for the past.

The colonialist's dress code contained both sets of this twinned imagery. In the colonialist imagination, the naked maiden in her forest paradise beckoned you to Africa. She inhabited an about-to-be-lost Eden. Ironically, it was about to be lost because you also brought with you the very things that might spoil this paradise. So you also imagined that the naked maiden called out for you to protect her against corruptions of tradition itself, as often as not in the guise of a man—her husband, perhaps who unfairly constrained her or used her selfishly. Saving her from the corruptions of traditional culture became a justification for colonial intervention.

Here, for example, are excerpts from a tract written by Frederico Pinheiro Chagas to drum up support for a final campaign against the coastal peoples of Guinea. He had served in a military campaign in 1908 to "castigate" the Africans who surrounded Bissau. The campaign had been technically a success. The Africans were subdued by superior military force. But Chagas worried that if they were not irrevocably pacified the situation would return to the status quo: local men taking advantage of local women and making fun of the Europeans,

> Tall, strong … they live a lazy life of drunkenness and *souteneurs*. They only fight. It is the women who work and sustain the men. … It is the women who come to the *praca* to sell water, fruit, eggs, milk … all the consumables necessary for the town. It is they who do the odd jobs of loading and unloading the commercial boats. It is they in sum who are employed in satisfying the particular wants of their men. … The husband waits at the gates of Bissau, wrapped in a type of toga—his *chic* outfit. After receiving the money, he goes to buy rum to get drunk, or buys gunpowder which he uses to celebrate his dead or to fight us.

According to Chagas, when such men did "fight us" they made fun of the Portuguese by mimicking them in their language. Invisible in the thick bush, they yelled insults, calling out to the governor, whom they knew by name, or they imitated the officers' voices, giving orders like "fire the cannon, fire the cannon. Cease fire!"

These juxtaposed images of the man who makes fun of you, using what he has learned of your culture to mimic you, and the maiden who waits for you to protect her from the unfair constraints that man imposes upon her also reveal a widely-remarked-upon paradox inherent in colonialist practice and discourse. Colonialism of the late nineteenth and early twentieth centuries differed from the period of colonization that brought Jefferson's ancestors to Virginia in that it was less about conquest and settlement than about political, economic, and cultural incorporation. The charter for colonialism depended on the belief that what the colonizer brought to the colonized would make the colonized better. The idea of colonialism depended on a vision of the world that was in essence Hobbesian. Savage beasts needed to be civilized. They resisted you and you often had to use force to civilize them. You needed to be sovereign so that you could give the savage civilization by teaching him to think and act like you.

Colonialists needed to modernize backward Africans in order to make the colonial enterprise a success. But do away with their backwardness, get Africans to "evolve" (as the French put it), to "assimilate" (as the Portuguese put it), and you destroy the foundations of colonialism. The problem for the colonialist inevitably became: What to do with the *evolué*, the *assimilado*? Were they proof that the civilizing mission had been accomplished? Or were they still savage beasts in disguise?

Bad Copies

One widely invoked solution was to ignore their presence or to treat them as exceptions and dangerous exceptions at that. This at least is what Portuguese colonial administrators tended to do with Manjaco. Manjaco were among the first labor migrants in the region that comprises the Casamance (in southern Senegal), the Gambia, and the rivers of Guinea-Bissau, and therefore were among the first in the region to count potentially as assimilated. In 1792, the British colonists in Bolama in southern Guinea-Bissau would not have survived as long as they did were it not for seasonal Manjaco migrants who worked willingly for wages. The peanut and rubber booms of the middle to late nineteenth century depended heavily on Manjaco labor. Concurrently, Manjaco became a prominent presence in the Euro-African urban enclaves that emerged out of this trade. In 1856, a Manjaco "named Domingo" was the "*porte a parole*" appointed by the French in the entrepot of Carrabance on the Casamance.

Meanwhile, further up river in Sedhiou, the sergeant of the garrison of native troops was a Manjaco. In 1849, characterizing the "rivers of Guinea" as a whole, the intrepid trader and amateur geographer Bertrand-Bocande noted that Manjaco typically worked as sailors or stevedores for Portuguese merchants on the coast. Becoming "fluent in their language," they "made others consider them as Portuguese in the French and English colonies." By the time Portuguese-led troops conquered the Manjaco kingdom in 1913, Manjaco had been a cosmopolitan presence in the region for well over a hundred years.

In the years after conquest, Manjaco became a constant headache for the Portuguese even though, to the Portuguese, the typical Manjaco was "a worker who had escaped, for the most part, the atavistic indolence inherent in the great mass of the negro population." The Manjaco region was rich in resources to be exploited for the benefit of the colony and its civilizing mission. Its forests were like natural oil-palm plantations, so numerous were the trees. Manjaco upland fields already produced more peanuts—the colony's leading export crop—than any other region. But according to Portuguese administrators, Manjaco had the disturbing propensity to vote with their feet against the colony and for French Senegal or British Gambia. By the 1930s roughly a fifth of them in any given year were hard at work in neighboring Senegal, their labor adding nicely to the French balance sheet, their absence frustrating Portuguese ambitions to make a colony as prosperous as the French seemed able to do. According to the Portuguese, Manjaco migrated because their own rulers were corrupt. They became tyrants, driving their subjects away. Or they were deposed with alarming regularity because their subjects were impossible to govern. By the 1930s as many as a third of Manjaco chiefships were either vacant or the current officeholders were embroiled in litigation. The upshot was that Manjaco were a particular embarrassment to a colony that—because it had been so hard to rule as specifically Portuguese—was routinely characterized by colonial authorities as an insult to Portuguese identity.

So in the mid-1930s, while Lyall was enjoying his brief stay among the maidens in "a native village in the heart of the jungle," it was not surprising that Antonio de Carvalho Viegas, the Portuguese colonial governor, warned future colonial officers about these same Manjaco—a people who were a particular nuisance because they were constantly crossing the border into Senegal and were, as a result, no longer loyal subjects to the Portuguese colony:

> In general, the colonizer judges the Manjaco from individuals of the race who live together with the white. Nothing is more misleading. The smart Manjaco— putting on the air of civilization that is belied by his ridiculous taste in fashion—

constantly questioning, shrewd in small matters, is only the Manjaco who has
lived in the urban centers. . . . The other, the one that represents the majority,
the one of economic value, the one that works and gathers the palm nut is as
savage . . . [as any primitive].

To Viegas, these "constantly questioning, shrewd" Manjaco were a dangerous aberration. They were a kind of cultural cancer let loose on the body
politic. They were "a nucleus apart, which does not represent, in the sector of
native politics and economics, a valuable element." He wished that they did
not exist, so he asserted that despite what amounted to more than a century,
throughout which migratory travel to urban areas had been a fact of Manjaco
life, that those who had been to "Dakar or Bissau"—those who had learned to
read and write and "petition"—were not "the majority." Moreover, while such
Manjaco appeared civilized, "their ridiculous taste in fashion" proved otherwise. Like the ruler Mollien had described more than a century earlier, they
could be dismissed because the clothes did not fit, nor would they ever fit.

Two decades after Viegas wrote his worried report about the Manjaco in their
off-putting suits, a local colonial administrator wrote a monograph on "Manjaco Bodily Mutilations" that carried a similar anxious message in the guise
of social science. The cover of the short book is decorated with a photograph
of a young Manjaco girl. It shows her scarified torso. A thick cross-hatching of
knotted skin runs from her navel up between her breasts, branching out to her
collarbones. The camera is focused on the belly. The image is clinical. The photo
of the scarified torso was taken for scientific reasons. It was one of dozens used
to illustrate a study of the decline in customary practices of scarification.

Artur Martins de Meireles wrote his monograph and took the photos that
illustrate it at the end of a long and frustrating association with the Manjaco.
For years Meireles had been an administrator among Manjaco when Manjaco
chiefs and rulers seemed so impossible to control because they were so corrupt
or feckless. Meireles had witnessed the ever-increasing exodus of Manjaco
from home villages abroad to the French colonies and burgeoning urban centers they contained. While he was researching the book, the revolution that
would eventually result in the Portuguese retreat from Guinea and indeed the
demise of the Salazarist New State itself was about to begin. Yet these facts only
obliquely appear in his work. Instead, a pretension to science overwhelms the
subject. You learn very little from all the work expended to gather so much
data. The science is big, its product small.

To conduct his inquiry of mutilations as comprehensively as possible,
Meireles used the opportunity another study provided. He had been ordered

to "concentrate" the local population so that a medical team could assess the extent of sleeping sickness among the Manjaco. Once the doctor, sitting at one table, was through examining a patient, she moved to another table, where Meireles's assistant asked the patient to face him and then turn around so that the assistant could record whether scarification was present or absent and where on the torso the scarification occurred. In a short time Meireles was able to collect data on 23,772 females, or roughly 56 percent of the total population. The tables he compiled were a map, as it were, covering almost the entire territory it codified.

Yet Meireles felt compelled to apologize that such an exhaustively illustrated sample was as complete as it could be—as if he were anticipating an audience that might doubt his science. He emphasized that most of the missing Manjaco were "residing abroad" and had "begun to detribalize," thereby losing "interest for an ethnographic study."

Meireles's thesis about tattooing or scarification was simple. According to him, as with other "unevolved peoples," Manjaco had a kind of skin that was perfect for tattooing. Tattooing, in the Manjaco case, was not a religious act. The lines and marks had no "ideographical" significance; they were merely decorative, "a kind of geometry." Scarification was an adolescent preoccupation based on "coquetry and fashion." Yet even as mere fashion, scarification was a quintessential sign of their primitive cultural identity. As Manjaco modernized, as they came into "contact with evolved populations," "this primitive fashion" went out of fashion. By tabulating the incidence of tattooing among women by age, Meireles was able to prove that this fashion was indeed in steep decline.

Meireles's monograph, like Viegas's tirade or even Chagas's angry call to arms, reveals the extent to which Portuguese administrators, an official policy of "assimilation" aside, needed naked Manjaco to practice a self-validating paternalism. For these men the naked maiden and the savage in a suit became the enduring images whose contrasts defined the colonialist's dress code. The images signaled the contradictions inherent in colonialism's civilizing mission and the aesthetic that went with this mission. The savage in the suit represented the "bad copy" which African postcolonial intellectuals such as V. Y. Mudimbe note is the objectification of colonialist disgust. The naked maiden by contrast was an objectification of colonialist desire. In the colonialist aesthetic the good native is invariably a woman, the bad copy is inevitably a man. She is the woman fettered by tradition—all those scars or that tyrannical husband who waits for her at the *praca* gait—she is a vulnerable woman who needs to be protected from tradition's savagery. He is the native who wears your suits, but the style is a little too flamboyant; he is the "unshod monster," the Hobbesian savage beast come to life. You can laugh at his imperfect attempts at imitation. Yet you are often anxious because you suspect that he might mimic you to make fun of you. But it is his presence that allows you to continue practicing an often brutally authoritarian form of government. You can kill, torture, and imprison to maintain an order he threatens to disrupt. Nothing bothered the colonialist more than the bad copy, the "savvy boy," the "wog," because he upset the implicit paternalism of the colonial enterprise. The bad copy violated the colonialist's dress code, while the naked maiden upheld it.

Portugal eventually lost its colonial possessions in wars of independence. Of all the wars—in Angola, in Mocambique, and Guiné—it was in the latter and least internationally known conflict that the government of Portugal suffered its worst defeat. Once they lost there, the officers who were in command mounted a coup that toppled the government in the metropole. Little Guinea-Bissau destroyed the grand pretensions of Salazarism. Between the early 1960s and 1973 Salazarist forces retreated or ceded control of more and more territory. By the end of the war, they held only a few enclaves and very little of the countryside. They had faced an army composed of bad copies and lost.

But throughout the war the scientist-administrators of the colony continued to produce a journal called "The Cultural Bulletin of Portuguese Guinea," which conveyed a timeless, changeless place, as if the war were not happening. In the back of the journal, which was made up of articles about parasitic diseases, quaint tribal customs, development projects—a catalogue of colonial science—there always appeared a set of photographs called "Scenes and Types of Guiné." The "scenes" were landscapes—forests, rivers, rice fields, images of bucolic beauty. The "types" were photographs of native villagers, almost all young women, almost always bare-breasted, almost all smiling into the camera as they kneeled and repaired a basket, or spun cotton, or stirred a cooking pot. As the Portuguese zones of control were overrun, as their power gave way to the revolutionaries, "Scenes and Types" was a constantly reiterated advertisement for Guinea-Bissau as a paradise Rousseau might have imagined. The guerillas who remained offstage, but who drove out the Portuguese, were, to them, the Hobbesian nightmare come true.

5

Taking Pictures in the Field, or the Anthropologist's Dress Code

Ever since there have been cameras, anthropologists have used them to make a record of the ethnographic material they encounter in the field. Before that (and even after) some people made sketches. Malinowski made photographic images of Trobriand canoes with their carved prows, and much else as well—a village of frond-roofed huts with his tent close by, a scene of men carrying a pig lashed upside down on a palm trunk: "Ceremonial destruction during a So'I feast." There are sixty-six such illustrations (and five maps) in his compendious *Argonauts of the Western Pacific: An Account of Native Enterprise and Adventure in the Archipelagoes of Melanesian New Guinea*. Evans-Pritchard punctuated his ethnographic analysis with photos of Nuer cattle, of girls milking cows, of men spearing fish, of leopard-skin chiefs in full regalia. He also used artful sketches of the gourds Nuer used to churn milk or to store cheese, and other implements of day-to-day life: "Bags made from the scrota of a bull and a giraffe," for example, or "Calf's bell-necklace of palm nuts." His monograph, *The Nuer: A description of the modes of livelihood and political institutions of a Nilotic people,* contains a dozen drawings and twenty-six photographic plates.

The sketch is a rendering of an observation. The camera is an extension of the eye. The camera takes visual notes. Anthropologists use these visual notes later to illustrate a lecture, to illuminate the words on the page in a book or journal article; we use these images to prove a point or as an aid to memory—we look at them to conjure up the place again, to recall it. Because the camera takes visual notes for us, and because those notes are a sort of document, we can justify the time we take snapping shots. But we also take pictures or make sketches for the sheer pleasure of the activity.

When I was in the field studying Lauje and Manjaco, I used to take pictures for fun even as I pretended to myself and my subjects that I was doing work.

Taking photographs gave me aesthetic pleasure. As I looked through the lens, I imagined the way the shot would compare to photographs I had seen in books, magazines, and museums. I enjoyed composing a scene, using light and shadow and color to create "art," and I enjoyed planning how best to convey a particular moment or mood or sensibility through a fleeting image.

Above all I took pictures for the reason any tourist takes pictures. A typical tourist shot has the tourist in the foreground and the object of the tourist's gaze in the background. Here you are at the waterfall. The waterfall flows right past your shoulder. Here you are at the plaza; the cathedral looms just behind you. Here you are in the town square in the quaint village on the mountainside. Your arm is around the shoulder of a smiling peasant. She is wearing a headscarf and her wrinkled face is tucked under your arm. Like the cathedral or the waterfall, she is a kind of trophy. If you can't get her to pose with you, you can stroll across the square to the café and buy a postcard of an old woman weaving a sweater while a cat lolls next to her playing with a ball of yarn.

At Colonial Williamsburg I used to take pictures of tourists taking pictures. There were certain scenes that everyone seemed to want to capture on film. In winter it was the doorways of the reconstructed and restored colonial houses, each door decorated with an elaborate Christmas wreath. The wife might pose next to the wreath while her husband snapped a shot. No matter what the season, people loved taking pictures of the horse-drawn carriages driven by a man in full livery. But most of all they all wanted a shot of the stocks in front of the courthouse. In colonial times the stocks were used for punishment. Someone who had been convicted of a petty crime would be forced to stand, their arms and head pinioned by the stocks, in plain view of passersby. To stand like that was painful and above all humiliating. Tourists would pose (usually grinning or laughing) as if they were criminals while a friend, a parent, or a spouse would take the photo.

Tourism is a quintessentially modern activity. Tourism tells us a lot about modernity, which is characterized by a thrilled and troubled relationship to authenticity, memory, and the passage of time. The tourist shots at Williamsburg signaled a sensibility Richard Handler and I came to call "nostalgia-progress." On the one hand tourists looked back on the colonial era as a better time than the present—a time signaled by the horse-drawn carriage and the Christmas wreath. But by the same token they believed that the past was somehow harsher, more crude and cruel, if perhaps more honest and true. The rough justice of the stocks symbolized that for them. Nostalgia-progress embodied the tourists' ambivalent attitude toward the past.

Tourism as a modern activity is about authenticity. We are compelled to visit other places because they seem so full of life, so real, so "timeless," so "untouched." Yet we worry that they might be fake—that the smiling peasant smiles for all the tourists and not for the pleasure of meeting just us. Worse, it is our presence that turns the real into the fake by a sort of malignant alchemy. Tourists pollute. They destroy and corrupt. What once was an exciting place to visit becomes a tourist trap. What once were beautiful baskets or blankets the locals made and used are now knockoffs they make for the tourists. Tourism turns gold into dross. It's a postcard, not the real thing. Postcards are always past tense, what the place used to be like before you got there, what the town square looked like before the tourists occupied the very seats in the café where, in the postcard, a group of old men are sipping coffee and playing with their worry beads.

If we are troubled and thrilled about authenticity and our complicity in its corrosion, we also worry constantly about forgetting, or about losing what we once had, and so we delight in recording and preserving. We scribble in journals or diaries, or we fill albums with photographs of ourselves, our families, our friends, and our travels. Photo albums, like diaries, are records of our existence. We possess a selfhood—a personality—because we have had experiences that we remember, because we have memories. These diary entries, these photos we take of ourselves, our families, and our travels, are objectified memories. Through the chemical magic of photography, experiences have been turned into possessions. Photographs make our experiences valuable. We can look at them again and remember. Or we can show them to others. They are tokens of the really real; like seashells or rocks or coins or stamps, they can be collected, stored, displayed.

Like any tourist, when I was in Africa and Indonesia, I took pictures because I wanted a record that I had been there: something to collect, something to display. When I returned from the field, I enjoyed showing my slides to family and friends and also to students. I was proud of the aesthetic qualities of several and I made sure to include them in my presentations. As I showed my favorite images, I became more and more fascinated by the gap between how the image was perceived and what I knew about the context of its production. Pictures, we all know, lie. They mislead. They hide as much as they reveal. And they do so unintentionally, not only because they are framed and selected and cropped, but because they are seen through the lens of the viewer's culture—in this case through the lens of the culture of modernity. After a while I began to show the images to illustrate to my audience this gap and what its existence can tell us.

Pretty Pictures

Take a look at figures 1 through 5. Three are of women, two are of the king. The first is not a photo I took. It comes from the pages of Meireles's monograph. Two Manjaco maidens look at the camera with perhaps fearful faces. The next is one I took of women fishing. The older women balance baskets on their heads as they bend into the water to scoop up the fish that swarm against the net. A man is in the middle of the frame. He stands in the water right by the net. His arm is thrust out in a forceful gesture, pointed at a young girl clutching a small net who rushes toward you. The camera catches her in mid-stride, almost in mid-air. Her breasts glisten with water. As she rushes toward the camera, holding the net with its fish, she looks straight at us. If it was not such a cliché you might say that she looks like a deer caught in the headlights.

In the next image, a girl is standing against a door made of an oil drum hammered flat. The door is rusted and glows with the rich patina of rusted metal brushed by sunlight. Decorating the door is a chalk drawing of a schoolboy in profile wearing glasses. Above the boy's head on both sides is the word "Stop" in English. The girl has one hand on her hip at the same bent angle as the arm of the drawing of the boy. On her wrist she wears a watch. She is dressed in a pair of very short white shorts, a red plastic belt, and a translucent black tube top. She looks directly at the camera and smiles. The girls in the two photos are the same age.

Now here are the photos of the king. In one image he is wearing a dark blue suit that looks too big for his thin frame, and his shoes are too small for his feet. The pants are flared and the white tie he is wearing is too wide—like a bib. He has a white cap on his head. He frowns and looks slightly to the side. In the other image, he is wearing a brightly colored cloth over one shoulder like a toga. He stares directly at you, from slightly above as if you were kneeling before him. His eyes gleam in the light. They are red. He frowns.

When I show these images to my family or to students I get the same kinds of responses, the same comments and questions. They ask why the king is wearing the suit. He looks so awkward, they say, so stiff, so uncomfortable. As for the other image, they wonder about his red eyes. Is he blind or merely intense? He looks so powerful, so angry, so mystical. The cloth, they tell me, looks beautiful. About the girls, they squirm when they see the scarified torsos. They ask how they were able to withstand the pain, and they want to know if scarifying was part of a ritual activity. About the women fishing, they tend to compliment me. "Like National Geographic," they often say. As for the image of the other girl, they are more ambivalent. "Was she your girlfriend?" someone once sniggered. There's something provocative about the way she smiles and poses. Compared to the other girl emerging from the stream, who seems so natural, so innocent, she looks, to some, a little like a slut.

Such responses to the images, like tourism itself, are about authenticity and the way authenticity endorses a certain idea about progress and tradition. The king in the suit and the girl in the tube top do not satisfy that touristic urge for authenticity; the king in his toga or the scarified torso, or the women fishing, do satisfy that urge. Those images are somehow more African than a picture of a king in a suit and tie. They are more African because they are more primitive. As for the other images, these betray what we take to be traces of us. The girl's wristwatch, the king's too-wide tie and his stiff suit—these are pieces of our culture. Seeing these objects, we assume that the king and the girl want to be like us, but that they don't quite do it right. As often as not this makes us sad. We pity them. But we also think their transformation is inevitable. It is the old story of the primitive giving way to the modern. It is happening everywhere, we assume, that it hasn't already happened.

When we look at those images and use them to tell that story, we are repeating the core myth of modernity. In this myth—and I am using the word myth to emphasize that the story has a persuasive power that goes way beyond whatever truth it contains—as the anthropologist Arjun Appadurai puts it, "our present is their future." Primitive, as Johannes Fabian pointed out, is always past tense. In the present, primitive becomes modern, and then disappears. History happens, and all the beautiful, exotic, natural places are gone, swallowed up, taken over. History happens in this way because the modern is more powerful than the primitive. We are stronger than they are. We are stronger because we are more advanced, evolved. But we are also ambivalent about our modernity. We are stronger, but perhaps they are better—closer to god, each other, and nature.

Now let's look behind and around the lens to get a context for the photos. Look again at that girl, standing in front of the door. I had seen the graffiti on the door. It was similar to many chalk doodles the kids in the village were always doing. They decorated their doorways or the exteriors of their huts with what I took to be self-portraits, or rather portraits of an idealized future when they would actually have glasses if they needed them, and shoes, and money for school books. These images of schoolboys, along with the drawings of cars and bicycles that also decorated the huts' wall, were all about aspirations. They often included snippets of English. Nobody spoke English really, although they knew what "stop" meant. A few people knew a few phrases. Kids would come up to me and say, "Time is money" and smile conspiratorially. That phrase, out there in the middle of nowhere, and those aspirational images of cars and schoolboys wearing glasses, fascinated me. They looked like art, like naïve or outsider art as it is often called—pieces of punk picturesque.

So when I was not busy interviewing or attending a meeting or ceremony I would sometimes wander the village with my camera, feeling a bit guilty that I was not really working as I should have been, but looking for the right moment to capture those images of the blurred boundary. Early on in my research I took my camera to the hut with the door at close to sunset. I had seen the door at sunset a few days before and I liked how the light made the rust glow with its own inner patina. I wanted to capture that glowing door and the rich white of the chalked words "Stop." When I got to the hut a young girl was bent over, sweeping up leaves in the sandy courtyard. She was wearing a "pagne"—one of those ubiquitous West African cloth wraps. It was stained and faded, matching the dull color of the dried leaves she was sweeping into a small pile. I saw her and suddenly realized that the picture would be better with a body standing by the doorway to give the chalk schoolboy something to be scaled against. I asked her if she would let me take her photo against the door. She said yes, but before I could focus my camera she disappeared through the doorway into the house.

I waited for her, a little annoyed because the light was fading. Then she emerged wearing those white shorts and the bright plastic belt. I asked her to stand by the door. She put her hand on her hip, displaying the wristwatch she now wore, and smiled at me as I looked through the lens. I quickly took the picture, thanked her, and left.

Many months later, toward the end of my time with the Manjaco, I was constantly struggling against an overwhelming lassitude, brought on in large part by the occasional squabbles I seemed to be having with Manjaco about what I could ask and learn. On one of those days when I was feeling especially lazy I took the photograph of the women fishing. The weather was hotter than it had been and the sky was a deep blue festooned with thick white clouds. I did not want to work anymore, nor could I imagine staying in my hut reading a novel. I had read more than my share already. This was because sometimes when I was tired of talking and listening to Manjaco I'd use the excuse of a stuffy nose or a vague ache to hide behind my mosquito net and read a novel in the space of a day. But on this particular day it was too hot for that, and so I decided to go on a photographic excursion.

The women of the extended family I was staying with were planning to go to the meanders beyond the rice fields to go fishing. They and their friends were gathering by the hut to head off down the path out of the village. A chance to wade in the cool water sounded like the perfect way to escape my lassitude; I asked them if I could come along and they agreed. I met them in the courtyard. My camera was around my neck and I had my daypack with my notebook, extra film, and lens. The older women looked at my camera and then began scolding me. "You cannot take your camera," they said.

We got in an argument. I really did not care whether I took pictures or not, although I had started to imagine what the pictures would be like, and I was also tired of always getting in little fights with Manjaco about recording, writing, or asking. People were always telling me not to ask that, not to write that in my notebook, not to take a picture of that. Once, I had been to a ceremony and a dog had been slaughtered. The dog hung by its rear haunches in a tree in the courtyard. I took out my camera to take a shot and the elder who was sitting beside me put his hand over the lens and shook his head at me. I put the camera away. I asked him why the dog was dangling there in the tree. He changed the subject. We talked of inconsequential things while blood dripped from the dog's snout a few feet from our faces.

So when the women told me to put my camera away, I was tired of always struggling with Manjaco over what I could and could not know, but I had also long since learned how to fight back as Manjaco do. I took their refusal as a kind of challenge. I explained that I had so many photos of the men in the village at work. Would these women want me to go home with no images of them at work? Would my students then think that only Manjaco men worked? They argued back. I was, they asserted, going to get rich off these photos. They had seen the kinds of photos I would take in stalls in Dakar (the capital of Senegal). All those postcards of naked women, naked women of the village, carrying baskets or water jugs. Someone shouted at me, "You want to take [a picture of] our assholes!" And suddenly the other women took that up as a chant. "Our assholes; you'll take our assholes! You'll sell our assholes!" But I shouted back, wanting to win this argument just for the sake of winning, that I wanted to take their photos only to show them working.

In the end, they let me bring my camera. And, in part to show them that I was serious about the work and also because I was curious, I asked them plenty about fishing. I learned quite a bit that morning about how they would divide the catch, about how much the owner of the net (that man in the photo) would receive, about how often they went fishing, and so forth. I did not notice, until months later when I developed the film and saw it for the first time, that most of the old women had kept their clothes on when they bent down and scooped at the water, their backs to my lens.

It also was not until I got back from the field and began showing these photos that I realized if I had asked the women many questions when we went fishing together, I had not asked the girl anything at all. Now all I had was an image and a mystery. Where did she get the white pants, the watch, and the belt? Did she buy them or did someone else? When? What was she thinking when she smiled at the lens all dressed up as she was? I realized, and I felt ashamed about this, that I had not asked her anything because I did not consider her to be as worthy an ethnographic subject as were the women fishing. I had missed an opportunity to understand Manjaco. Like my students and family, I too was blinkered by my own desires and prejudices.

Because of those desires and prejudices, Manjaco sometimes disgusted me, or at least made me feel a kind of sympathetic embarrassment—a feeling I got when I took the photograph of the king in his suit because he seemed so awkward in that suit, a feeling I did not have when I took his picture in the cloth toga. I visited the king often. Sometimes, when it had been a while since our last visit, he would send one of his grandchildren to fetch me. He would usually be alone, sitting under the eaves of the crumbling veranda of his house—a dark shadow, shaded by the eaves of the thatched roof. He was a smaller man than most of his peers, and he wore a long black raincoat and a tattered black fedora. His face looked bitten, the nose cut short and the eyes constantly red and watering. When he laughed or smiled, his lips dragged downwards at the corners as if betraying more bitter emotions. We would sit together on the veranda. I'd have brought some palm wine or he would have had some and we would have drunk a few glasses—his sometimes mixed with cane rum because he was an old man and needed something stronger "to grab the veins." People would pass by. The king would call out a greeting, but they would hurry by, never stopping. Even though old Manjaco men generally seemed to spend much of their time alone—they farmed alone, they "guarded" their fields alone, they tapped palms alone—the king was more alone than most. Vincinti Nai was a man in internal exile. In part his exile was self-imposed. He was angry with the community for forsaking him, and they, in turn, were not pleased with him. So he visited no one and had few visitors himself.

Because he had so few visitors and was bitter about the way the villagers treated him, he was glad for my company. He loved to be interviewed, to speak into my tape recorder and to then listen as I played back his words. Mostly he told me about the business of being a king, often digressing to disparage his erstwhile subjects. But he also did not mind talking about other things. I was interested in Manjaco funerary practices, for example, especially the economics the elaborate funerals entailed. Elders were buried wrapped in dozens of expensive, locally made cloths; during their lifetimes elders collected cloths that would be used to wrap their bodies when they died, investing in the future, as it were, much as responsible elders in our society might put money aside for their retirement. I wanted to see how many cloths an old man might have ready and hear the details about how they were acquired. Yet most Manjaco were very secretive about wealth of any kind. They worried that others would become excessively envious of what they had and that those people might harm them in some way, through witchcraft for example, because they were envious. The king agreed to show me the contents of his chest of cloths. I was fascinated by one cloth in particular. It was so brightly colored. I had never seen such a cloth. He told me he had bought it at a European trade depot up north in Senegal when he was working there before World War Two. He remembered who had made the cloth. "Germans" he said. "They made it to look like our cloth, but it is not same, see?" As he talked, he draped the cloth over his shoulder. "Take a picture now, Eric. This is how the elders in those days would wear such a cloth." I took the picture as he posed like an elder in the old days.

Just as the king liked that I recorded our conversations, so too did he want me to take photographs of him. He wanted to frame the photographs to decorate his grave after his death. He told me that he planned to construct an elaborate tomb for himself. It would be of "cement." "The villagers will pass by when it is being dug. They will ask, 'What are you making?' I will say, 'It is a latrine.' They will think I am making a latrine with walls of cement, the floor of cement." He laughed as he talked of how his neighbors would be fooled. "No one will know until after I am dead. My body will go there in the hole of cement. The ants, the termites—they will not eat my body. The earth will not touch my body. I will make a door of cement. In the door will be a frame, in the frame your photograph. Glass will keep the rain from the photograph." Other kings, he explained, had all been buried surreptitiously in the patch of tangled sacred forest that abutted the court, and their tombs were ephemeral and invisible, but his tomb of cement would last forever. And "everyone going on the path will see it."

The photo session with me was to be conducted secretly. The king chose a time when others would not be around, and I was to keep my camera hidden in my bag until I reached his courtyard. He said he needed help dressing for the occasion, so I followed him into his room in the hut where he kept his clothes in a large dresser. I was surprised that he had several suits, and, as he showed me each one and asked which would look best, he told me that all of them were gifts from "sons in France." He found a white cap he told me was a part of the uniform the Portuguese had given the chiefs and rulers. It was of cheap white cloth, so thin it had the consistency of crepe paper—a hat a child pretending to be a sea captain might wear to a costume party. He selected a tie and he asked me to knot it for him. His fingers were bent with arthritis. The light had faded. I had not brought a flash. But we took the picture anyway as he stood by the carved wooden images of previous kings.

To me, he looked so pathetic, especially because of that flimsy cap he was so proud of. The colonizers had given it to him. His country had recently won its independence in a long and violent struggle against the Portuguese. I felt embarrassed for him because he did not realize how pathetic he looked in that hat and ill-fitting suit. Other elders annoyed me just as much. I felt embarrassed by the elders in their overcoats and odd headgear (a Tyrolean hat, a fedora, a bright yellow plastic hard hat). They seemed so pitiful decked out in their tokens of travel. I was enervated by the middle-aged men in sport coats with too-wide lapels cut out of cheap cardboard-like material, who all were eager to speak French with me even after it was clear that I could not speak French well enough to understand much of what they were saying. Equally off-putting were the teenagers at the Saturday night dance, shuffling awkwardly to the not-quite-latest tune from Senegal or Zaire played on a battery-powered record player. But these were all Manjaco, and if I wanted to understand Manjaco I would have to understand them, even if mainly in retrospect.

Manjaco Neo-Traditions

When you take a picture, you tell a story, whether you aware of the story you are telling or not. When you are curious or fascinated by one thing and not another, you also frame and edit the story you will eventually tell without necessarily being aware that you are doing so. Looking back at my field notes and at my collection of photographs, one set of practices clearly fascinated me, made me curious. This was the Manjaco funeral. Funerals were a ubiquitous event in the village I inhabited. They were noisy and beautiful. They fascinated me because nothing seemed more enduringly traditional than a Manjaco funeral. All those crowd-filled days of drunken dancing to the incessant rhythms of the funeral drums. All those cattle slaughtered, their carcasses left on ostentatious display in the bloodstained sand of the household courtyard. All that locally woven cloth wrapping the corpse like a corpulent mummy. During the funeral, the cloth-covered body was carried to a communal tomb where it was stripped to be stuffed into a small hole in the ground to join the desiccated remains of its forebears. In this way another individual was consigned to the earth, eventually to re-emerge from the ground as a revered ancestor, who, as

Manjaco put it in their orations at the ancestor shrine, would "work for the company now." When he emerged as an ancestor, his carved image would now be among the cluster of such carvings—the collective employees of the household as corporation.

Those ancestor figures, like the photos of the king, spoke to the mystery and ubiquity of the blurred boundary, because they were portraits of men in suits with white or pink faces, who looked like Portuguese people, not at all like Manjaco. Likewise too, the cloth Manjaco made wove images of pieces of European material life into the fabric of traditional cloth—steamboats, brandy bottles, flags, and so forth.

Manjaco funerals are what some scholars of Africa, such as Anthony Appiah, call a "neotradition." Neotraditions are new activities, recent practices that, however, have the patina of age, of tradition. Rather than a holdover from the past, or a kind of fossil, they appear so lavishly traditional because, for decades, Manjaco living abroad have signaled their commitment to home by paying for such ceremonies. Indeed, when I was doing research, it was because far more Manjaco lived and died abroad than in Guinea-Bissau that there were more funerals than bodies to bury. Local funerals allowed emigrants who died and were interred in distant places like Paris and Dakar to return, if only ritually, to households of origin in rural villages. During the colonial era, when Manjaco were "crossing the river" (as they put it) from villages in Portuguese Guinea that were rich in wet-rice fields and oil-palm groves to farm peanuts for cash in the Casamance or Gambia, or to work as stevedores and household help in Dakar, every effort was made to circumvent colonial laws of hygiene to bring the actual body back to the home village. But for decades after that, Manjaco had made their accommodations to circumstances, replacing literal corpses with virtual analogues.

Years after I did research in Guinea-Bissau, I spent a summer studying a shantytown in Lisbon, where I attended a gathering of expatriate Manjaco who were lamenting the loss of a middle-aged comrade. As one of my companions punched numbers into his cell phone so that I might speak to a mutual friend in Guinea-Bissau, he emphasized that to announce this death, they would make arrangements to hand-carry the clothing of the deceased to present to the villagers as a physical sign of the person's passing. It was that bundle of clothing, the *uyeman,* or sacred thing, as it is known, that made it possible to hold a "real funeral"—with its lavishly excessive conspicuous consumption— in the village.

Meanwhile, living emigrants, the offspring and consocates of the deceased, not only paid for all those cattle, all that palm wine and rum, but they transformed the space of the funeral ceremony into a theater of cosmopolitan accomplishments. The household courtyards where the dances to the dead are held, the ancestor shrines where the carved effigies of the illustrious forebears are kept, became stage settings for emigrants to celebrate themselves. In the Manjaco region I was familiar with, home village populations had declined by more than half in the fifty years prior to my fieldwork. Yet household ancestor shrines were packed. Manjaco houses looked like mausoleums. Empty of the living, they were full of the dead. Death had become a kind of repatriation.

Yet if mortuary ceremony was ultimately a ritualized repatriation, the celebrations of cosmopolitan accomplishments that had become a routine part of the funeral were often enacted and embodied in explicit opposition to what the local household and homeplace seemed to stand for: travel as opposed to stability, antagonistic individuation as opposed to social solidarity. It was as if emigrant Manjaco wished to use the funeral as a setting for celebrating a fundamental tension between the desires of individual persons and the imperatives of corporate sociality.

It is often the case that we assume individuality is itself associated with modernity. Tradition, we feel, is about the group's hold over the individual, while modernity is about the triumph of the individual against, as often as not, the constraints of society, of custom. So one way of explaining or interpreting what the Manjaco funeral tells us is the story we already know by heart about the transition from tradition to modernity. But I will suggest a different interpretation: that the funeral opens up a space for emigrants to celebrate their accomplishments as a personal freedom of movement, as a capacity to leave the village at will, because the format of the funeral allows for assertions of individuality, which are routinely portrayed as destructive. I will do so by juxtaposing celebrations of cosmopolitan worldliness with other celebrations of personal accomplishment enacted during a funeral. Cosmopolitanism can become the costume of choice at home as well as abroad, not because Manjaco are becoming more modern and less traditional, but because this kind of practice is quintessentially Manjaco. Destructive individuation is a Manjaco tradition. If emigrants "invent" tradition, they do so in a way that makes room for modernity as tradition.

Most of the action of a funeral takes place in the courtyard of a Manjaco house, or *kato* as it is known in Manjaco. *Kato,* or house, is not a single building; rather it is an abstraction linked to a residence. House is the name for the kinship corporation that is both the location and motive for the mortuary ceremony. When I was doing fieldwork, most "houses" in Manjaco villages

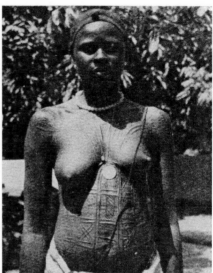

Figure 5.1. Image of Manjaco girls in the pages of Meireles's book

Figure 5.2. Women fishing

Figure 5.3. Girl posing in front of graffiti-covered door

Figure 5.4. King posing with trade cloth draped over his shoulder

Figure 5.5. King posing in a suit

were made up of one to three multiroomed rectangular cement residences with zinc roofs, yet the house was invariably described as a cluster of huts around a circular courtyard or *bolai*. The *bolai* is the site for the funeral celebration. It is in the courtyard that the corpse is displayed. It is in the courtyard that the funeral dances are performed, as a pair of talking drums call out the praise names of the male ancestors of the house and house members dance in accompaniment.

The house, as corporation, controls certain properties, which have a kind of emblematic status: wet-rice fields, cattle, funeral cloth, and the buildings that make up the house as actual place of residence. More amorphous, and more contestable, are claims the house has on the incomes of its members. Control, or "ownership," of these material manifestations of the house as corporation is inevitably communal. While one male elder is called the "owner" of the house, he makes his decisions about how to use household property in consultation with the ancestors and with other adult members of the house. These adult members of a house are a group of agnates, around forty in all, including women who leave the house at marriage, and men who emigrate and spend their entire lives elsewhere. Out-migration has been so heavy in the last decades that there may only be two or three married men, along with their wives and children, and the wives and children of absent brothers actually in residence in the house in the village.

Manjaco in the village I lived in routinely spoke in bitter and disparaging terms about absent emigrants. They accused them of betraying the household corporation out of selfishness. Out-migration, many Manjaco habitually asserted, had turned the village into a "broken land"—a place which could no longer sustain itself as a viable community.

Listening to these complaints, I came to assume that the exaggerated lavishness of funerals and the population explosion in the ancestor shrines reflected the guilt, or should I say fear, that those who had left the village for better prospects felt about those who stayed behind and acted as their go-betweens in interactions with local spirits. Or at least this seemed to be the pervasive subtext in the letters emigrants and stay-at-homes exchanged—letters to which I had adventitious access. Armando, the host of the house where I lived, was the village postman. He not only sorted and delivered mail but read and composed letters for his neighbors. He did this work at night in the privacy of the room that was also my office, so I listened as Armando wrote down a fellow villager's perfunctory greetings followed by halting requests for money, or I watched as a letter opened to eager anticipation followed by Armando's low voice as he read from the thin sheet of paper why such a request could not at the moment be fulfilled. Or the letter from a distant emigrant might contain a request in a roundabout way so that the message would be suitably opaque to stranger's ears.

On one occasion, a distant daughter who had been laid off from a job in a canning factory asked her father to "baptize" a written request for assistance at a local shrine. In the letter she explained that her "name was on the list" for an upcoming position in the factory but that a diviner had told her that "someone is working behind my back." Indeed, after waiting at the "factory gate" for several days her name had finally been called "but someone else took my place"—stealing her very name. The daughter closed the letter by asking her father to "return to that place" (that is, to an unnamed shrine) and pour cane rum for her there. "You know what to say" (she did not want to spell it out). She had enclosed 1,000 CFA—at the time about three dollars—enough to buy the initial offering of cane rum but no more. She'd apologized: "I have no work. I have no money."

If emigrants occasionally asked stay-at-homes to act as go-betweens in their dealings with local spirits, villagers also seemed to insinuate that they might use such spirits and ancestors as convenient agents to enforce, if tenuously, their will upon more fortunate kin who had escaped the restrictions of rural life to emigrate abroad. Reminding them in letters that "our fathers remember you," "watch over you," and so forth, they would then make their various requests. Consider an excerpt from a discussion I had with one of the younger and poorer household heads. He is explaining to me how an ancestor forces the living to install an effigy in his honor.

You are a father and you have sons. Some of those sons go away—to Senegal, to France. You have fed them, cared for them. Now you are dead. Your sons who are at home write a letter. 'Our father has asked to have an ancestor post planted in his honor.' The letter asks you to send money for your father [and] if you do not send money, this is bad. You, who work in an office, you might one day go blind. . . . Your brothers may have gone to the spirit shrine carrying a bottle of wine . . . or one day you arrive at work and before you can enter the door, your boss says, 'out.' You ask your boss why, but you know why: Your father waits there under the ground. He who has fed you, provided the oil [that makes you attractive] that has led you to your job. If you have money you send it. You go to your boss to ask for your money. You sign your name. He gives you your money. You send it. You feel happy in your soul. Your work will go well. Some are paid a wage; others are not paid a wage. Some stay at home and are sad. Who will help them work the fields? You have left.

In this excerpt of a taped conversation the accusative "you" is the emigrant who has escaped the house and forgotten the tie he has to the brother who stays behind. The young man who told me this had no one to help him in the fields. He depended on money his several brothers who resided abroad could send him. One brother had recently nearly been killed in an auto accident and the children of another had suffered illnesses. They had eventually consulted diviners and been told to "remember" one of their mutual fathers by installing an ancestor post in his honor. The agent of this remembering—the one who suggests persistently and persuasively that one see a diviner, the one who in fact sees a diviner at your request and then relays or interprets the message for you—is the stay-at-home. Thus I assumed that the population explosion in homeland ancestor shrines reflected the success stay-at-homes have had in extracting funds for rituals of repatriation in home villages, even as those emigrants spent their whole lives abroad.

At the Funeral

Villagers invariably emphasized that a funeral or a ceremony to plant an ancestor post was "expensive" (*anyat*) when they talked of the quantities of cane rum that would have to be procured for libations and number of livestock animals that would have to be bought for slaughter. But compared to new zinc for a roof, or cement for flooring, such ceremonies might count as fairly cheap. Indeed, the Manjaco I met that summer in Lisbon tended to downplay the cost of the burdens repatriating the dead placed on them. Nor did they act or talk in ways that revealed the kinds of tense guilt, fear, or conflict I expected. When I, for example, remarked to my friend with the cell phone perpetually pinned to his ear that it must be hard to afford that trip to deliver the bundle of clothes to the inhabitants of the ancestral home, he scoffed. A round-trip plane ticket was less than five hundred dollars, cheap really, hardly a burden. The trip home would count as a kind of vacation.

Indeed, many emigrants made frequent trips home to pay visits to local spirit shrines or to participate in funeral ceremonies. At funerals, emigrants would join in with fellow household members in dances that accompanied the praises of their ancestors. They also paid the drummers to beat out, in the language of the drums' rhythms, their personal accomplishments, and they danced in pantomimes meant to embody those accomplishments. As with most of funerary ritual, such dances tended to privilege men. Women danced, but only as a group, moving from one end of the courtyard—the veranda where the drums are set up—to the other—the gateway leading outside the courtyard. This dance is known as a "running" dance, and the women shuffle or trot at different tempos. Picture it as an endless film loop of a crowd on a sidewalk at rush hour, some of the crowd in a hurry, others ambling, all preoccupied, yet despite the chaos managing not to collide as they pass back and forth. The dance is visual equivalent of a Philip Glass piece: a certain voice endlessly repeated but at different speeds. The women's dance privileges their collectivity.

By contrast, the men's dance in praise of the ancestors is more agonistic and individuating. The dance, called *fongat,* or "rage," begins as men of a particular lineage rush into the courtyard as a group and claim it with sweeping whirling gestures that clear the courtyard of spectators. The drumming is much faster and louder. Soon most men are worn out. Only the best dancers remain, whirling, almost colliding. Manjaco today dance with a stick to make slashing gestures when in the "old days" (*uwal uyek*) they used swords, making the dances genuinely dangerous to unwary spectators. Nevertheless the swirling dancers, getting ever-closer to the boundaries of the cleared space, force the audience to focus their attention on the dancers. As the dancers pause to refresh themselves, their mother's or father's sisters or wives come out to the dancers to embrace them, to kneel before them, or to cover their shoulders with cloth, or use the cloth to fan them and to wipe their brows. Ostensibly the men dance to glorify the names of their ancestors. But they also glorify and individuate themselves as the mass of dancers is reduced through time to single dancers.

Men can further individuate themselves by paying the drummers to sound out their personal praises, or by getting an age-mate to play their praises on the flute as they pantomime the story the music conveys. Before we look at particular individuating performances, it is worth opening a parenthesis here to give a sense of what Manjaco praise names entail.

Praise names are compact alliterative phrases—fragments of a longer narrative—that characterize the person by alluding to a particularly dramatic moment in his life, or, more generally, an activity the person performs that is distinctive or noteworthy. In general, "praise" entails competitive comparison, and names often refer to the act of boasting or bragging. A common praise name, "You all stop your bragging, let's really see" (*Dawatan upiitch Jakaten*) uses the root *piitch,* or "brag." But there is also the parallel construction, using *brik,* "river," in place of praise. For example, "stop your 'rivering' (bragging), let's farm" (*Duwatan brik jakajar*) substitutes *brik* for *piitch.* Indeed, "river" is the iconic term for the act of bragging or aggrandizing the self or, by metaphoric extension, to "praise name" itself. Thus the common way to ask someone their praise name is to say "your 'river' name how is it said (*katim brik jaum*)?" "River" refers by way of synecdoche to two possible "praiseful" activities—the "opening" of new rice fields in the salt-water tidal marsh, or crossing a river (*pepat brik*)—that is, emigrating—to seek one's fortune.

For men who came of age in the early twentieth century there are several instances of names referring to river fields and agricultural work. Examples include "I pass [you all] in diking the river"; "You all brag of farming have you measured your fields?"; "Stop trying to farm me, I gave birth to farming"; "You cut a dike you try to imitate me"; "You bragged of river fields; I cleared it." By the 1930s and 1940s these names using the word "river" to refer to farming gave way almost entirely to names using "river" to refer to emigration. The most common praise name for this era—the name "chief of the drummers" glossed as "just a migrant's name"; "He left infancy to take up the paddle" —implies that by the early colonial era, emigration had become a de facto rite of passage for young Manjaco men. "River," that shorthand for praise, which once drew its connotative power from diking salt marsh to create wet-rice fields, became simply an allusion to "crossing the river," or emigrating.

Manjaco recognize two kinds of praise names. One they call a "distinguishing name" (*kapitch pepiitch*), the other they call a "disparaging" or "complaining" (*kakanar*) name. Both stress competition and conflict among consociates. Both exalt antagonism. What is perhaps most revealing about the names is the close link Manjaco make between praise and destruction. In general, a distinguishing name refers—in often exaggerated and occasionally comical terms—to glorious victories and vanquished foes. Thus, for example, a popular name for a great hunter is "Beats the Grass Eaters" and its humorous analog is to a renowned palm-wine tapper who "Beats the Elders" with strong wine that makes them stagger.

Typically a disparaging name is an insult or affront, recast and flung back at the insulter. It transforms mockery into challenge and enshrines antagonism between peers. An example is "White's Ears Are Whiter." First used in the 1940s, "White's Ears Are Whiter" became a common praise name in the region where I did fieldwork, referring to any educated Manjaco—a teacher, a bureaucrat. It originated as an insult—one man accusing another, who was a low-level clerk in government office, of putting on airs by dressing and acting like the Portuguese. "Ears" can refer to appearance, but "ears" also indicates intelligence. The clerk, so the story goes, responded to the insult by claiming that "the white's ears were whiter" (that is, a white will always look more white than any Manjaco) but that he, the Manjaco clerk, was in fact smarter and more educated than the Europeans who were his ostensible superiors. Contrast this "disparaging" name with a "distinguishing" name for a colonial-era clerk, a name that was used in the late 1980s as a generic praise name for educated emigrants—"Little Twigs, You Hear Them in Cacheu"—Cacheu referring to a Portuguese enclave fifty miles north of Bassarel and well beyond the range of the talking drums. Here the little twigs are a humorous play on the differences and similarities between drumsticks and writing implements. When Manjaco sent long-distance messages exclusively by drumming, the stronger the arm and the bigger the stick, the louder the sound. But an educated man had only to write a letter and his quiet message would be "heard" in the distant district capital.

The Bad Copy Again

Manjaco praise names are pantomimed in performances during the funeral. I will describe three such performances and the praise names associated with them—one to the generic farmer, another to the generic emigrant—that oc-curred during funerals I witnessed in the late 1980s. Note the juxtaposition Manjaco make between praise and destruction, as if that juxtaposition were an inevitable human condition.

One popular pantomime men perform is known as "the farmer's dance." The dancer literally plows away at the dirt of the courtyard, flinging sand from his fulcrum shovel. He begins slowly, pausing to position his shovel, stressing in that gesture the "heaviness" of the work. At this moment women may come up to him and make planting gestures in front of his poised shovel, as if they are putting seeds in the ground. Or they may simply bend down to look at the fulcrum shovel, making admiring noises as they do. After a few deliberate cuts into the sandy soil the dancer begins to move more frantically, shoveling spasmodically at the ground, spilling the sand in all directions, moving faster and faster but without precision. As he works thus, the women come up to fan him or to cloak him in cloth. At which point he stops.

The drummed praise name that accompanies this performance is "You all carve mounds; they crumble" and it refers to a particular event. A great farmer is a man who can build mounds with a fulcrum shovel faster than his peers. During work parties organized among the young unmarried men of the village, the young men lined up in a field and raced one another to see who was best. Such races were said to be "good" because they "make you forget the pain of the work." But they also were "bad," because the slower men, in trying to catch up, often built their mounds sloppily, "ruining" the field and making it less productive. The pantomimed performance that accompanies "You all carve mounds; they crumble" captures in mimetic gesture the moment when a victorious farmer taunts his peers who, in struggling to catch up, make a mess of their work.

Emigrant's pantomimes also play on this theme of social destruction that comes with personal success. The "emigrant's dance" is a mimesis of what might count as the exaggerated lassitude of a flaneur. The "dancer" dresses in a suit and walks in a casual way around a bottle of "white man's wine"—brandy or whiskey. Again, the women will come up to cover him in cloth or to embrace him. And he will pay them for their compliment with a glass of the brandy. Here the drummers might be beating out several praise names to emigrants. One such, for example, harks back to a praise song which was composed in the early 1960s for a ruler's son who returns from his sojourn abroad with a motorcycle. The refrain goes "[the motorcycle sound], the goats break their bonds," referring to the young man's triumphant entrance into the village at the height of the harvest season when everyone must tether their livestock lest they wander into the rice fields and graze on the ripe grains. Tethering livestock is the perfect image of individual responsibility to others in the community. You constrain what is yours for the benefit of others. The song therefore offers a compact encapsulation of one of the paradoxes of praise. The emigrant's triumph is socially destructive; the goats break their tethers and wander into the neighbors' fields to eat.

Another performance for men who served in the military involves the pantomiming of parade ground gestures. I once witnessed such a performance where a middle-aged man named Jorge, who had served in the Portuguese army during the revolution, paused to pay the drummers and began to orate, rather than simply act out, his accomplishments. Consider Jorge as he stands in front of the drummers as if at attention. He begins to speak, almost as if he were reciting a poem in a Manjaco, but a Manjaco heavily laden with Portuguese terms:

I was the first, the best
No one was better than me
I know every border of Guinea.
I fought on every frontier.

He speaks, then pauses, as the drums repeat his words in tattooed rhythms on hollow wood. Then he begins again:

Me Jorge Teixeira. Nobody else.
I was *primeiro cabo.*
I was their leader.
You talk of generals, commanders of the battalion.
Me, Jorge, the best. No one was better.

He goes on like this, speaking, pausing to let the drums catch up, and he finishes
his praise poem to himself with:

My passport is complete, my papers are complete.
I can go anywhere.
Me [he pats his chest for emphasis]! Me
the *primeiro cabo.*

What Jorge enacts when he chants that his passport is complete, or what
the emigrants perform when they strut in their awkward suits and toast each
other with "white people's wine" at the funeral, was the mimetic equivalent of
what many Manjaco—men Jorge's age, men who were much older and younger
men—did daily. Of the forty or so heads of households in the village where I
stayed, only a few dressed routinely in garb that wasn't clearly European. One
I knew well wore a long white Muslim-style tunic and had a pointed goatee in
the style of the young warriors of the 1930s. When he strode barefoot through
the village, he carried a machete cradled in the crook of one arm. His name
was Faran Balé, or "Francois Bullets," a name his peers had given him to
commemorate a long sojourn in the French army along with other Senegalese
recruits—first in France during the Second World War and next in Vietnam.
It was this experience of war that Balé underscored by carrying the machete
and wearing a warrior's beard. Most elders were not nearly as theatrical in their
presentations of self as Faran Balé, but when they dressed up, they pretended to
cosmopolitan accomplishments. Some clothed themselves in talismans of their
own time abroad. I used to visit one who almost constantly wore his denim
colored coveralls with the "Esso" emblem stitched above a breast pocket, a relic
of his time working as a mechanic in France. Others donned borrowed finery;
thus the erstwhile king, whom you have already met, who never ventured from
his courtyard without wearing his fedora and a raincoat or one of the several
suit coats those children "in France" had sent him as gifts.

Yet when the Manjaco king wears a suit or when returnees such as Jorge
celebrate, through drumming and dance, their accomplishments during a funeral ceremony, or when Manjaco pack ancestor shrines with effigies of absent
emigrants, they become a problem for anthropology precisely because our dress
code is not all that different from the colonialist's dress code as exemplified

by Meireles and his preoccupation with the scarified Manjaco maiden. For Meireles and for his fellow Portuguese administrator, Viegas, the Manjaco in the suit was a "nucleus apart," while the scarified maiden meanwhile was an always-about-to-disappear avatar of a bucolic authenticity. The bad copy is also a problem for anthropology.

Pristine Primitives

At first glance this is not surprising. After all, it is sometimes argued that anthropology and colonialism are merely two versions of the same Western practice and discourse. Fieldwork-based anthropology emerged as a disciplinary practice in America and in Europe in conjunction with late nineteenth-century colonialism. Anthropology, based on "being there" ethnography, was only possible because of this dramatic and pervasive penetration and expansion of Western societies into the terrain of primitive societies. During this period, anthropologists often argued for the utility of their discipline in terms of colonialist interests. If colonial administrators wanted to rule colonial subjects, then they needed anthropologists' help to understand them better first. Yet anthropologists tended to be more sympathetic to the colonized than to the colonizers with their civilizing missions. But in being sympathetic, they often inadvertently replicated the colonialist's dress code in their own explications of culture theory, especially when they talked about cultural change. If nothing bothered the colonialist more than the bad copy, the "savvy boy," the "trousered African," because he upset the implicit paternalism of the colonial enterprise, then the bad copy also upset the enemies of colonialism, among them anthropologists, for the "black man who wants to be white" is proof positive of colonialism's pathological effect. For both camps, and even for anthropologists who should know better, the bad copy is often an aesthetic abomination, an embodiment of a troubling inauthenticity.

Part (but only part) of the reason has to do with our long history as a discipline that was constituted in the study of primitive people. Early on, anthropologists often explicitly couched their work as if it were a kind of "salvage." Anthropologists claimed it was important to study the natives before they disappeared, or lost what made them unique or different and became merely cruder, more impoverished versions of Westerners. In America, for example, Franz Boas and his students began collecting as many of the myths and legends of American Indians as they could, capturing these stories in their languages, before these people and their languages were swallowed up and destroyed by the corrosive forces of Manifest Destiny. Boas and his followers imagined that they were salvaging what was good and valuable from the wreckage of intercultural contact. They sought out reservation Indians for what they remembered about a past on the verge of dying out, but they were less interested in what reservation Indians were doing in the present. They sought out old men and women, because such people were thought of as cultural repositories. They were far less interested in young Indians.

Soon Boas's students, Margaret Mead among them, would venture forth to New Guinea, Samoa, and the Philippines because these places too had been "pacified" and could now be studied in that crucial period before they too disappeared. In these places, the present was still the past. New Guinea, they assumed, was as close to the Stone Age as one could still get.

In Europe, an ethnographic urge that involved collecting customs and artifacts of a disappearing indigenous peasantry, as that peasantry left villages to migrate to the cities and the life of the proletariat, was eclipsed by social anthropological fieldwork in the newly acquired colonial territories of Africa and elsewhere. In those places, people still lived as they once had in the country in Europe—perhaps as far back as in medieval times, although again, because of the corrosive effects of colonialism, they too were starting to migrate to the city. In the European anthropological tradition, the city was often opposed to the country, as tradition was seen as the opposite of modernity.

Pristine, or close to pristine, primitive societies made for good science because they were a "natural laboratory" of human difference. E. E. Evans-Pritchard, for example, used the Nuer to demonstrate that the human sense of time was not a universal but was instead relative to social structure and practice. He argued that notions of "time and space depend . . . on structural principles which belong to a different order of reality"—different that is, from nature experienced directly and empirically. He quoted Nuer to demonstrate that "time" in general was experienced in terms of "social activities" and time was communicated in terms of those activities—e.g. "at the time of harvesting, at the time of weeding" or "I shall return at milking." He used this kind of data to draw a contrast between us and Nuer in order to remind us that our sense of time was also a social construct. For us time has been fetishized as a "thing"—a quantity external to us. We can waste time or use it wisely; "time is money" as Benjamin Franklin famously put it, and as Manjaco used to repeat in English to show off to me and to make (slight) fun of my cultural peculiarity. Not only do we think of time as a quantity that might get scarce lest we are careful, but we embody such thinking by "hurrying." Make a film of an American working at a task, say, chopping wood or washing dishes, and the action will appear hurried, frenzied, jerky. Follow a Nuer as he works and his movements will seem frustratingly slow (especially if you're a colonial officer or a development worker) or (if you are a romantic) wonderfully relaxed and unhurried—as if the Nuer had "all the time in the world." But that's not what Nuer are imagining. For them time does not exist except as an activity. Cattle and people—society in its broadest, most concrete sense—are Nuer clocks.

For Evans-Pritchard a Nuer sense of time was determined by their way of life. So too with ours. In the West, clocks and watches are everywhere. But this is not because time exists as a natural fact we have discovered and learned to monitor. Rather, we objectify time as a quantity because we live in an industrial society that makes time into money. The ubiquity of clocks and watches are an outcome of that attitude based on those social practices. By the same token, Nuer would not have been such a perfect laboratory to study the social relativity of time if Nuer routinely consulted their wristwatches. If everyone everywhere had watches, it would have been very hard for Evans-Pritchard to prove the cultural constructedness of time. He needed contrast to reveal constructs.

The desire for boundaries between "us" and "them" was reflected in the way ethnographic descriptions were edited—what they left out as much as what they put in. Evans-Pritchard lived among Nuer who at first treated him as an enemy because they associated him with British, who had bombed them from the air and shot at them on the ground. Pacification also brought pestilence. Before Evans-Pritchard arrived, a rinderpest epidemic had decimated the Nuer herds. Yet when he wrote about the Nuer way of life, Evans-Pritchard erased these searing facts in favor of images of Nuer before the scorched earth of colonialism, when a bride price exchange required forty cattle, when feuds were still the way disputes were settled. Evans-Pritchard's Nuer occupied a timeless place. He wrote about them in the present tense: Nuer "are" rather than Nuer "were." Likewise with Malinowski. The Trobrianders he lived with traded with Europeans; some of them worked on their plantations. They even enjoyed playing cricket! But what we saw and read of them portrayed a self-contained world—the archipelago of the Kula trade—as if the islands and the objects that circulated between them in exchanges never involved cash or work for wages, but exclusively entailed barter, trust, debt, and obligation.

Neither Malinowski, nor Evans-Pritchard, nor the Boasians who collected and catalogued all those myths and legends hid modernity's effects because they were complicit with the colonizers and the "only good Injun is a dead Injun" types who had slaughtered and hounded them. Rather, they tried to bracket off the corrosive present from the past because they found this past at once more compelling as science and more appealing.

The pristine primitive was not only scientifically compelling, primitives were also appealing in a less immediately rationalizable sense. Anthropologists like Evans-Pritchard were, in a sense, romantics. You don't go to the field to discover poorer, more miserable versions of yourself. You go there to celebrate them and their way of life. Nuer quickly took Evans-Pritchard in as an "equal," and this made him far happier than anything specific he learned from them. Margaret Mead carried a carved Samoan staff she had been given by her natives until the end of her days.

Anthropologists of that era and since have wanted to be like their interlocutors, to see and feel their world from, as Malinowski put it, the "native's point of view." They also wanted to be liked by them. But they did not want them to be like us, to end up like us, to lose what we had already lost. For most anthropologists, modernization and colonialism meant that the people with whom they sympathized were being hurt, damaged. The desire to protect merged with the desire to preserve.

Not long after Malinowski enjoined anthropologists to see and feel the world from the "native's point of view" in order to better explain it, American cultural anthropologists used the idea of "culture shock" to talk about how hard that was. Culture shock was what happened to you when you had to live as others lived. Inhabiting a strange environment, you became estranged to your psyche and you felt a nagging malaise. Becoming annoyed, feeling annoyed, disgusted without really being able to put your finger on the why of your annoyance, were signal symptoms of culture shock. But the idea of culture shock always implied that what would cause such a sense of malaise was the absolute difference that existed between what you took for granted and what they took for granted.

Modernity and the Trouble with History

Anthropology has changed quite a bit since Malinowski sailed in an outrigger with the Trobrianders and Evans-Pritchard shared tobacco and the promise of friendship with the Nuer. In my era, it was more likely that our annoyance with our natives had more to do with perceived similarities than differences. When anthropologists of my era went into the field, we still craved authenticity, but it was a deflected authenticity. When we got to the field we hoped to encounter natives who were as compelling as those Malinowski met. We still wanted to see the world from their point of view. Most of us hoped their point of view would be a critique of modernity's relentless march. We hoped they would express in culturally evocative ways their displeasure with their displacement. That would make them authentic in our eyes. By speaking for them, we would (so many of us wished) enact our own critique of the excesses of capitalism and the state. We would help them to speak truth to power by having their voices heard through us.

When we got to the field we expected a "ruptured landscape"—a place marked and scarred by colonialism and its aftermath. And we expected to find people preoccupied with that rupture. The Manjaco village I chose to live in should have been just such a place. After close to fourteen years of violent revolution and a decade-long drought, that village had lost roughly half its population. Manjaco claimed that the "land had broken" as their kin fled the village for safer and more prosperous places elsewhere—Portugal, Senegal, France. Migrants returned for brief visits. The village was shadowed by their distant presence. It was a place of blurred boundaries rather than clear differences—not anything close to Eden.

To understand ruptured landscapes we assumed that we would have to account for history. In anthropology two views of history have emerged as paradigms to account for natives who look a little too much like us for comfort. One vision of history that became the dominant one among anthropologists working in Africa was to imagine history as a global transformation associated with "modernity"—which stood for the when and how of the onset of capitalism, the beginning of colonialism, and the rise of the nation-state. Or "history" referred to "recent" "transformations" of the same—of the rise of "millennial capitalism" or "neoliberalism," for example. History, in this sense, is rarely good and is usually bad, so an analysis of historical transformation becomes a story of the "malaise of modernity." In this narrative, it is best when natives eschew cosmopolitanism in favor of localism. They should not want to be like us and the story we tell about them should focus on how forces beyond their control make them do what they do not want to do. But Manjaco cannot be made to fit into that narrative frame.

There is another way that anthropologists have accounted for history that seems to make more sense of the Manjaco experience. What if we take it as a given that the attitudes the funeral enacted are "quintessentially Manjaco" and not merely reflections of recent events, of history in that sense? Could we talk about a Manjaco "ethos of modernity" that has entirely different origins from our modernity? Here I am signaling my affinity for the work of Clifford Geertz, who pioneered what we might now label a "culturalist" approach to modernity in his several book-length and shorter essays on modernization in "out of the way places." In these works Geertz consistently argued that "whatever its outside provocations, and whatever foreign borrowing may be involved, modernity, like capital, is largely made at home." By exploring modernity in Indonesia and Morocco, he tried to show how societies might experience the same or equivalent histories, yet interpret them in dramatically different ways, revealing in the process the contours of culture. A Javanese Muslim or bureaucrat or leader of a nation-state might seem to occupy the same moment in history and the same sociological subject position as a Moroccan Muslim bureaucrat or leader, but they would remain above all else a Moroccan or a Javanese. Cultural difference would trump social subject position.

Geertz was following the lead of Ruth Benedict, whose portrait of Japanese modernity in *The Chrysanthemum and the Sword* made much the same point. Japanese could occupy the same kinds of social positions associated with a modern society. They could have a modern army, a modern bureaucracy, department stores, schools, and yet they would use these institutions in ways that revealed difference rather than similarity. Benedict found authentic Japan in the guise of a people seemingly mimicking the practices and institutions of the West. I would say that the same applies to Manjaco.

I have suggested that to really understand the blurred boundary of the ruptured landscape among people such as Manjaco requires that the fieldworker take what his interlocutors say and do at face value, even when what they say dissatisfies. Malinowski's basic idea remains valid: We still have to see things from the native's point of view, not ours. Manjaco were not critics of modernity even though I wished they had been. Rather, they wanted us to let them join in modernity's pleasures. They also fully expected that if given the chance, they would thrive in our land just as they thrived in theirs. For them there was no sharp contrast between the city and the country, because in both places Manjaco expected the same attitudes and worldviews to work. They figured that if they could crow of their accomplishments in homeland courtyards, they could also make accomplishments real in Lisbon, Paris—anywhere.

My goal in this chapter has been to offer a glimpse of that worldview. Yet that goal, despite me, despite or perhaps because of all that I had learned in anthropology, almost eluded me, maybe did elude me. The girl in front of the doorway endlessly looks at me, and because I failed to ask her about herself and to listen to what she might have to say, I will never know what she was thinking.

6

Beyond Belief

When Thomas Jefferson was president, his opponents stoked the rumor mill with stories about his keeping a slave mistress, "Dusky Sally," and they accused him of foisting atheism on the American public. What Jefferson did or did not do with Sally Hemings is a story I will take up later. How Americans through the years have told that story, or interpreted its meaning, tells us a lot about what we assume about love and love's odd relationship to modernity. What Jefferson believed, or rather did not believe, about God also tells us much about modernity and, by extension, about anthropology's peculiar preoccupation with religion.

If Jefferson wanted to move the religious sensibility beyond fickle belief to a set of enduring moral principles based on reason, anthropologists have argued that to understand the religions of people like Manjaco and Lauje we need to get past our assumption that religion is a belief of the kind we are used to given our own cultural traditions. For so-called primitive religions, we have tended to think of religion as primarily composed of acts—as ritual, as performance— not as primarily composed of ideas—beliefs, reasons, morals. And in order to understand religion in modern societies as well as in so-called primitive ones, we have, as usual, to get beyond our tendency to dichotomize and to imagine them as either simpler or more quintessential than us. They are not our ancestors. Nor are they closer to truth than we are. By the same token, they are also no more mired in superstition and credulity than we are.

Jefferson was notorious as a foe of established religion. In his era, Americans were deeply divided about what religion was. New and more populist forms of Christianity were gaining adherents. As the historian Fawn Brodie notes in her insightful biography, Jefferson attacked established religion head-on in *Notes on the State of Virginia*: "since the introduction of Christianity," sectarian differences meant that "millions of innocent men, women and children . . . have been burnt, tortured, fined, imprisoned; yet we have not advanced one inch toward uniformity." This probably made sense to the adherents of the new sects. But then Jefferson added that it was better to accept that there will never be agreement about the nature of God, for "it does me no injury for my neighbor to say there are twenty gods or no god. It neither picks my pocket nor breaks my leg."

No god or twenty gods. To practically any believer, whether a member of the established church or not, this was blasphemy. Yet in Jefferson's day there were plenty of influential atheists or Deists who might have concurred with him. Deism and atheism were in a sense Enlightenment faiths. There had been deists and atheists before the Enlightenment, but not until the Enlightenment had there been such a systematic and pervasive set of arguments refashioning the relationships among God, nature, and man as there was in Jefferson's era. Deism turned God into the great clockmaker, an animating force that created a universe based on principles of reason and order, leaving it up to humans to use their capacity for reason to discover that order and to order their lives and their social practices accordingly. God in Deism was nothing more or less than nature writ as spirit. One could talk of natural law and not need to resort to the Bible to describe what self-evident truths such a law contained. Meanwhile, atheism, or at least radical skepticism about religious authority, went hand in hand with the revolutionary political visions associated with the Enlightenment. Voltaire, for example, had said that he would not rest happily until the last king was strangled with the entrails of the last priest.

The philosophers of the Enlightenment recognized their peers in earlier civilizations. Jefferson admired republican Rome. His house with its dome was modeled after a Roman temple. Romans worshipped at least twenty gods, as did Greeks and Hindus. All the ancient admirable civilizations were polytheistic. More exciting, if more troubling still, were primitive societies of Africa, aboriginal America, and the Pacific. What was the status of their beliefs? Did they count as beliefs at all? One solution was to consider such religions as even more primitive than those based on belief itself. If science was an improvement over mere belief, then belief was an improvement over primitive religious practice, which was more like a habit or a routine retained out of fear of the unknown or out of inertia than it was a product of individual human sentiment and thought. In this view primitive "religions" were hardly worthy of the name. They were characterized by "ritual" and "taboo." Savages were slaves to customs and tradition. They could not think for themselves, and they were often fooled by the cheap magic tricks of the ritual specialists who preyed on their credulity. Religions, by contrast to these "superstitions," had texts associated with them, with skepticism as a by-product of literacy because texts could be scrutinized for inconsistencies. Thus it was that the first Western scholars who were skeptics were biblical scholars. By contrast, it was assumed that people who practiced traditional faiths could not be so relentlessly skeptical. They did things out of habit. They tended to assume what everyone assumes. Belief, as it were, shaded into erroneous "knowledge."

The religions, or rather superstitions, of people in these places therefore supplied Western skeptics with the vocabulary they used to excoriate the errors of their peers or to emphasize their credulity. Skeptics like Voltaire and Jefferson found much useful in the kind of anthropological data that Enlightenment scholars were also amassing as they explored the world and brought back stories of the varieties of religious practice among human beings in exotic places.

When Jefferson was writing *Notes* and when explorers such as Golberry were bringing back hippo bones to further the scientific and pedagogical projects of the European nation-states, other explorers were importing words like "taboo" and "mumbo jumbo." Skeptics and cynics in the Age of Enlightenment quickly deployed such words to define what was wrong with the beliefs or practices of their opponents. Mumbo jumbo was a West African term from the Mandinga people of the Senegambia. It perhaps first appeared in print in Francis Moore's account of his travels in Africa: "At Night, I was visited by a Mumbo Jumbo, an Idol, which is among the Mundingoes a kind of cunning Mystery. . . . This is a Thing invented by the Men to keep their Wives in awe." More famously, Mungo Park wrote in his *Travels in the Interior Districts of Africa* that "A sort of masquerade habit . . . which I was told . . . belonged to Mumbo Jumbo. This is a strange bugbear . . . much employed by the Pagan natives in keeping their women in subjection." Mumbo jumbo came to define religion as legerdemain. You could accuse a political or religious foe of using mumbo jumbo. But you might also recognize the utility of a little mumbo jumbo now and then. For the flip side of Enlightenment skepticism, as the anthropologist Marshall Sahlins has noted, was the recognition that "there is no God, but don't tell the servants." Legerdemain—using one's subjects' credulity to keep them in check, to make them act altruistically and against their own interests or to remain quiescent in the face of exploitation—was a recognized part of statecraft.

How quickly such loan words entered into the European vernacular reveals the fraught relationship that was emerging between belief and theories of knowledge. The relationship is complex, full of contradictions, but there are certain broad patterns of thought that emerged and came to be increasingly pervasive as religion and the problem of religious pluralism became a topic for scientific scrutiny. The word "belief" came to take on the tones of what later would become cultural relativism. If other people tend to have "beliefs" that differ from what you know to be true, then as long as you assume that the individual is not mentally impaired, you are compelled to come up with a cultural or sociological reason for their "error." That other people have them and that you recognize this fact makes for a culture theory, because your skepticism about their beliefs compels you to explain why they might have such beliefs even though such beliefs are clearly (from your perspective) fiction. Other people's gods came to be perceived as reflections of social structure—society writ as spirit(s). Other societies, other gods.

Another common pattern was the idea that belief could be opposed to ritual or custom, personal as opposed to habitual or routine. You had beliefs because you had thought about things, and your beliefs were often at odds with what those around you took for granted. Beliefs were interior, a product of thought.

Yet another common idea was that beliefs were in general inferior to reason as ways of thinking, with the former giving way to the latter as a part and parcel of the progress of human civilization. In the Enlightenment, civilization was characterized as a utopian vision of a future society that would be governed entirely by reason and not at all by blind faith. To the Enlightenment philosophers, reason was a universal human capacity. Reason was at the core of what it meant to be human; it distinguished humans from animals. Some people and some societies had it more than others. But reason could be taught and enshrined in social institutions through laws and regulations. It could become the foundation for better science that provided better health in the broadest of all senses. Reason could also become the foundation for better government as reasonable citizens joined forces with reasoning bureaucrats and legislators to enact better laws and make better institutions. Civilization in this view was not yet accomplished but was an ongoing project experienced as the movement toward reason and away from mere belief. Science, in this view, articulated reason. As the explanatory power of science expanded, religion associated with belief receded, although it retained moral authority and its emotional appeal.

Long after Jefferson published *Notes*, when he was president and often under vicious attack for his atheism, he wrote his own version of the New Testament to remove the bits that were about superstition. He wanted a Jesus who embodied an exemplary ethical and moral code. He envisaged a smart, wise, and morally exemplary Jesus, not a magic Jesus. He could not stomach a Jesus who performed miracles like he was pulling rabbits out of a hat, much less a Jesus who was actually God incarnate. Jefferson wanted Americans to move beyond belief toward a society based on reason, a shared body of accepted knowledge, and a set of agreed-upon truths. Toward the end of his days he confessed that he doubted there was a heaven. But he also understood that others might find solace in the sentiments of superstition.

In the century that followed, the idea of progress based on the passage of consciousness from belief as a set of superstitions to knowledge as a set of reasoned and demonstrated facts about the world came to define the ambivalent sensibility of what came to be known as modernity. If Jefferson tended to be sanguine about reason's triumph over superstition, philosophers and intellectuals in the early twentieth century were not as optimistic about progress's power. Early social scientists such as Emile Durkheim argued that social solidarity at once depended on and produced group rituals that created a sense of a power beyond the individual person—a sense that was not rational or even consciously thought out, but directly experienced through the body as a profound sentiment of togetherness. For Durkheim, "primitive religion" entailed collective ritual practices that created in the ritual's practitioners an embodied sense of belonging he called "collective effervescence." This sense of belonging to something greater than the self was the outcome of such ritual action, and while modern societies were in danger of losing their embodied sense of the belonging, they too depended on collective rituals to create an all-important social solidarity. Durkheim's utopian vision for the future of modern societies entailed a return of sorts. In order to thrive, modern societies needed to manufacture collective rituals as an antidote to the atomizing tendencies of modernity.

Other social philosophers in the early twentieth century assumed that the passing away of belief to be replaced by knowledge would have its psychological costs, for belief at least brought comfort. Magic enchanted the world, made it a sometimes scary but also a thrilling place. The sociologist Max Weber would articulate this emerging central theme in modernity. As moderns increasingly rationalized their ideas of what the world was, as they increasingly used rationality to model the social order, they increasingly confined themselves to the "iron cage" of disenchantment.

Nevertheless, the upshot was that progress could be mapped out in cultural or in sociological terms. In these maps, which traced the trajectory from enchantment to disenchantment by way of the increasing power of rationality to explain and order everything, the savage or his local sociological analogue the servant, the working man, the peasant, was assumed to have kept his beliefs— be wedded to them or mired in them, take your pick. "We" by contrast, that is, we enlightened people, we educated people, we who rule and administer them, have lost ours—"thank God!" or to our chagrin, again take your pick. Beliefs—that other people have them, that you don't anymore but might feel a nostalgic pang of loss about them—from Jefferson and Voltaire by way of Durkheim and Weber and a host of others, came to define the essence of the modern condition.

These ideas would also inform anthropological investigations into the religious practices of so-called primitive societies. Anthropologists would borrow from Durkheim and Weber to interpret primitive religion, but they would also disrupt and call into question the dichotomizing paradigms of Western philosophy and social science. Anthropologists would argue, for example, that if they have rituals, so do we. Indeed, ritual, as a routinized action, as we have already seen, would be one of the foundational ideas in an emerging theory of culture. But in contrast to Durkheim what would become important to anthropologists was not just how rituals embodied unconscious if deeply felt sentiments, but how rituals could serve as models which prompted thought. Rituals were in this scheme "good to think" as well as good to feel. Anthropologists would also subvert the distinctions the intellectuals of modernity tended to make between belief and skepticism. Evans-Pritchard would use his research among Azande to demonstrate that if we have beliefs, or can be skeptical, so can they. We will return to these anthropologists, but first an excursion into the beliefs of the Lauje and then Manjaco skepticism by way of contemporary America.

American Belief

It is sometimes hard for my students to accept the proposition that religious belief and modernity are opposed—that progress was not only imagined by people such as Jefferson as a move away from religion and toward reason, but that religious belief according to sociologists such as Weber has declined as we have become more modern. The facts, at least in the United States, do not seem to square with the theory. While I was writing this book, we were in the second term of the presidency of George W. Bush. President Bush spoke openly and often of his belief in God, and he linked his Christianity to his political program. Without this kind of frequent talk, and without some political action reflecting this talk, Bush likely would never have been elected or re-elected. That he was elected, that he talked so much about God, that he could mix religion and politics in a state ostensibly founded on the principle of the separation of church and state, was not remarkable to my students. During his second term in office his approval ratings hovered at just above 30 percent, but he still had overwhelming support of the more than 25 percent of Americans who claimed to be evangelical Christians. This number, large in itself, was dwarfed by the more than 70 percent of Americans who claimed to be religious.

The religiosity of the majority made religion itself an unremarkable fact of life to most of my students, not to mention the many students who were themselves evangelical or the children of evangelicals. Many of them, if not most, believed. Belief to them was not anathema to progress. America, most of them also assumed (without, however, reviewing the evidence, for this is the essence of ethnocentrism), was the most advanced nation on earth, or at least the most prosperous. To them, if large majorities of Europeans had given up God, if most academics and scientists the world over were equally agnostic, then this might explain why such people and places were not quite as prosperous as Americans were, why those other seemingly modern nations were so weak, so immoral, so incapable of helping America make the world a better place for all.

Belief for the modern American had become an idea clearly inflected by an all-pervasive ethos of individualistic pluralism. Many of my students were loath to talk openly about their beliefs, lest they be construed as trying to foist their beliefs on others, or, worse, that they might reveal that their beliefs were superficial or without much substance. Belief, they would say, was "personal." Just as everyone was an individual, unique like each snowflake is unique, so could there be an endless variety of beliefs, all different, yet all the same in their difference. Just as everyone should have a distinct and strong personality, so too should everyone have a belief. To say "this is what I believe" was to express your core. You could easily imagine "laying down your life," losing a friend, getting fired from a job, all because you stuck to your beliefs. Likewise, to merely go through the motions would mean that one was a phony, a poseur, not a real person. For this reason, and because Christianity, the dominant faith, put a premium on an interior or mental view of what religion was, my students tended to assume that religion itself was a belief—that it was mainly about thoughts and feelings and not primarily about acts. Thus too all religions were imagined to be assorted according to the sentiments they called up or the ideas they expressed, not according to the rituals and actions they required. Some of my students, for example, claimed to be Christians but found it not to be a contradiction to admit that they no longer went to church. Belief, like personality, was something inside you. It might be revealed in what you did— what you wore, how you acted—but it did not have to be. Religion to them was more quintessentially a prayer rather than a set of food taboos or a veil. These, they often assumed, could even be discarded and yet religion—that is, belief—would still remain.

For many students as well, belief was opposed to knowledge; in this they were similar to their peers in European universities, who by and large thought of knowledge as a product of science and belief as associated with religion. My students did not draw the distinction in order to imply that belief was inferior to knowledge. Sometimes having a belief meant that you recognized or asserted that what others took to be knowledge was merely a belief. Thus for some students, "the theory of evolution" was a belief, a matter of (misguided) faith. Some people believed in science, some people believed in the Bible. In short, you have your beliefs, I have mine. Belief, that idea that you have yours and I have mine, dovetailed with a general idea of American pluralism—we are all equal if different—and it allowed for covert disagreement without overt argument.

More significantly, for many of my students belief implied maintaining a faith in something even as empirical evidence seemed to contradict those beliefs. To maintain a belief in the face of facts or without the corroboration of facts was a kind of test, a demonstration of one's faith. Some of them knew the kinds of tragic but inspirational stories that are the stuff of so many sermons, so many acts of "witnessing." The car you are driving crashes on the way back from church because you had to swerve to avoid a drunk driving a truck in the wrong lane. You survive, but your children die. Years later, you retell the awful story to explain how your faith was tested and how you became even more of a believer than you had been before. Belief is what you have even when the evidence isn't there to corroborate it.

This idea that belief is a higher form of consciousness than knowledge is widespread, if perhaps mostly cloaked in a kind of modernist nostalgia. No student would admit to believing in Santa Claus, for example, but they remembered with much emotion reading such books as *The Polar Express*. The message of this story and others like it is that enchantment is a good thing, and that enchantment can be recovered or protected if only one believes. In *The Polar Express* a boy is transported on a magic train to the North Pole, where he receives a present from Santa—a bell from Santa's sleigh. Later, he finds the same bell wrapped up as a present under the Christmas tree. As he grows up, he loses the capacity to hear the bell, but he later recovers that capacity. As long as he can hear the bell, he occupies a special magical place in the world. Belief acts as a kind of bracket around the passage of time. You used to believe. Now you don't. If you could only get yourself to believe again, then progress would be a return of sorts—a return to the comforts of childhood. On the surface that notion seemed to share much with the cynical enlightenment view that God doesn't exist but don't tell the servants, transposed to

Santa and don't tell the children. But it had a twist: If one could convince the children, then the parent too had to become convinced. Belief was a good thing, if a fragile thing.

Lauje Enchantments

Anthropologists are not immune to this way of thinking about belief. When I read *The Polar Express* to my small children I always cried. Every Christmas Eve I showed them the carrots we were going to leave out for Santa's reindeer, and after they had gone to bed I would chew up the carrots, spit out some bits in a trail to the door, and enjoy the bittersweet pleasure of their joy when they discovered the traces of Santa's visit the next morning before we opened the presents. One upshot of our modernity is that we assume that the enchantment of belief is at once pleasurable and somehow past tense—belief is what children still have, what our society used to have, what primitive people still have.

A cynic once said that anthropology was religion for atheists because, if nothing else, a field trip among primitive people allowed you to experience, if mainly touristically, the enchantments of belief. That enchantment is one reason Lauje were so exciting to me. There are so-called primitive societies whose members seem to express a religious sensibility we associate with that protean term, belief.

In Taipaobal—that ridgeline community that was ostensibly so close to the navel of the earth—our neighbors, closest friends, and best research informants were the family of Siamae Senji (Father of Senji), a famous shaman. Siamae Senji could cure most illness by passing his hand over the infected region of your body while blowing on his hand and reciting a secret prayer. He knew hundreds of prayers, each with its arcane significance, and he had collected these over several decades from other great shamans, all of whom were, by the time we met him, long dead. Siamae Senji also had what the Lauje called a "bolian," or spirit familiar, who "sat beside" the great shaman and guided him when he took invisible journeys to distant Mecca or other magical places to acquire healing powers or to do battle with the spirits of illness.

Siamae Senji was a very old man when we arrived in Taipaobal. From the stories he told us about his dealings with the Dutch and Chinese, we estimated that he was close to a hundred years old. He could no longer walk. His sons had to carry him when he needed to defecate. He told them that he would soon die and that they would need to make a grave for him with a covered roof, lest his spirit be desecrated by rainfall or sun, and the surrounding land suffer drought or awful storm as a result. When he knew death was upon him, he called out to his family from the surrounding mountains to come to him so that he could divide up and pass on his prayers and, above all, his spirit familiar. His youngest son, his most gentle son, inherited the spirit. The others received prayers, most useful for curing, but some that made a person impervious to bullets and blowgun darts or made enemies flee in terror. Siamae Senji had been a gentle man. He had once saved his entire community from a smallpox epidemic by drawing a large circle in the dirt around his house in which the people gathered, forbidding the smallpox to cross the line. He had also cured several prominent "foreign" officials in Tinombo of severe illnesses, of "cancer," one of these officials told us. But Siamae Senji had also been a warrior. He wielded a sharp machete and he had used his blowgun against foreign invaders. He was both feared and loved as a man of power, a "To Baraka."

By morning he was dead. We buried him in a grave covered by a roof—an honor Lauje reserved only for its rare "To Baraka." Then we went home to eat a meal in his honor. A rainbow appeared in the clear sky; from where we sat on the veranda it looked like it was coming out of the grave. I took a photo. After I took the shot, Siamae Senji's sons remarked that the rainbow was their father's spirit returning to heaven.

A week or so later, I was returning home to Taipaobal after an excursion to another ridgeline community to visit another shaman. It was late at night, but there was a full moon, so my companion (who had come with me from Taipaobal because he too wanted to add to his collection of spells and prayers) and I could easily see the slick path through the tangle of leaves in front of us. As we forded the last crossing of the river before the steep ascent up to Taipaobal, my friend suggested that we use the opportunity of the moonlight to catch crayfish to eat. He showed me where to look for them around and under the river rocks, but warned me not to keep any crayfish that was missing a claw or arm. When I asked why, he responded, as if it should be obvious, "Would you eat a chicken or rooster than had lost its comb? Would you point at a rainbow?"

Later, as we trudged up the steep hill, I pestered him with questions about the rainbow and the rooster. You cannot point at a rainbow, he explained, or you'll get leprosy. Hook your finger when you point and you will be safe. If you slice a rooster comb and eat the rooster, your blood will begin to flow out of you like the blood from the rooster's comb. Eat a crayfish that has lost its claw, and that claw will come back to etch at your insides, killing you. Then, as we approached, he made a loud noise, he told me once we had reached the safety of my house on stilts, so as not to startle and offend the shaman's ghost with our sudden arrival.

Lauje lived in an enchanted world. It was a world in which the enchantments all seemed to circle about one another, making uncanny connections. The whole wide world was always being connected in startling ways to the smallest things. Saimae Senji, a man, was also a conduit for the powers of the universe. His small, roof-covered grave would become a shrine, a place to spend the night in anxious but brave meditation in the hope that the power would fill you up and make you powerful. A "simple prayer," his son once told me, a prayer with names in it, "only five names," could hold up or destroy the five pillars that anchored the earth in space. The ultimate truths, so many Lauje believed, were the truths of the placental spirit, the ultimate all-encompassing thing (and idea) that one could "grasp in the palm of your hand."

To pursue the logic of such beliefs was a pleasure. Even though I did not believe them, I liked the feeling of believing. I had seen the rainbow. It felt good to entertain the feeling that it was Siamae Senji's spirit's passing that had conjured up that rainbow in a clear sky. For me, too, the intricate simplicity of Lauje belief was what made it so compelling. With them I felt closer to God, closer to nature, and closer to humanity—cozy and thrilled in our mutual journeys to pursue another piece in the spiritual puzzle. As the outlines of this puzzle took shape, the main message, endlessly repeated in different forms and scales, was a sort of paradox. Humans were connected to the whole of the world, but to live they had to sever, at least momentarily, such connections. Yet the connections you severed always threatened to come together again, and this caused problems. Thus, recall that most illness, chills and fever, or diarrhea, were caused by "connection"—by, that is, the inappropriate rejoining of the placenta or the birth fluids with the person who to live had to be detached from its "twin." Thus, too, it was dangerous to travel during "*huja huja eleo*"—a time when it rained yet was also sunny. Worse still would be to have sexual intercourse during such a day, or to fart while having sex. So too, we were told, should you never laugh at two dogs in coitus. That would cause a typhoon or an earthquake. Cosmology always was connected to the close at hand.

We were warned never to laugh at copulating dogs by one of our friends, whose serious lips seemed to threaten a smile even as he warned us not to laugh. As he told us, we too began to smile, suppressing the compulsion to laugh, while he sketched for us the image of two dogs caught in the midst of sex. Dogs once so engaged cannot easily become disengaged. That image of two dogs struggling to disengage, each pulling in the opposite direction, cannot help but be funny.

Later we would learn in one of our frequent late-night sessions with a shaman that during the world's beginnings the ancestor of dogs had cursed the ancestor of humans for laughing at him, and that the curse entailed that they exchange sex organs. From then on, the shaman explained, "to laugh at a dog's sex was to laugh at your own sex organs"—to do so, therefore, was to commit a cardinal sin of "connection."

Connections seemed to be everywhere and always all-encompassing. If you should not laugh at dogs copulating, you should rejoice when dogs begin defecating on the pathways, because they did this when the constellation "Many People" (Pleiades) was directly overhead, and this was the time of rice planting. To prepare a rice field, the Lauje made a sacrifice in the field's center, or its "navel," placing among other objects half of a coconut turned over to resemble a skull. This object, plus the "seven" kernels of rice planted around the shell, were meant to call up the memory of "Nabi Adam," who had sacrificed herself—yes, herself—for her starving people back in the earliest of days. When she died and was buried, out of her hair and part of her skull bloomed the "Many People" constellation, while out of the other half of her skull and bones sprouted the first rice, and out of her teeth the first corn, and so forth. Around the edges of the field, around, that is, the field's head and feet (or Nabi Adam's body), the Lauje planted a variety of seeds—seeds whose plants were to be left for the pigs or rats or insects, all refractions of the spirit of Nabi Adam. When they ate the edges of your garden, this was the tribute you paid to "connection." When you planted the moment the Pleiades were directly overhead, you reconnected the disassembled skull of Nabi Adam, resurrecting her, as it were, reconnecting her in that act.

Rice planting was a festivity associated with human sexuality as well. A line of young men moved across the field's body, each man poking holes into the earth with a long and heavy teak staff. As they did this they sang songs filled with double entendres equating poking the earth with procreation. Meanwhile, a line of girls waited for them to approach, responding in turn with bawdy songs of their own. Once the boys had prepared the field, the girls moved across it, dropping seeds into the holes. Human reproduction thus was connected, by way of mimetic acts and songs, to rice planting, and the rice planting Lauje did every year was connected mimetically, through rituals and coconut shells, to the first rice and the first sacrifice. Life and death: connection.

The ritual of rice planting is a quintessentially cultural act in the sense that Clifford Geertz defined the cultural as a slurring interchange among "models of" and "models for." To perform a ritual in Lauje meant to make mimetic models of connection itself. Boys and girls planting rice and singing about sex embodied in their actions a complex set of ideas about connection. Thus models of the world became a part of a personal, sensual experience. The sexual desire you felt for him, or he for you, endorsed the "reality" of Nabi Adam's ancient sacrifice.

Many of these models became puzzles to be solved, for Lauje and for us. Thus, for example, at harvest time a large platform was built in the fields, and on it a shaman placed circles of sticky and regular rice of a variety of hues. The circles of rice mimicked or modeled the way a body was thought to form in the womb—the skull first with its hard bones encompassing oily brain matter, and later bones containing marrow, and finally darker but softer layers of muscle and flesh, packaged in skin. The circles of rice mimicked the human body, but also the earth's body. The egg at the center of the offering mimicked at once the beginning of human life and the origin of the earth and heavens. When shamans studied with one another, they learned how to place the rice, the offerings of tobacco (at "the earth's center, and its four corners"), antique coins, and egg, while also learning secret names for spirits occupying the earth's anchoring corners and the anchoring parts of the human body. To think, in short, about a body or the earth entailed thinking with the models one learned to make. In thinking this way, though, the shaman conflated the model with the reality it was made to represent.

As Geertz has said, elaborating on Weber, we inhabit a world that weaves us into a web of meanings we make for ourselves. To see this web as a web we make, it helps to see it being made by others. So it was for us with the Lauje. We could experience their web making touristically and feel a kind of deflected pleasure in the ethnographic quest for knowledge that, in its way, mimicked a Lauje shaman's quest to understand and use "connection." For shamans, truth could be grasped in the palm of your hand. It was as small and all-encompassing as a human placenta. It was as all-encompassing yet compact as a rice offering.

Such an all-encompassing connection fulfills a pervasive Western fantasy about knowledge and faith that is signaled in our endless fascination with stories like *The Da Vinci Code* or *The Lord of the Rings*—that comforting and thrilling idea that you can grasp, in something small and self-contained, the entire truth. But religion, even primitive religion, has a history and has been transformed. Lauje shamans, we eventually realized, were always concerned to make sense of local beliefs in the context of a more globalizing Islam.

Islam was monotheistic but hardly monolithic in how the Qur'an and other texts were to be interpreted. In Indonesia, for example, there had been a long struggle between Muslims who followed the interpretations of Sufism and those who were influenced by what were becoming the more mainstream views associated with Sunni readings of the Qur'an. A crucial sura—a meditation on Abraham's willingness to sacrifice his son for God—states that "God is closer to you than your jugular vein." For Sunnis that is a reminder that God is the ultimate arbiter of one's fate, so that one must always submit to his will because one never knows the time and place of one's death. For Sufis, the meaning is different. God is inside you, and you can discover God's power by meditation and so forth. For Lauje this idea confirmed their belief in "connection." What was inside one's body—what was as intimate as your blood and bodily fluids—was as universal as God.

Even Sunni Islam made room for "connection" as Lauje interpreted things because, in its legal codes, it also allowed for "custom" to coexist with "religion." Lauje used the philosophy inherent in the idea of connection to argue that, just as humans had to pay their respects to the "older sibling" that was their twin as embodied in the placenta, so too did good Muslims have to pay respects to custom, for custom was Islam's "older sibling." The upshot, though, was that over the years that Islam became more popular in the region—first as a hodgepodge of mystical beliefs associated with Sufism and later as a more rationalized faith tied to mainstream Sunni scholarship that eventually came to be taught in schools in a more clearly rationalized and articulated form—local shamans became more articulate about "connection" and "custom," streamlining a welter of local beliefs and practices so they became in effect more coherent and more monotheistic. Lauje shamans could find in Islamic beliefs echoes of their beliefs in connection. In studying Lauje religion, we were not getting a glimpse into a kind of primitive fossil of beliefs of earlier and ancient times. Rather we were witnessing the contemporary invention of a new faith that allowed a marginal people to imagine themselves as part of a globalizing world defined in part by the apparatus of a state-sanctioned religion. To understand this belief, we had to get beyond our tendency to think of Lauje as holdovers from a distant past—as a kind of living ancestor to ourselves or to contemporary Indonesians.

Manjaco Faith

Arriving among Manjaco after less than three months' rest "at home" in the United States inevitably meant that I thought in Lauje terms when I tried to understand Manjaco. If most anthropologists try to "make the strange familiar" by recognizing what is odd or unusual about what their subjects take for granted, contrasting it to what is routine or ordinary "at home" (thereby also making "the familiar strange"), I tended to find most strange those things Manjaco did that would have been out of place in Lauje country. I have already mentioned the noise; the aggressive gregariousness of Manjaco felt odd and

unexpected to me after the willful quietness of Lauje. You approach a line of
Lauje coming your way on a forest path, and neither they nor you and your
group change pace or offer a greeting as you pass each other quickly and in
silence. You might nod your head, but that is about it. Lauje, to use one of our
clichés, seemed especially concerned with "privacy." Manjaco, by contrast,
were always quick to greet and often greeted with aggressive inquisitiveness.
"Where are you going?" "What are you carrying [in the bag]?" You, under the
[mango] tree, lazy today?" You were required to respond; sociability in Manjaco
felt like interrogation.

Manjaco religious practices made for the most startling contrasts to Lauje. If
Manjaco were louder and quicker to assert themselves than were the standoff-
ish and shy Lauje, then they also were routinely expressing overt skepticism
and irreverence in public. For example, Upa Nanguran, an elder and the ruler
of one of the six satellite villages of Bassarel, told me, in a loud voice right at
the moment we were participating in a public ceremony at the most sacred
of Bassarel's shrines, that he had "no faith in" the spirits. It was my first visit
to that shrine, and it was during the community-wide ceremony that marks
the transition from planting to harvest season. He motioned me to sit by him
and share his bowl of wine. We sat together a few feet from the spot where the
shrine priest poured to the spirit, and Upa said loudly, "This is of the spirits,
is of the left hand. Dirty. Bad. The left hand is the dirty hand. What hand do
you eat with? What hand do you use to wipe your ass?" I asked him to tell me
more, but he replied, "We can't talk here at the shrine. That is why the shrine
is dirty, bad. Look at us. We are drunk. We'll forget tomorrow what we say
today. Words spoken here are the words of wine."

The next day I visited him and he explained, "The spirits are like street merchants." Itinerant merchants "want to sell you something. You buy it. But you
don't know if it's good." He emphasized that "the spirits want to cheat you just
like the merchants. . . . The words spoken with the spirits are unclear (*jintat*).
This is why the shrine priests die so fast. . . . I see you sitting in front of me. We
are of different countries. . . . But we see each other. If we agree on something,
we see that we agree. But the shrine is different. We speak. We pour wine. We
say that the spirit agrees, but does it agree? The shrine priests die because they
are working with something unclean."

After my years with Lauje, when it sometimes seemed that everyone was a
part-time shaman, or wanted to be, or at least collected a spell or two much as
we might keep a well-stocked medicine cabinet, I was constantly made aware
of how many Manjaco openly criticized the spirits as untrustworthy, even evil.
I also came to know a few men who publicly doubted their very existence. A

chance conversation with Tomas, who was in his early forties and had spent most of his life in Senegal, where he had converted to Catholicism, exemplified an extreme version of a lack of faith in the spirits. After a funeral, as we watched the men interrogating the funeral bier for the causes of death, he remarked to me in disgust: "I am *wokat*. A tree dies; we don't accuse the father of the tree of witchcraft. Termites eat the tree. Fever kills the child. I have no faith in the interrogation. Does the deceased speak? No, the bed moves. People carry the bed. They move the bed."

Tomas was doubting a paradigm, not just a particular practice. But the word *wokat* in general meant to not have faith in a person's action, not in their essence. In English, when we say "believe in me" or "have faith in me," we are asking someone to trust us. If you don't have faith in someone, you still know that the person exists; you just aren't going to lend them the money they've asked you for. When Manjaco said that they had no faith in spirits, were skeptical—*wokat*—it was usually in that sense. They usually still assumed that there were spirits, but they also assumed that because they could neither see nor communicate with spirits, that it was counterproductive to trust their fates in the hands of such entities. One youth explained that to request something of the spirit was like playing *totobola*, the popular and ubiquitous soccer lottery: The spirit might grant one's request, or it might not, but in any case the outcome was beyond human control. Another told me that he and his companions wished to avoid dealing with the spirits because the elders, who spoke at the ceremonies and asked "for signs" (*iik*) from the spirits, "exceeded the spirits"—that is, spoke to others invoking spiritual authority or sanction when no evidence of sanction or authority was present.

If Geertz thought ethnography is part philosophy and part confession, I would add that a good deal more of it is biography in disguise. We tend to reflect upon a whole people through the individuals we meet and who have the most effect on us. The Lauje I knew primarily through the sons and daughters of Siamae Senji became my guides to Lauje life. They believed, as it were, in shamanistic truths. If they were skeptical, it was about the efficacy of this prayer or that, about the honesty of this shaman or that. Theirs was a piecemeal skepticism. They never doubted their father. They also craved the quest for connection. Connection was both a fact and a mystery to be pursued and discovered. By contrast, what I learned about Manjaco I learned most through a charismatic if angry young man named Armando, who was my host, my closest friend, and my intellectual collaborator while I lived in the "land" of Bassarel. What intrigued and disturbed me most about Armando was how little he seemed to care for, need, or want authority of the kind my anthropological ancestors deemed to be essential for the mental health of an inhabitant of a traditional village. Nothing, or more accurately nobody, was sacred to him. Armando was perhaps extreme in his skepticism, extreme in his urge to be openly, even defiantly critical, but he also seemed profoundly at home in what I euphemized as "Manjaco society," and he was in many ways a paragon other Manjaco respected and admired. Whether or not I could legitimately characterize his kind of pervasive skepticism as a Manjaco ethos, I could certainly claim that it typified a homegrown youthful attitude and that Armando at least exemplified such an ethos.

If when I was among Lauje I focused on belief to understand an ethos and to make sense of religious transformation in the postcolonial era, among Manjaco I focused on this skepticism. It happens that one of the most important anthropological accounts of an African religion—Evans-Pritchard's *Witchcraft, Oracles and Magic Among the Azande*—focuses on the idea of skepticism. Evans-Pritchard explored the various ways religious practices persist despite considerable skepticism about, for example, the efficacy of particular diviners, the accuracy of particular witchcraft accusations, and the efficacy of particular rites and charms. Evans-Pritchard's monograph explicitly blurred the boundaries between Western and African modes of thought. For Evans-Pritchard, Azande were just as suspicious of the truth claims of others, just as likely to empirically test forms of curing, and so forth, as were Westerners. The rationality of their skepticism was, however, piecemeal, and therefore the exposure of charlatans or of medicines ineffectively administered had the unintended consequence of reinforcing their general belief that the world indeed contained witches and medicines useful for countering their deleterious effects.

In light of Evans-Pritchard's work, my quest became to consider Armando's typicality. What can we learn about a society by focusing on total skeptics? I watched Armando interact with his circle of young emerging leaders in this postcolonial village who were at the vanguard of revolutionizing village-level religious practice, pushing the community at large to modify or outlaw certain religious customs and to do away with certain village spirit shrines. Soon I became habituated to their irreverence, and what became even more intriguing was that such youths also continued to participate in community ceremony and ritual. More interesting still, they made offerings (without the supervision or even the encouragement of elders—as a kind of play, but at real shrines) to local spirits before intervillage soccer matches, before school entrance examinations, during courtship, and the like. By looking at how youthful religious play both promoted skepticism and habituated juniors to traditional religious practices, we can see how belief and skepticism are entangled, and we can start to think beyond belief as we think about religion in a comparative context.

Manjaco Skepticism

For most of the time I was in Bassarel, I shared rooms and meals with Armando. We lived together in an almost empty compound in a large, cement-floored structure with a zinc roof paid for by absent emigrants. The women of the household—the two surviving wives of Armando's father along with Armando's wife and two small children—lived in a smaller, thatch-roofed hut. Tomas, Armando's fifty-year-old father's brother, occupied (with his small family) a cramped little house in the center of the village, one of dozens built by the Portuguese during the revolution to make (so the Portuguese claimed) village life more sanitary, and built also, of course, to make the village more compact and therefore easier to guard and monitor as the Portuguese fought their losing war against the "bandits" as they called them in the bush. Gabriel, Armando's younger brother, also usually slept in such a hut with other bachelors temporarily back from school or work in Bissau, the country's capital.

Armando was always giving me impromptu lessons in Manjaco "customs"— our shared space becoming a kind of spontaneous theater for his skepticism about much of that custom. Here is a fairly typical occasion. Armando has just entered my little room. I am sick with a high fever, and I wake up to find one of the old mothers in my room, making a fire. She has shut the windows I habitually keep open. I ask her to leave, and not long afterwards Armando appears. I am not yet out of bed. As Armando opens the window shutters to let in the light, he notices the beginnings of a mud-wasp nest high in the corner of the ceiling. He pokes at the nest with a broom he'd brought to sweep up the ashes. He knocks the nest down. "The elders say the mud-wasp is taboo to kill," he tells me as crushes the nest with his foot.

I had recently become preoccupied with cataloguing Manjaco beliefs about "sacred" insects, and Armando had been with me on several occasions when I had asked this or that old woman or man about them. One such insect called "God's Blood" became a particular obsession for me. A bright red droplet, it appeared in droves as if from nowhere under the silk cottonwood trees at the beginning of the rainy season. To me its name and provenance seemed to hark to the kind of all-encompassing cosmology I had come to crave after my time with the Lauje. Once, when I was walking with Armando along the narrow path to our house, I paused to photograph a cluster of the little crimson drops.

Armando remarked, as I knelt beside the bugs, which seemed to swarm out of a dent in the sand, "The elders say they fall from the sky, but they come out of the ground." Now, as Armando crushed the wasp nest with his heal—gloating, I swear, at me—he listed, as if he were a teacher reciting a lesson, the other insects that were taboo to kill, among them "the spider," which he introduced by mimicking an elder scolding a child caught in the act of stepping on one, "Do you want go to heaven to get a shroud for its funeral?"

On another occasion we are eating a meal of rice and a particularly succulent long-jawed fish. Armando holds up one of the fish heads to get my attention. He puts the head in his mouth and makes loud sucking sounds. He removes the long jaw and smacks his lips loudly—a mimesis of gustatory delight—and tells me that when he was a child he would watch the elders eat just like that. "We could not eat the heads. They told us it was taboo." He put another fish head in his mouth and sucked and smacked.

As he savored the meal he told me how as a child he'd subverted such rules. Eggs, he told me, were supposed to be especially forbidden. According to the elders, eggs were the favorite food of the *nanjangurun*—the mischievous but also malicious bush spirit that a diviner had to cajole to become the diviner's spirit familiar. When Armando was a young boy, he and his friends had discovered several clutches of eggs hidden in the tall grass behind the compound. They had set fire to the grass, "an accident"—he grinned at me—that roasted the eggs, which they then ate.

For some reason this childhood memory elicited another—of learning to use the tall grass stalks to make the buzzing sound of the diviner's spirit familiar, or *nanjangurun*. As Armando told me how they "played diviner" as children, he cupped his hands and imitated the way they blew through the split grass stalks. "The diviner goes into his hut where you can't see him," he explained. "You hear him ask a question. You hear a noise—the *nanjangarun*'s answer." When Armando and his friends played diviner, "our parents became angry, told us it was taboo, told us to stop."

On yet another occasion Armando and I were waiting for a bush taxi in the district market town when a group of older men passed by—each dressed in a huge overcoat, each wearing a tattered hat, and each with a large satchel, somewhat like a postman's bag slung over the shoulder. Armando commented, "See the sack. An elder cannot travel without his sack." He then conjured up a conversation with an imaginary elder, playing the role of the poker-faced man. "You ask the elder what's in the sack. He looks and looks at you [Armando pauses for effect] and says, 'It's taboo to tell.' But there is nothing in his bag; just an empty bottle, a pipe, a wad of tobacco."

Armando did not restrict his cynical skepticism to local authority alone. Once when we listened to political speeches on the radio, he parodied the president's remarks, turning an address to the nation into an invocation an elder might make at a local shrine. Or he made fun of the incompetence of Cuban doctors at the hospital in Bissau. "They send them here to practice on us. Once they learn, they send them home."

Indeed, Armando's desire to expose the emptiness of authority in general—it hollowness—seemed to be an all-encompassing obsession. Once, for example, when Armando, his brother Gabriel, and Gabriel's age-mate Marcel were quizzing me on the hypocrisies of Christians, Armando began to tell a story about a local outbreak of millenarian Catholicism. Late in the revolution, a ceramic saint had (miraculously, so it was claimed) appeared in a nearby village. "They said when it first fell, it talked. But when we saw it in Calequisse where they built a little house for it, the saint was just a piece of clay the Europeans had made. After the war some drunk boys tipped it over and it shattered." To Armando the ceramic saints of Catholicism were just as empty as the satchels Manjaco elders carried.

Armando's tendency to dismiss the authority of others dovetailed with a certain charisma. As his peers and many elders put it, he "had soul" (atiji uas). He was (if there is such a thing) a natural leader. Peers and elders alike sought him out for advice. At public meetings, while other youths yelled rashly, or while drink-addled elders seemed to orate incoherently, endlessly, Armando spoke with a succinct calm that made others nod their heads in agreement.

Armando seemed to have a key role in every postcolonial decision-making body or power platform there was in Bassarel. On his own initiative he had become the village postman. He made periodic trips to the district capital to gather the mail. Illiterate elders trusted him to compose letters to distant relatives for them, or to read aloud (in the privacy of our shared hut) the letters they received from emigrant sons. He was among the handful of young men who had been trained to run the local infirmary, a place only haphazardly supplied with the medicines Armando and his peers distributed. He had become the favorite interlocutor of the various agricultural extension workers that visited Bassarel. He was often dismissive of them to me once they left, whirring off on their fancy off-road motorcycles. But he played polite and generous host to them and listened to their schemes; he sometimes used or redistributed the seed or fertilizer or insecticide they promised and occasionally delivered.

Armando had been one of the founders of the Development of Culture Club and was still in many ways its de facto leader. The prototype of "the Club" (as it was commonly called) had been introduced by Portuguese Catholic missionaries in the last years of the revolution, when Bassarel, on the border of the Portuguese zone of control, was selected to benefit from development programs under the rubric of "Guiné Melhor," or "a better Guinea." "A better Guinea" brought to Bassarel those closely packed huts with their zinc roofs I mentioned, but also a clinic, a deep-water well, and a Catholic school; it was the priests who encouraged the students to perform culturally uplifting plays in local costumes and idioms. After the revolution, the "Club" became for a brief time a local chapter of the Nationalist Party's version of the Young Pioneers, the Nationalist Party being itself heavily influenced by similar movements in places like Cuba and Vietnam. But by the time of my sojourn in the village, the Club had long since broken its ties with the government because Manjaco, who had remained for the most part neutral during the war, often found themselves at odds with the state. The Club had a double agenda regarding what they called "culture." They wished to protect and promote certain elements of Manjaco culture (e.g., dance, cooperative labor) in order to make village life attractive to the young. But they also wanted to eradicate certain elements of Manjaco culture they deemed destructive. These included, for example, funeral divination, witchcraft accusations, the inflated costs of certain "traditional" sacrifices, and so forth.

Armando was also one of the younger members on the postrevolutionary Bassarel community council, called (after the French word for bureaucratic office) the "Biro." This council had no official sanction from the state government. It was entirely a local innovation. It served, however, as a local governing body. If, for example, one village was complaining that the cattle of another village were polluting their wells, the issue would first be discussed among the Biro members. Then certain policy options would be outlined before the issue was presented to the general public for their consent. The Biro had considerable influence in shaping policy in village affairs.

In short, Armando had actively sought or had thrust upon him a host of leadership positions in the postcolonial village. Yet ironically Armando would always be a kind of jural minor in his own "house" or kinship group. There he would have to defer, in important and ongoing decisions of daily life, to a series of "uncles"—the younger "brothers" of the house's recently deceased patriarch, Armando's father. By Bassarel's rules of kinship succession, where brother followed brother, Armando would probably never become a house patriarch as his father had been. He would never be the master of his own house.

Moreover, while so many of his peers had solved that kind of problem by emigrating, Armando was, for complex reasons, stuck in the village. Armando was oldest but belated son of the house patriarch—Wrink—a man of considerable local power. Wrink had made Armando stay close by to act as his factotum while younger siblings and cousins moved to distant cities in pursuit of a better, more autonomous life.

Armando was his father's protégé, yet, as Armando kept telling me, they had never been friendly. Their life together had been one long test of wills. Armando had always wished to emigrate, but just when he thought he might be able to leave, Wrink and the other elders had forced him to marry a girl (Armando had several girlfriends) he had made pregnant. After considerable pressure, Armando agreed to marry the girl, but he swore to his father never to speak to her again. A few months later Wrink died. Armando could not take back his oath.

Armando's uncle Tomas, a short skinny man given to loud outbursts that everyone ignored, hated Wrink and resented Armando. He had returned from the Gambia during the revolution when he received news that Wrink was sick, probably dying. When the Portuguese built the "Guiné Melhor" (a better Guinea) huts in the center of the village and ordered those "in the bush" to move there for safety's and sanitation's sake, Tomas went gladly while Wrink refused, staging a one-man protest against Portuguese paternalism. Wrink recovered from his illness, so Tomas continued to stay, with his wife and children, in the hot, cramped building. He told me that "a man should have his own house." With Wrink finally dead he was eager to claim his ancestral home. He showed me a space near the courtyard where he would build his house with money from brothers in Senegal. "I am the owner of this now," he reminded me. "Not Armando."

Although Tomas may in theory have been the rightful heir, Armando continued to contest his authority, to Tomas's consternation. For example, on the eve of the first dry season ceremony at Penau, the shrine of the "king of the below," Basserel's guardian spirit, Armando and Tomas got into an argument about how the house would make its required offering. Each house was to bring wine and a clay pot of cooked rice and sauce to share with the rest of the community. Armando and I sat together finishing our dinner and chatting when Faran Balé arrived, staggering and slurry from too much rum. Balé was the oldest member of the clan Wrink's house belonged to; his house was a few dozen yards away and he visited Armando daily to consult with him about village affairs and to flirt with the women. As usual he wished to speak of "something important" and leaned over to Armando and said, "I am old. Soon I will be dead. You will be the one to continue." Armando interrupted him by pouring him a drink. Balé drank one glass of cane rum and then another.

Soon he had fallen asleep, his bearded chin against his chest. Armando woke him and Balé staggered for home. Tomas, who must have been sitting under the veranda with the women, entered just as Balé left. He brought a bottle of palm wine. "My bottle which I tapped in your father's name" he said. He then told Armando that tomorrow he would send his ten year-old son, Edward, to fetch and carry to Penau the rice offering from the Wrink house. Armando cut him off: "I've already tapped wine to take." Let Edward carry your offering; I will carry the offering from here."

Tomas left, but not before depositing his bottle on the table. Armando picked up the bottle and exclaimed to me, "This is stupid. If the wine is good we'll drink it now." He took a sip from the bottle, pronounced it good, and poured me a glass.

Later Armando told me that Balé had been talking to the women about preparing the offering. Balé had told them to make two—one for Armando to carry "for his father" and one for Tomas, which Tomas's wife was to make on her own.

The next morning when Armando and I went to Penau, Armando told me to carry the rice. "Who's older?" he said, imitating an elder's forceful tone. "You are," I replied, playing along. So he said, "You're the child, you carry the rice." We entered the forest with Armando in the lead carrying the bottle. The elders laughed. Balé, who was sitting at his spot next to the shrine, laughed and exclaimed, "There is Armando and his younger brother, my son!" Without acknowledging the elders, Armando sat with the young married men about fifteen yards from the shrine, and I followed. I watched other groups enter the forest and noted that, unlike Armando, most of the men would genuflect on one knee after they had deposited their bottle in front of the elders at the shrine and before turning to find their place along the twin rows of tree-trunk benches that jutted out from the shrine. Most would bend one knee and bring their hands to their chests or their forehead—a gesture I found faintly Catholic. Armando, ever my interlocutor, explained, "It's to respect the spirit." But he added, "I never bow."

Elder men such as Balé and Tomas sat closer to the shrine. Each elder was served a clay pot of wine. They talked, drinking at their leisure from the pots that were sitting in the dust at their feet. Once they had drunk their fill, and before the younger men had received their "share" of the wine, individual elders called upon favorites among the younger men to come up and drink from their pots. Some of the younger men were squatting in front of the elders, drinking from the pots as the elders looked down at them from their perches on the bench. Balé and Tomas both called to Armando, but he ignored them, telling me, "I don't go there when they call me. You drink more, but you don't share the wine with your friends."

Once the elders and the young men had drunk and eaten their fill, the boys Tomas's son's age, waiting for us under the shade of a large tree at the edge of the sacred forest, were called in to eat the leftovers. Then the elders ordered their children to take the empty pots home. Tomas told his son Edward to pick up the pot the women of the Wrink house had cooked. If Armando had denied Tomas an authoritative entrance, at least he could engineer a telling exit.

The ceremonies at Penau went on once a week for the rest of the dry season, but Armando stopped going. He would give his bottle to me. "You take it Eric; you be the elder," he would joke, and I would ask him why he did not want to go. "I don't like it—it's just an excuse to drink," he'd say. But I suspected he did not like the constant reminders of the authority of the elders and ultimately his conflict with Tomas over who should inherit the headship of the house. Armando was a natural leader; Tomas was, as Balé once blurted out to me, "a fool." Yet while elders like Balé may have wished that Tomas would not succeed to power, they would support his "traditional" right to the headship.

Performing Skepticism

Armando's biography, as I have sketched it, could be used to illustrate a certain interpretation of Armando's skepticism about "traditional" authority. The wasp's nest he smashed with defiant delight, the elder's "empty sack" he made fun of for my edification, the way he savored the appropriated pleasures of a long-jawed fish—these could be interpreted as reiterations of a deep, perhaps oedipal dilemma. A struggle with a powerful father, a sense of unfair entanglement, a sense of entitlement earned but never to be received, all leading to an escape, therefore, into a skeptical distancing. But there was also something quintessential, even typical about his skepticism, or at least how Armando's consciousness of his skepticism was as much enacted, or embodied, as narrated: Memories of childhood play and subsequent punishment; pitch-perfect imitations of an elder's orations or of a diviner's gestures. Belief, or in this case skepticism, was not just thought but act, performance.

As a performer, Armando seemed to me to be fairly typical in his ability to play elder for a laugh. Indeed, his peers in the Culture Club deployed such theatrical skills for comical effect in a series of skits they performed on Independence Day for the children in the village. The members of the club borrowed the idea for the skits from similar productions that the party youth organization used to put on to commemorate the revolution and foster its beliefs. But the format for the skits and the skits themselves were a local invention. One skit, I was told, was a perennial favorite. New skits are done each year, but this one had become the centerpiece of the performance.

In the skit a young wife rouses her decrepit husband to go visit a diviner because her child is ill. The audience—children and teenagers—is gathered on the veranda of the open-walled village schoolhouse. I am with some of the young unmarried men, among them Marcel, who is studying to be a school-teacher and who was one of the original creators of the skit. As the skit begins he reminds me that the performance is supposed to make the people "doubt the diviners."

As with the performances in general, the youths are able to create comically accurate characters with the fewest of deftly deployed props. In this case a teenaged boy is dressed in an oversized tattered overcoat and wears an absurdly large fedora—headgear and overcoat being an elder's uniform. He lies on top of the teacher's desk—the desk here serving as a bed just as in a previous skit it had been the back of a bush taxi, and just as in a few minutes it will become a diviner's hut. A simple prop transformed into something else by a deft gesture. The "elder" is so crippled with age that he cannot rouse himself from his bed. He tries to prop himself up, coughs, and collapses. The "wife" tugs and pulls at the long arms of his tattered coat and ends up drag-ging him to the "diviner." The elder clutches at her shoulders from behind while his gimpy legs trail along on the ground as they circle around the desk, imitating a long journey.

The couple finally reaches the diviner, an equally decrepit man wearing a yellow plastic hard hat and an equally tattered overcoat. He too takes a long time to be roused from (what Marcel later tells me is supposed to be) a deeply drunken sleep. After coughing and hacking in an exaggerated manner, the diviner begins his interrogation of the couple. He orders that each grab a low roof beam and then asks each, in turn, if they are witches. I learned later that a according to diviners a witch will find that he or she cannot release their grasp from the roof beam and will be left hanging. Both the young wife and the old man say "no." The diviner, satisfied with their response, beckons them to follow him to the diviner's hut. The wife follows, but the old man, struggle as he might, remains glued to the post.

The diviner returns, pries the old man's fingers from the post, and then car-ries the old man on his back, his own tottering frame supported by a hopelessly rickety cane. They enter his "diviner's hut," which is again the table. Underneath the table and only partly hidden from view by a screen of cloth is the spirit familiar, played by another youth.

The diviner goes through a typical routine. He asks questions and the youth within responds, imitating perfectly—and to howls of laughter—the high-pitched sounds a spirit emits when in real life the diviner disappears behind the wall of the inner sanctum of his hut to converse (ostensibly) directly with the spirit in the spirit's "foreign" language.

The diviner asks every question imaginable but the obvious one: Is or is not the old man a witch? The couple leaves, the diviner again dragging his buddy on his back. But as they pass the table the spirit familiar's arm reaches out from behind the screen to grab the old man's coat. There is a comical tug of war, with the old man being dragged under the table. His buddy the diviner returns and with his rickety cane begins to swat at the spirit's arm until it releases the old man. With the old man freed, the three actors leave the stage, the woman first, followed by the old, crippled diviner who drags the old "witch" clinging to his back.

Later, the youths of the Culture Club told me that when the skit of the diviner was first performed, the whole village had come, not just children. Marcel, who had originally played the diviner, said that "after [the show] a diviner from Baramb held out his hand and said to me, 'Give me your hand [to shake]!' It was exactly like a diviner." But a friend of Marcel's recalled it differently: "The diviner said, 'I'll hit you' and held up his hand." They laughed.

Marcel doubted contemporary diviners and conveyed his doubt to others by deft mimicry. Others, in turn, copied his original performance, turning it into a kind of tradition. Marcel's capacity to mimic so well is predicated on considerable observational skill, on close attention to the artifices of a diviner's performance. Indeed, he was able to articulate for me in considerable detail how diviners performed feats of legerdemain to fool unwary Manjaco into thinking they possessed "eyes" or the capacity to see and to communicate with the invisible world.

Not long after I had witnessed the skits with Marcel, I participated in what might count as another kind of mimesis, another kind of play. Marcel and Gabriel had invited me to watch the village youth compete in a soccer tournament against other neighboring Manjaco "lands." They themselves would not be players—they were too old now for that. But they would maintain order on the sidelines, and they, along with the rest of the Culture Club, would organize, they promised me, a display of "traditional" dance to be done by the village girls. The girls were supposed to dress in traditional garb, and just as in the "old" days when the nubile village maidens coaxed a line of young men plowing a field, each man racing the others to complete his row of mounds first, so too were these girls to encourage the soccer players to compete and win. Such were the "traditions" the kinds the men in the Culture Club wanted to maintain.

When I arrived at the game the girls were also there. But perhaps out of embarrassment, they never danced. As I watched the game I was intrigued by the way my companions did their job of crowd control. As the hundreds of fans pushed and jostled right up to the edge of the dusty field, they would stride in front of them, their faces angry masks. They each held a long thin stick which they would raise straight up in the air above their heads and whip down to the ground at the space just inches in front of their feet in the narrow space in front of the crowd. The snapping noise of the stick cutting the air, the slap and puff of dust as it hit the ground—these gestures were accompanied by squeals and laughter as girls and young boys moved just in time out from under the slashing stick. The angry faces of the young men as they shouted at the children to move back were echoed by the crowd laughing at them as they strode and grimaced. All this looked to me like a kind of dance, crowd control as theatrical performance. As I watched I remembered police in Bissau using similar sticks, making similar gestures, as they pushed back the crowds during a carnival. The trick is to look fierce, to swing the stick hard and fast but to always miss. So this enactment of crowd control at the local tournament had the air of parody, young men playing the role of policemen and transforming for our collective enjoyment a little dusty field into a big stadium in Dakar.

That night after the victory, several of the players arrived at my compound. Armando told me they were there to make an offering at the household shrine because "the spirit had helped them win." I asked why they had chosen this shrine and he told me it had a reputation as the second most powerful in Bassarel. It was, he reminded me, the shrine to which the initiates collectively made an offering after they emerged from a similar encounter at the shrine of Penau in the sacred forest.

Armando joined them outside at the shrine—an ancient tree whose tangled roots had grown over and incorporated the skulls and jawbones of dozens of goats and pigs. Gabriel and Marcel were there too. They gave Armando the bottle of rum, which he put in the gourd bowl and then dribbled over the earth at the base of the tree. As he did, he orated in the elaborately elliptical way that elders do. Then each of the players in turn made his oration, each ending with an implied or hinted promise, again each making a pitch-perfect imitation of an elder's speech: "Should what we have asked for—you know what that is—be given, should we receive what has been asked for then. . . . [a pause] He who works is paid; he who does not work is not paid!" They giggled and sniggered as they made their promises.

I was so surprised—despite the laughter the imitation was so perfect—I had to ask them then whether they really "promised the spirit something." They assured me that they had, but they laughed at my puzzled look: "It is a game Eric, just a game. We'll kill a pig, have a dance. We are just playing."

Beyond Disenchantment

Thus it was that playful mimicry and youthful skepticism interacted in Bassarel. In witnessing such interactions I came to assume that if Armando was exceptional—a kind of homegrown Thomas Jefferson—he was also somehow typical of his peers and of Manjaco in general. A standard way to explain such skepticism has been to link it up to modernization. As so-called primitive people are exposed to our ways of explaining the world, they lose faith in old ways and beliefs. In this scheme, Armando reminds us of Jefferson because, however indirectly, he has been exposed to the kinds of ideas Jefferson spoke so eloquently about. But I think we can learn something far more interesting than that from Manjaco people such as Armando and his peers. We can use what we learn from them to get beyond another recounting of the story of modernity in which belief gives way to reason, or in which the rest succumbs to the West and the world is disenchanted as a result.

From the colonial era to the present, anthropologists of religion in so-called traditional societies have been preoccupied by what happens when there are two belief systems occupying the same social terrain. Just as colonialism required that two political systems—a Western one and a local one—would overlap, so too did colonialism invariably result in religious juxtaposition. In the colonies, administrators let missionaries do their work. The alliance was at times uneasy, but usually it entailed a kind of mutuality of interest. Missionaries used modern medicine, for example, to entice potential converts, and administrators could depend on missionaries (as was the case in Bassarel during " Guiné Melhor") to provide schools to further the colony's modernizing project. The goal of the missionary and the administrator were in a sense conversion, and conversion had to be total. As many scholars defined the collision of local and Western systems, "Christianity and local spirits" were conceived as competing or conflicting thought systems. You could subscribe to one or the other but not both. Yet for the colonized it was more likely, as Anthony Appiah has so succinctly put it, that "juju and aspirin" could coexist in mutually accommodating juxtaposition.

Juju and aspirin are instantiations of ideas. We might think of them as religion or superstition and science, but they are also tools you might use without thinking about them as coming from contrasting belief systems. So recently scholars have been much less interested in exploring local religious practices as manifestations of thought—as a logically coherent system of beliefs. Most scholars today assume that they have gotten "beyond belief" and are working on something at once much more essential about local religious practice and also less obviously ethnocentric—its embodied factuality. Here they develop a tradition in Western thinking about religion that goes back to Durkheim. But such a literature tends to take persistence of religious practice for granted. If you do a ritual—say, if you bend your knee or cut into yourself—then you "inscribe" thought into your body. With an experience so tangible, so sensible, it is assumed that this sensibility is not subject to a kind of endogenous challenge. Body trumps mind.

Such an argument has several virtues that make it nearly unassailable. In the first place it easy for its proponents to play the ethnocentrism card. If the West is generally assumed by its faithful natives to be the seat of the power of reason (an exaggerated and complacently arrogant assertion), and if belief is itself a narrowly Christian (and modern at that) concern, then discussions of religious practice which begin with bodies and embodied experience seem not only universally more applicable, but less ethnocentric as well. It also works well as a culture theory because almost all culture theory, whether professional or vernacular, assumes a certain embodiment of knowledge. Culture cannot reside solely in the head. It has to get under the skin to be that incredibly powerful force we claim it to be. Cultural anthropology would disappear as a discipline without theories of embodiment. We have known this since Durkheim came up with the idea of collective effervescence. This is also central to Geertz's idea that models are experienced as if they are empirical realities—how worldview becomes ethos, how thought becomes attitude or sentiment.

As Geertz suggested, though, embodiment cannot simply be taken for granted. This has become especially obvious as anthropologists have tried to make sense of practices such as possession, masquerade, performance, parody. Among so-called traditional societies the world over, spirits are often made manifest by dancers in masks and costumes. Likewise, throughout the colonial era colonized people often performed masquerades or possession rites in which they embodied their colonial rulers. Most anthropologists writing about such colonial-era practices assume that such forms of embodiment entailed the mimetic appropriation of foreign powers, but they also portray such performances as parody. This allows anthropologists to appropriate mimesis as mimicry in order to use native performances of colonial powers as an allegory of our own cultural critique of colonialism. By contrast, we rarely grant the same knowing or witting qualities to the mimetic embodiment of endogenous spirits and authorities. Here the reverse side of the double standard applies. Mimicry is assimilated into mimesis, so the embodied act's potential for fostering a sense of critical distance rather than identity is erased.

Yet "play" has ambiguous connotations in Manjaco as it does elsewhere in so-called traditional societies. In Bassarel, young people learned religious activity by largely unsupervised imitation. If elders had their secret societies and rites in which they embodied spirits, then juniors developed parallel institutions. Young people made offerings to shrines of their own invention; they initiated still younger people in cults they created and maintained. Play, in short, can make belief as easily as it can unmake it. Embodiment, even when it is explicitly parodic, can, if it does nothing else, lead to an atmosphere of believability. Manjaco people mimic both to parody and to appropriate. They "play" in a range of ways.

If we really want to understand the repercussions of these forms of embodiment, we have to get beyond the dichotomies we routinely make between the mind and the body and between belief and reason. When Manjaco imitate elders, even to make fun of them, they act in ways akin to what we do when we play Santa for the benefit of our children. We can disbelieve and make believe at the same time. This is because, as Geertz said, we are enchanted by the models we make, so the line between a performance and reality is always blurred. This is the lesson we learn from Manjaco. It forces us to think in new ways about ourselves. To understand how religions work, we have to get beyond belief and into a realm where performance works its magic.

7

The Sex Life of Savages

Sex and politics are always intertwined in America. In 2006, the Democratic Party won back the House of Representatives and the Senate in large part because of the public's disillusionment with the Iraq war, but also in some small measure because Mark Foley, a Republican congressman from Florida, had been caught sending sexually explicit e-mails to a young congressional page, a teenaged boy. In 1998, on the eve of the U.S. congressional elections, *Nature* published an article by Eugene Foster outlining the DNA evidence that Thomas Jefferson and Sally Hemings had children together. In the same issue, the historian Joseph Ellis wrote a sort of editorial comparing Jefferson's liaison with President Clinton's sexual dalliance with a young White House intern, Monica Lewinsky. In Ellis's hands, Jefferson's illicit sexual relationship with a very young slave made Clinton's peccadillo seem slight, unremarkable. His article and others like it changed public opinion and rescued both Clinton and the Democratic Party. A potentially damaging scandal dissolved into mildly prurient spectacle—something for the tabloids, but no longer politically dangerous. By the same token, that Clinton found Lewinsky's thong-clad behind so compelling, that she liked it that he did, and that we learned so much about the shape of Clinton's penis and what fun you could have with a cigar, not to mention why Lewinsky wanted not to wash the semen stains out of her dress, made Jefferson's desire for a young slave who was his dead wife's half-sister and a kind of *au pair* girl for his daughters seem tame and sweet by comparison. Indeed, what had once been a scandalous rumor that dogged Jefferson during his presidency, and a "myth" that Jefferson scholars were constantly compelled to puncture, dissipated into the fuzz of a feel good romanticism as soon as it came to be widely accepted as fact. The Thomas Jefferson Memorial Foundation at Monticello quickly accepted the DNA findings as definitive and received much positive publicity for their honesty. Not coincidentally, a made-for-TV movie followed the lead of the facts, turning Sally Hemings and Thomas Jefferson into a sympathetic couple—lovers trapped in a society that kept their love illicit.

That the chiasmus of these twinned scandals mitigated each other, while sex with boys cannot be so easily explained away, tells us much about what Americans think about sex and power and that crucial third term, love. Both Clinton's and Jefferson's actions seemed ordinary, understandable, normal in their own way and therefore not transgressive, if perhaps technically illegal or otherwise unethical. It humanized both men while doing something slightly different to the two women, making Monica and Sally perform the roles assigned to women in the sexual scripts society writes. By contrast, Representative Foley's desires did not elicit empathy but rather, for many, disgust.

Nowadays most Americans accept that homosexuality is a fact. Gay characters are common on TV. Most Americans, according to recent polls, see nothing wrong with having an openly gay professor teach at a university. Yet on the very day I am writing this paragraph, General Peter Pace of the Marine Corps stated publicly that as far as he was concerned homosexual acts were as immoral and reprehensible as adultery. Several pundits immediately took up the cudgels in defense of what some of them claimed are thousands of gay soldiers doing their patriotic duty in the "don't ask, don't tell" armed services. They argued that the general would eventually have to get with the program. Gays are here to stay and he and others like him would just have to deal with that fact. Yet, if to be sure most Americans are more publicly tolerant than General Pace, even if the boy had responded to the congressman's flirtations with a love note of his own, for many Americans the disgust would have still remained.

Because these scandals tells us quite a bit about what we think about sex and love and what is natural or ordinary or not, they are anthropologically fascinating. As we have already seen, anthropology's business is to make the familiar strange, usually by making the strange familiar, by using the savage slot to rub our noses in our own complacencies. To most of us, the connection between Clinton's desire for Lewinsky and Jefferson's for Hemings is not a cultural fact but a natural one. Human nature is revealed in the rawness of sexual passion. It is there waiting to come out when the lights are turned off, the door closed, and the clothes yanked off. Boys will be boys. All men have a wandering eye. Older men go for younger women. There is, so we assume and so we constantly tell ourselves, a certain calculus that averages in waist-to-hip ratios and the spread of eyes and the shape of lips that drives all those men to lust after young girls the way they do. Sex is biology and biology is destiny. Some sex is natural, some is not. Likewise, powerful men are attractive to young, impressionable women. They are alphas in the pack. It is all about reproduction. Sex like that is written in the language of Darwin. Sex as game. Winners, losers. Or so we assume.

But what if sexual passion were dramatically different in different places? Just as the diversity of religious experiences and beliefs—other places, other gods—would lead to a theory of culture, so too would other places, other passions engender a need for theories of cultural difference.

Not surprisingly then, anthropologists early on in the history of the discipline studied and wrote about sex, usually to disrupt our tendency to universalize as human nature what were, from the anthropologists' perspective, our cultural proclivities. For example, Malinowski used what he learned during fieldwork in the Trobriands to write *The Sexual Lives of Savages,* which disrupted several common prejudices about the nature of sexual desire. In Malinowski's day it was commonplace to imagine that so-called savages were more sexually promiscuous than were people of civilized societies. Westerners assumed that sexual desire was associated with nature, and that civilization entailed repressing or deflecting natural passions and channeling them for better purposes. In this view, we gained civilization by sacrificing "ardor" (to return to Jefferson and a theme we reviewed in an earlier chapter); savages, by contrast, still wallowed in the pleasures of the flesh without guilt or shame. Malinowski set about showing that Trobrianders could on occasion be as prudish as we were. But he also attacked the universalizing pretensions of Freudian psychoanalytic theory, noting that since it is "essentially a theory of the influence of family life on the human mind," a culture with a family structure dramatically different from that of the West would not generate a Western-style Oedipus complex, but different neuroses, different repressions— in short, different "psychologies." Trobrianders were a matrilineal society. Fathers were insignificant as compared to mothers' brothers. Fathers were unimportant as far as procreation was concerned. Among Trobrianders, the verb "to father" did not exist. So much for the universality of the facts of life and for a psychology that emerges out of a particular family galaxy. The oedipal complex makes sense, but only, Malinowski stressed, among "the overfed and nervously overwrought people of modern Vienna, London, or New York."

Margaret Mead made a similar argument in *Coming of Age in Samoa.* Westerners assumed that adolescents went through a period of emotional stress having to do with hormonal changes. Biology made teenagers what they were, society didn't. Their chemical stress manifested itself in rebelliousness, depression, and excessive excitement—the "Sturm und Drang" of youth, German psychologists called it. But adolescents in Samoa were seemingly unaffected by hormonal shifts. They were neither rebellious nor anxious. Mead linked this difference to differences in attitudes toward youthful sexuality. Samoans were far more permissive about sex, but they also put less emphasis on sexual passion as a symptom of deep affection or sentiment—of what we called "love." Samoans were more than willing to "play"—give and receive sexual pleasure—and they did so with a variety of partners. Girls, for example, "played" with girls with as much pleasure as they "played" with boys, but they were not encouraged to develop lasting or exclusive relationships with their sexual playmates.

A little more than a decade after *Coming of Age in Samoa* became a best-seller, Mead used the authority of two years of intensive fieldwork among three dramatically different New Guinea societies in *Sex and Temperament* to make a more sustained argument about the cultural construction of core temperaments associated with core experiences of sexuality, of the body, and of pleasure. Like Malinowski's *Sexual Lives of Savages*, hers was a critique of common Western assumptions about human nature. In her day (and I would argue to large extent today as well, although the landscape may be changing) it was assumed that men and women naturally had different, if complementary, temperaments. If men tended to be passionate, violent, creative; then women were nurturing, tender, loving, cooperative. Women were "from Venus," while men were "from Mars," as the current pop psychobabble has it. Mead also noted that Westerners could imagine other possibilities, but they tended only to reverse the oppositions. Thus they could picture a society of Amazons and docile, henpecked men, but they found it far harder to imagine a society in which men and women did not differ at all in terms of basic personality and attitude. In her fieldwork in three New Guinea locations, she found such societies. Arapesh men and women tended toward a nurturant tenderness. Strong passions were an anathema. Among Mundugumor, by contrast, men and women tended to share an aggressive and violent temperament, "and the man who wishes to beat his wife takes care to arm himself with a crocodile jaw and to be sure she is not armed." Meanwhile, in contrast to both Arapesh and Mundugumor, Tchambuli men and women split temperaments to reverse the American standards of Mead's day. The men "are catty . . . and go shopping while the women are energetic, managerial, unadorned partners."

In *Sex and Temperament* and in *Coming of Age in Samoa*, Mead used savage sexual practices and desires to develop what has become a standard form of cultural criticism. First, fieldwork provides data showing that what was once taken to be a human universal is a cultural norm. Then a different set of cultural practices is demonstrated as leading to a different set of basic human motivations and attitudes. Mead showed that Arapesh women and men do not experience or seem to desire sexual "climax" or orgasm. In Mundugumor "love affairs of the young . . . are expressed in intercourse. . . . Foreplay in these quick encounters takes the form of a violent scratching and biting match." But she also noted that Arapesh, unlike Mundugumor, practiced the "true kiss." For other societies in New Guinea, by contrast, to put your lips together, much less to stick your tongue into each other's mouths, was a practice most would find abhorrent and disgusting.

Mead and also Malinowski (and others such as Ruth Benedict, who wrote with incisive candor about Japanese attitudes toward masturbation, pornography, and homosexuality in ways that could at best annoy the arbiters of morals in the United States) were pioneers in an emerging critique of what they might have euphemized as "the missionary position"—the phrase that refers to the height of missionary intolerance, to the idea that there is only one kind of sex that is natural and moral as well. In the missionary position, the man is on top and the woman submits to him because they are in love. Mead's and Malinowski's exercise in cultural critique was intended to lead to the acceptance of alternative ways of being, as well as the recognition of one's implicit prejudices. If there were a plethora of sexual practices out there, why could we not come to accept a variety of practices here as normal? If a society labeled as deviant what we called normal or vice versa, and, as Mead stressed, if there were deviants in every society, why not be more accepting of what anthropologists such as Mead and her mentor and friend Benedict were claiming was a vast arc of human personalities and proclivities? In Mead's day homosexuals were assumed to be deviants, just as women who were pushy or ambitious or too obviously interested in sex were also deviant. In theory, back then you could cure homosexuality just as you could cure (or manage at least) schizophrenia, or agoraphobia, or, for that matter, nymphomania. In practice, homosexuals suffered from shame and were treated as pariahs. Their illness, if you will, was caused by their treatment. When Mead wrote about the sexual practices of Arapesh and others, her hope was that we would become, through reading about others, more tolerant of difference among ourselves. We would live up to the lip service we paid to pluralism. That was the goal of American anthropology as it made the familiar strange by making the strange familiar, and it still is.

So let us go back to Thomas Jefferson and Sally Hemings to make a familiar picture strange, or at least to see that picture from a more distanced, estranged perspective. For those of us who can imagine them in an embrace, the picture most of us see, of course, is of a surreptitious but loving couple. A few of us might imagine a more lurid scene: Jefferson the master taking advantage of

Sally the slave, using her like men always do, and using her like white people used black people. This would be an image that is also as old and plausible as the love story: Tom as sexual predator; sex as power; sex as politics writ on the bodies of exploited and disenfranchised women.

Love and Modernity

Yet it is very hard to know what Jefferson and Hemings did with each other back in the beginning of the nineteenth century. Imagine that they had sex together, and that Jefferson's sperm and Hemings' egg met not once but several times, engendering offspring. DNA samples from descendants through a line of males of Hemings' last child, Eston, match the DNA of a line of male descendants of Thomas Jefferson's brother, meaning that they also would match the same DNA sequence from Jefferson's Y chromosome, but also therefore meaning that they match other male relatives as well. We can take this literal and physical trace of the past, replicated into the present, as evidence that Jefferson and Hemings had a child together, and then extrapolate that if they had one child, a last child, and plenty of opportunities to have others, that odds are they had several children together.

Imagine that they had reproductive sex; wouldn't it be nice if you also could read a letter or several letters, traces of an exchange of thoughts and feelings between Jefferson and Hemings? Jefferson wrote thousands of letters. He wrote about love and passion to women in his day. But we have no letter from him to Hemings or from Hemings to him. And if they had surreptitious sex not once, but often and over a period of decades, would not there be other traces of their affair? Again, a letter from a worried daughter to a confidante or something like that would be nice. Such traces would help historians, but their absence would not indicate that sex did not happen. Jefferson burned every letter he wrote to or received from his wife. Jefferson did this, so it is now assumed, to protect his privacy and the privacy of his dead wife. It is not hard to imagine him burning other letters, or others burning letters for him after he was dead, to protect his reputation, for example. So much of history requires imagination.

Anthropologists are historians of the present. The past, as far as we are concerned, is—whatever truth it contains, whatever traces of actual lives lived long ago it contains—a myth. The past is a story we tell ourselves today. And in general, that story is a reflection of our current preoccupations. The past changes as we change. When anthropologists write our histories of the present we use the histories our natives write, read, perform, and tell to illuminate what they think and feel about what is real and true. Beliefs, as the philosophers put it, are true in their consequences.

After *Nature* lent its authority to the story that Hemings and Jefferson had children, CBS made a film that aired in prime time—"a world premier mini-series event" starring Sam Neill as Thomas Jefferson and Carmen Ejogo as Sally Hemings. In this film, we see the imagination at work because all those letters we long for are there. We see them being written; we get to read them. History is to fiction as desire is to its fulfillment.

Here is a crucial scene at the end of the film. Jefferson has just died. Martha, his oldest daughter, and Sally have a confrontation. Martha wants to drive a wedge between her father and Sally. Reading his will out loud, which leaves, she emphasizes, no property or valuables or money to Sally or her children, she also notes that her father gives freedom to the children but not to Sally. Sally then snaps back: "I am your aunt. Your mother and my mother were half sisters. We are family." Then she pulls a letter of her own from out of a drawer. She tells Martha that it is a letter Thomas wrote her after their time in Paris (when, according to film's imaginings, the teenaged Sally and the middle-aged Thomas began their affair), in which he gave her her freedom. But she stresses that she stayed with him all these subsequent years voluntarily out of love.

This is a sentimental story. It's a kind of romance novel, and it gives shape—using the real, or what we assume to be the real—to a would-that-it-were fantasy. In such a fantasy, race divides us, as separate kindreds, but it does not have to. Because Sally is right: We are family, and family, so we like to think, is a unit based on an all-encompassing altruistic affection—on love. In the sentimental imaginings of the film, Tom and Sally loved one another and that made them equals. Sally is a beauty, but this is not why Tom wanted her. She learns to read what Tom reads—the great philosophers and the poets, Shakespeare, Voltaire. She is his intellectual equal and emotional anchor. The gap in their ages and the gulf in their social statuses is a source of tension that makes the viewer continuously realize how matched they are.

This is how love should be. Love in the American idiom this film illustrates is an egalitarian word. Even though you love your dog and Jesus loves you, love tends to signal a fundamental equivalence. If Tom loved Sally, then he had to also think of her as somehow kindred, as equal, as equivalent. At least that is what the popular movie on the subject signals.

There is an old saying, still heard occasionally because it still seems so apt, that "love and marriage go together like a horse and carriage." When I tell my students about the made-for-TV miniseries, they understand, without really having to think much about it, the idea of love the show conveys. For most of them—natives as they are of a vast civilization with a long history, Americans, yet also Westerners, Americans yet also members of a quintessentially modern society—love is a peculiar yet crucial emotion. On the one hand, we believe that love is a kind of social super glue. Families become families because of love. Girl meets boy and they stick together through thick and thin because they were once in love. They make babies whom they in turn love because they are in love. In short, love makes little micro-societies, little models of social perfection. When and if such little societies break apart, it is because the founders have fallen out of love, or have forgotten that they once were in love. They've lost faith, as it were. If only they could regain it.

In fact, when we look at the social problems that surround us and seem to threaten to tear our country apart, we often believe that if we just loved one another more—recall Rodney King's still wounded face as he made his televised plea to Los Angeles at the height of the riots that scorched the city—these problems would be magically resolved, and that we could, as if by magic, live happily ever after. "Love, love, love," The Beatles sing. "Love is all you need." In that sense love is a crucial catalyst. It creates and maintains communities—families, neighborhoods, whole countries.

On the one hand then we imagine that love is crucial to culture, even as we believe that it arises naturally—that it is a result of a kind of chemistry, as a kind of fate. Yet paradoxically, love in this sense has nothing to do with culture. Indeed, this is why on the other hand our conception of love is also peculiar because love and culture are almost antithetical. Love may be fate, chemistry, biology, but it is also about personal freedom, about transgressing, about the individual against society and against convention. Somewhere out there is Mr. or Ms. Right, and when I meet that soul mate my knees will turn to jelly and no amount of seeming incompatibilities that arise out of the different social positions we occupy will keep us apart because our bodies—our souls—are prewired for entwinement. Love conquers all. You are rich, I am poor; I'm from this side of the tracks, you're from that side; you are black, I am white; I like break dancing, you like ballet; you are a Catholic, I am a Jew; you are a northerner, I am a southerner ("I say tomayto you say tomahto, I say potayto, you say potahto . . ."). The list of seemingly insurmountable social differences is endless, the permutations endlessly fascinating, yet also in their way so predictable. Class, race, religion. The walls society erects to keep us apart. Cliché—delectable cliché.

Think here of the row upon row of romance novels, their covers capturing that first swooning kiss. The buccaneer, the cowhand; the nanny and the young widower. Think here of the countless movies that play on this theme of love as only an apparently inappropriate transgression made right by the stars. There is of course Romeo and Juliet, but also Beauty and the Beast, Pocahontas and John Smith, and let's not forget that huge hit *Titanic*. Love stories used to be tragic. The first kiss was often the last. Lips touch only to sip poison cups. In *Titanic,* love and an impending catastrophe keep us on the edges of our seats, and somebody still has to die. The lover's body sinks into the icy sea. But love creates. Years later she's a successful artist (because love freed her) just as he hoped he'd one day be. Love is creative but also intrinsically transgressive because it comes out of a far deeper place than mere social convention. Tom and Sally cannot help themselves. Love is a force greater than they are. They risk all by acting on their love.

When Jefferson was in Paris as the new nation's ambassador to France, America's closest and most important ally, he began a flirtation with Maria Cosway, a beautiful and talented artist who also happened to be married and a Catholic. We know this because we have their letters to prove it. We also know that Jefferson was at once fascinated by and repelled by the sexual goings-on in the French court. Adultery was commonplace. Sexual dalliances were a kind of game. Everybody seemed to be playing it—keeping score, competing, comparing. Nobody seemed to take transgression too seriously. You had a spouse, and you had a mistress or a lover, and your spouse knew all about it but kept up appearances. That was civilization, the very civilization that so sickened Rousseau. Jefferson took to calling himself a "savage" by contrast. On the one hand, he seemed to mean, judging from his letters, that he was a man with passions, or ardor—a savage in this sense, and that this was a good thing. On the other hand, he meant that, like a good savage, a noble savage if you will, he was repulsed by the way civilization channeled and corrupted human nature. Savage passion was fine. Civilized games of passion were not. Such passion was inauthentic. Political revolutions in modernity are often a response to such corruptions. They are portrayed as a cleansing. But political revolutions are also often signaled by the release of the sexual from the constraints of the artificial. Sex and radical politics are always about Jefferson's savage.

Moderns can either be optimistic or pessimistic about progress, and they can be either optimistic or pessimistic about human nature. Nowadays my students tend to be more optimistic than pessimistic, although they are less optimistic than their parents were. Nature is good, and so too is human nature. Yet to be a modern and to believe in progress does not mean you have to be an optimist about human nature. Human nature can be a bad thing. Think here of Hobbes and the savage beast that lurks inside all of us. In this scheme, love might be the kind of emotion that requires a certain refinement in order to be properly expressed. Love without civilization is merely lust—chemistry in the crudest of senses, transient.

By contrast, optimists—and here Rousseau is an early example—about both progress and human nature might see progress as a kind of return, via an ever-greater exercise of personal freedom, to what is natural. In this scheme love is a natural emotion that is squelched by social convention and custom. In this scheme modernity is about freedom—the freedom to choose a mate rather than have one chosen for you, the freedom to defy convention and to find oneself in an entwinement with another rather than to lose oneself in endless obligations. Indeed, historians of modernity have argued that one of the motivating factors that drove peasants out of villages and into cities— those great engines of progress—was the desire to exercise precisely that kind of personal freedom.

Given that for us love seems to arise out of our very biologies, and that love can act as a kind of social super glue, it is ironic that for a long time Westerners have entertained the possibility that among so-called primitive people love may not exist or at the very least may not thrive. This is because for us love also has a history. Love requires a social transformation. Indeed, we might say that modernity itself is a product of love. The authors of modernity—men like Rousseau and Goethe and others—all wrote novels that were love stories. Others such as Jefferson seem to many of us to have lived such stories. If we imagine our civilization progressing and evolving, we can't help but think in terms of contrasts—nature versus culture, for example, or primitive versus modern, with our tendency, of course, to conflate these contrasts. In general, whether one is an optimist or a pessimist about human nature, all of us tend to agree that savage or primitive or traditional societies such as Lauje and Manjaco are ancestral to us. They are analogous to those long-left-behind villages. They are places where people still marry who they are told to marry, places where love is not put on a pedestal, where love is not the subject of endless poetry and song, but where love might even be viewed as a threat—as a corrosive agent rather than as a binding glue. Some might even go further, arguing that primitive societies will be loveless societies. Primitive people will lust after one another, to be sure. But they will not love one another.

Lauje Love

What about love in Lauje or in Manjaco? Lauje certainly loved one another; they made love a sort of obsession. But love hardly created a stable society. Instead it meant that Lauje were constantly falling out of love, having illicit affairs, getting jealous, fighting. Families were as likely to break apart because of love as stay together. Manjaco, too, talked about love and composed love songs, memorializing youthful passions. But they relegated love to "childhood" and downplayed its importance in forging and fostering the bonds that were the business of adults and that knit families and societies together. To perhaps stretch an analogy a bit too far, Lauje were romantics. Manjaco weren't. To Manjaco, Hobbes would make far more sense than would Rousseau.

Lauje youths had a fairly idyllic life. Teenaged boys and girls routinely spent several nights in a row sleeping at the houses of friends or kinspeople, often in villages a ridgeline away from where their parents lived. They formed their own little society that had its own routines and rules, little affected by the lives and concerns of adults. Their parents could not seem to exert much authority over them. Youths helped intermittently with household chores and with household gardening, but they also tended to their own fields of garlic and shallots. They organized work parties from among friends, whom they paid with a share of the crop, and they made sure they had enough help to take their harvest to market in the coastal town of Tinombo, again by offering shares of produce or profit in exchange for help. They earned from this kind of work, and, when we were there, many of the more brave boys and single young men worked in the distant forest gathering rattan. This kind of work was dangerous and scary. Coastal merchants would provide them an advance paid in rice and other goods for the rattan they would eventually carry out of the forest after a few weeks of hard work. The money youths made they spent mainly on themselves, or they gambled it away, sometimes losing or winning what amounted to the entire profit of a crop in a night. Girls and boys alike visited the coastal hairdressers or bought makeup or new dresses and shirts. They also spent money on "foreign" (that is, Chinese, Bugis, and other) medicines, such as birth control of various kinds—usually, from our perspective, entirely useless—varieties of love potions, such as mermaid's tears, which itinerant merchants in the market sold in small vials. Some of them bought lyrics or words from a song cycle called Dero, which came from another region in Sulawesi. It had become popular throughout the region through the efforts of the Japanese in World War Two to spread a local but unitary set of "customs" in that part of Sulawesi.

The Dero dance was an excuse to get out of the house at night. Groups of young people from one village would host a Dero party in a cleared space away from the prying eyes of parents. They would invite friends and kin from other villages. The dance involved a sort of competition. The host group formed a semicircle and moved side to side in a slow, swaying motion. The guests formed a similar semicircle across from them. The hosts would sing a verse, in Bare'e—that is, a foreign language—that was laced with double entendres. The guests were prompted to respond, and each side tried to keep the dance going, while also engaging in a ritualized courtship. The ostensible goal was for the guests to get the hosts to give up one of their girls in a kind of parody of marriage. The dance could last for hours, and the ones we watched seemed incredibly tedious, if also innocent. Slow sliding feet; long pauses. Sometimes many participants. Sometimes only a few. We grew bored of the dances and left early. Part of our boredom was that the Dero dances were "new"—an introduced custom—and "foreign." What we witnessed didn't seem ethnographically interesting.

What we did not see, but learned about later from our young friends and neighbors in Taipaobal, was that the dance was just an excuse for a far more interesting set of encounters. While it was going there would usually be a gambling game or two with sums large by Lauje standards at stake. Meanwhile, girls and boys would pair off and head into the darkness surrounding the dancers, who were usually illuminated by a kerosene lamp. Our friends assured us that many of the girls were especially sexually aggressive. Dancing side by side with a boy from somewhere else, holding hands, a girl might let go and drop her hand to his groin, touching him to signal her interest. Indeed, girls in Lauje were notorious for playing the field. The sweet, shy girls we knew by day sometimes turned out to have several boyfriends at once, usually living in different mountain communities.

Many of the girls we talked to could not fathom why anyone would want to get married. They'd point to their mothers or other older women, hungry and burdened by children, and ask why anyone would want that. They primped themselves, wearing their hair down when they wanted to show how loose they were, and up and tied when they were a little more modest. They had special salves to keep their breasts small and not too developed; they had birth control. Abortions, so we were told, were common, though abortion was also thought to be a dangerous thing. As one commonly told story had it, when you eventually died, you needed to cross a narrow bridge over the blood pond to reach heaven. Waiting for you in the blood pond were the aborted fetuses. They would reach up to pull you into the pool of blood in revenge.

Girls worked hard to keep their freedom—from boyfriends and marriage. Meanwhile, boys bought love magic, composed love songs, and made sure, just as the girls did, that their hair was just right and their makeup on just so. They too, with a lot of pushing from parents and future parents-in-law, tended to be the ones who pressed for marriage. Girls, by and large, were reluctant brides.

Marriage happened as a kind of gradual accident. A boy might start visiting a girl at her parents' house. At first he might only come during the day, perhaps bringing her a gift, helping his future parents-in-law with chores. He might sit on the veranda of the house, his feet and legs dangling over the ladder, exhibiting in that body language an appropriate "shyness." Bidden to "eat," he might join in the family meal, if reluctantly. And when he left he could leave behind, as if by accident, his shirt or a spare *naus*—the cloth wrap all Lauje slept in and cloaked themselves with against the evening chill—or a prized machete; each possession was an excuse to return, and a sign of impending possession. Over a period time, if she liked him, he would then spend the night, sleeping with the young people of the house in the front room while the mother and father and very young children slept in the back room around the hearth. A relationship could go on like this for a long time, and often only reached the next stage when the girl got pregnant and could no longer hide the fact. Then she was forced to marry. Or rather her parents—especially her father—and brothers and other male kin would lash out in anger at her suitor, precipitating a Lauje version of a shotgun wedding. Generally the boy she married, she loved, and usually too the boy loved her. Once married, they lived for a time—one or two years—with her parents and worked with them, but they eventually built a house themselves, usually close by. Lauje food taboos required that a son-in-law not eat ceremonial meals with his parents-in-law, and this he felt as a burden. Again it was the boy and not the girl who had to make the effort to build a nuptial home, and the boy, not the girl, who had to convince her that moving out of her parents' house would be worth her while.

The feminist anthropologists Jane Collier and Michelle Rosaldo (who worked with a group similar to the Lauje but in the Philippines) compared a number of hunter-gatherer and horticultural societies and found a remarkable similarity in how they imagined and talked about love. Building on the work of earlier pioneers in gender studies such as Mead, these anthropologists and their peers were also compelled to critique assumptions about the nature of what it meant to be a woman or a man. If Mead was primarily a pluralist, feminist anthropologists of this later era were more concerned with questions of equality and fairness. It has long been argued that in a modern industrialized society at least, women are less empowered than men because they are relegated to motherhood. Yet if motherhood is a natural condition, a state of being women want because of their nature, then, if because women cannot earn as much as men or work in equally publicly empowering positions because they must act as mothers, then this is not the fault of society and therefore not a question of social justice. Feminist anthropologists such as Collier and Rosaldo argue that women's natural desire to "mother" is a "fact" we often take for granted because it is endorsed by our images of primitive and therefore more natural societies. Yet Collier and Rosaldo discovered that, rather than affirm our collective image of the primitive in which "man the hunter" is paired with the contrastive but complementary "woman the nurturer," in these societies women were seen as sexual beings, not as mothers. Men in these societies were often violent, as our myth of masculinity has it. They hunted and they fought one another, often over women. Men, too, were as likely to be nurturant as were women. They shared child care duties as much as they divided them.

Collier and Rosaldo explained this pattern in terms of social structure. Men needed a spouse to compete with other men in the political arena—to prepare meals and so forth for social events. But because society was egalitarian and there was little in the way of incentives to make people follow or listen, people had to rely on friendship and affection to engender cooperation. Spouses were partners, companions, friends. Children for both men and women were more a burden than a boon. So their care was seen as an obligation, or it could be seen as a result of a kind of spontaneous affection. Women could only be convinced to marry if they loved, yet love itself was a weak if compelling social glue. Your companion today might not be your friend tomorrow. Men and women frequently fell out of love, or found better more compelling love in transgressive extramarital affairs. Wives left husbands, and jealous husbands attacked their wives' surreptitious lovers.

The pattern Collier and Rosaldo described fits what we found about the Lauje, albeit with modifications. Lauje were less concerned with hunting than were men in many of the societies Collier and Rosaldo reviewed. But this could have been an effect of the conversion to Islam, as pigs, which had been the primary prey for Lauje hunting parties, had become taboo meat. But Lauje men (and women) were certainly as violently jealous. Lauje men also had to demonstrate to their future spouses that they could be good providers. They had to woo them, attract them, and be attractive. Young men used what they earned selling shallots or rattan to go to the hairdressers in cosmopolitan Tinombo. They bought and used makeup, and they purchased love magic. Girls too dressed up to look good. And above all, Lauje did not subscribe to the notion that a woman was primarily, and should be primarily be, a mother.

When a woman gave birth, this too was a sign, a culminating sign that she and her mate were, as the Lauje put it, *ipaipal*—like two index fingers, the same, equivalent, matched.

Lauje had other words for the perfect couple. Such words always stressed their equivalence and used the everyday experiences of bodies moving in the landscape to make metaphorical sense of this ideal psychosocial state. Couples should be "side by side"—a word that harked back, by contrast, to the standard fact that people walked together on trails too narrow to walk any other way but single file. When groups of Lauje went on their various excursions, they always walked single file, the older or slower people first, the faster and younger ones following. But couples were described as ideal if they were "side by side," as if they were together even when they walked alone.

Ipaipal, that common term for a well-matched pair, also always had sexual connotations, for it was assumed that a matched couple was also sexually matched, as if, as it were, their sex organs were matched. This did not mean they were thinking literally of size. Lauje used to joke with us that a vagina after all is very accommodating: "It is like your nostril; you can stick in your pinky or your thumb." What they meant instead was that in the sex act itself there was an equivalence. To be *ipaipal* in life also implied that when you had intercourse you were also equally pleasured. Indeed, to conceive required that both the man and the woman have an orgasm—*ipaipal* in orgasm, they both ejaculated a fluid that swirled together, meeting like two index fingers inside the woman to swirl together to congeal into the beginnings of a fetus. For Lauje conception could not happen unless one had *ipaipal* sex. No amount of intercourse would lead to conception if the girl or woman did not have an orgasm when the man or boy did. Such sex was barren sex.

Native Biologies

If anthropologists tend to treat history as a myth that we read to learn about the present, so too do anthropologists treat indigenous science as a kind of myth. What human beings know or think they know about what goes on inside the body—the verbal or pictorial maps they draw of organs and blood and bones—are as much a product of the cultural imagination as they are a result of empirical scrutiny. This is especially the case with how the interiors of bodies are mapped in sexual terms. You can see a penis and testicles and a vulva, and you can see the fluids they excrete and link these to the sex act, but you cannot see the womb and what goes on inside it to make a baby. Or, even when you can see these hitherto invisible entities, you still project a cultural template onto what you see.

This at least is what anthropologist Emily Martin argued in a series of studies of modern medicine in the United States. One enduring trope of science revolves around vision, with scientific progress imagined as new ways of making visible what was once invisible. Here the microscope and the telescope are quintessential objects that hark back to this process. We now see farther or peer deeper than we ever have before. In obstetrics, we have the "miracle" of ultrasound and other technologies that allow us to gaze into the womb and see the fetus. And of course the microscope gives us pictures of the agents of reproduction—egg and sperm. But images, no matter how seemingly clear, require interpretation. Photos need to be cropped, edited, placed on a page. They are always representations, and as representations they objectify culture.

Martin studied how these images were used in medical school textbooks and how stories that emerged from the images and paralleled the images influenced the biomedicine of conception. What she found was that scientists tended to project onto microscopic sperm and egg what Mead would have called the temperaments of the sexes in modern America. Egg was a passive entity, helpless, waiting. Sperm was an active swimmer, aggressive and competitive. Sperm, as it were, was the agent of conception. Sperm penetrated, egg was penetrated. "He"—scientists routinely anthropomorphized these little one-celled entities—acted, while "she" was acted upon, and as such the one-celled drama of conception mimicked a modern cliché of sexual seduction. Martin demonstrated further how such a model clouded the vision of a group of scientists working to develop a clinically useful form of birth control that would thwart the sperm from fertilizing the egg. After many false starts, the scientists on the team eventually realized that sperm were not as active as they had assumed, nor was the egg a passive target or prize in the spermatic endeavor. Martin showed that even science is cultural, and that what we see, even when we use a microscope, is in a sense what we assume we will see.

When Lauje talked about procreation, their story of invisible interiors matched their actions and stories of love and marriage in the visible of human beings and bodies. Productive intercourse was a symptom of a couple's compatibility—Geertz's "models of" blending into "models for," creating the webs of mutually reinforcing meanings we humans, always cultural, never natural, confuse with reality.

Not surprisingly, what Lauje imagined happening after conception, and what they imagined and did up to and into labor and birth, confirmed and conformed to what they assumed to be natural for what a man and a woman would naturally do. Their imaginings were various, but they all tended to erase the maternal agency of women. How did a fetus grow in the womb? It fed on itself, or rather on its placental twin. It sucked its own thumbs, drawing from them the fluids of god itself.

In downplaying the maternal agency of the woman, they also, though, tended to privilege the agency of the man. They believed, for example, that to have a healthy birth you needed to have sex throughout the pregnancy. Sex "opened the door" of the birth canal, promoting an easy delivery. When a woman gave birth, Lauje downplayed the significance of this act, making them very different from societies where it is assumed that motherhood is natural to the feminine condition. In such societies the act of giving birth is often treated as a heroic and dangerous endeavor and a significant rite of passage, if not the *most* significant rite of passage for a woman. This is how it was for Manjaco. For a woman to become an adult required that she give birth. She did so in secret, at least away from her husband and other men and in the company of other women. Birth was, as Manjaco put it, the "pack" or the "coven" women shared that was their exclusive property. If men did dangerous things, did things that put their lives at risk, so too did women. Thus the commonly phrased couplet that Manjaco elders recited when they were asking the ancestors or spirits for safety and prosperity in their households: "A man has the palm tapper's belt; and the woman has her belt too. Don't let it be said that the belt has broken"— that is, do not allow an accident to befall a woman in labor or a man climbing a tall palm tree; let them both survive their ordeal.

Manjaco imagine birth as a dangerous act, one that requires heroic fortitude. To be a mother is to be an adult. Lauje women, however, claimed that birth was relatively easy. Several had stories of working in the fields or traveling on a trip from one ridgeline village to another, and suddenly feeling a desire to defecate, and then squatting on the side of the path or in woods by the cleared field and delivering a child. Most delivered at home, though, almost always squatting, using the central house pole as support, and often with their husband's help. If he was experienced, he knew certain secret prayers to ease labor, or at least he had learned how to massage her stomach to shift and coax the fetus.

Once she gave birth, it was her husband's job to separate the infant from its placental twin and to gather up the cloths that were soaked in the fluids and blood of afterbirth. Once the umbilical cord stopped throbbing, the husband cut the cord with a sharp sliver of bamboo, and after marking the infant's forehead and cheeks with umbilical blood, he wrapped up the placenta and took it into the forest to hang it in a state of suspended animation in a fruit-bearing tree.

These acts, and I simplify them here, all conspire to make the man into a nurturant actor in the birth scenario that Lauje create. From our perspective, much of what he does is unnecessary, magical. To us, cleaning and wrapping the placenta has nothing to do with the health of the child, even if to Lauje this is a crucial embodiment of their belief in Umpute, or placental connection, as the source of virtue and cure. But some of his actions might indeed do something concrete and beneficial that we too would recognize, even if our cultural models initially might blind us to their benefits. For us, for example, intercourse during pregnancy, especially late in pregnancy, does not immediately strike us as salutary. Indeed, it used to be that common sense counseled avoiding sex during pregnancy, probably because of the assumption that motherhood and sexuality were opposite conditions. Sex during pregnancy, especially late, felt wrong, dirty. Yet according to current medical wisdom, intercourse near the end of pregnancy can be used to stimulate the onset of labor, while massage is a technique Western midwives also use. And both the increasingly common practice of midwifery and their advocacy of sex late in pregnancy are in turn connected to recent shifts in cultural models reflecting feminist thinking and practice.

In any event, for Lauje, all these practices taken as an ensemble make sense because they are actions that put into practice a model of the sexes and what they should be and do. When a woman gives birth, you are not supposed to see her vagina. She keeps herself covered. This fact surprised me. More surprising still were the claims our interlocutors made that you rarely see a woman's vulva, even in having sex with her. The word "vulva" is also far more embarrassing than the word "penis." It was thus that Lauje did everything in their power to deny or erase difference between male and female.

Manjaco Masculinity

If the Lauje surprised me by their denial of difference between the sexes, Manjaco, by contrast, were not surprising at all. Indeed, if I had not been with the Lauje before I was with Manjaco, much of what they said about the bodies of male and female would have struck me as routine, obvious, familiar, if slightly off-kilter. Unremarkable to me, for example, was the fact that Manjaco initiated boys into social masculinity in an elaborate, expensive, and time-consuming ceremony that entailed circumcision. Every quarter-century, more or less, the boys and young men of a given "land" are herded off into the sacred forest, where each one has his foreskin cut off and where the bloodstained leaves that are used to protect the boys' wounds are eventually gathered, dried, and burnt into ashes. The ashes are mixed in the palm wine the initiates collectively drink before emerging as "men of the village" from their long sequestering in the sacred forest. This all was unremarkable to me, not because we had such ceremonies—we don't really, even if you count fraternity initiations and the fact that circumcision, until recently, has been a routine medical practice in the United States—but that masculinity was so obviously manifested in the penis. Men were men because of their penises. They were a social body because they shared in a kind of collective penis, marked by a shared heroic ordeal.

Women in turn, as a woman famous for her singing put it in one of her popular songs, were "scarred the gazelle's hoof" and therefore "could never be warriors," only wives, sisters, and mothers. Their vulvas made them second-class citizens. What prestige they garnered, they acquired through their connections to men. Even motherhood required a man.

For Manjaco a woman's womb was likened to a palm wine gourd. The man filled it with his semen or, as Manjaco put it, his "blood." Her blood, her menstrual fluid, was also necessary. It mixed with his blood in her womb. But the dominant image was that she was the receptacle, with the man the agent of her pregnancy. If a woman could not get pregnant, people assumed one of two causes for her misfortune. Either envious co-wives had put a spell on her or made a bargain with a spirit, or her husband was somehow deficient in blood. That latter possibility was a shameful one, a problem people whispered about in private. But there was a cure. In many villages the women constructed a special hut where midwives gathered. You could leave your village and go to spend a month or so in a distant village under the watchful care of the midwives. They would protect you from the magic of your female foes. They would also, though, provide you with a secret surrogate husband. "The bull of the village" such men were called. Famous for their sexual prowess, they were local celebrities. Men had penises, or should have them. Women had vaginas that led to the womb that men filled.

Manjaco, in short, stressed the differences between male bodies and female bodies and put these differences to work in justifying other differences as well. So they were more familiar than strange to me. But surface similarities hid deeper differences. Recall Jefferson and Clinton. If we forgive them their social transgressions, as often as not we do so by resorting to a vernacular paradigm in which nature is imagined as superior to or at least more powerful than culture. In our view Clinton's transgression is primarily a demonstration of masculine power. We might shake our heads at his foolishness—how could he have risked so much?—and we might even see such an act as immoral and unethical—but we also recognize, and to some extent exult in, its manifestation of power: the penis as nature incarnate. We are, to be sure, ambivalent about this power. But it is a power also tinged with freedom. For us, freedom, especially masculine freedom, is also as often as not coded as social transgression. Society holds men back. And society is often embodied in the form of a woman who is too concerned with social conventions, with what the neighbors will think. If freedom is a sort of god term to us, then freedom is also exemplified in the power of the penis to take what it wants and damn the consequences.

What I am saying here about freedom, transgression, and Clinton is not of course what everybody believes. I used the pronoun "we" to provoke thought. I would venture that what I say about "we" at least applies to the thinking of many men in America. It is a reflection of a host of taken-for-granted attitudes about masculinity that come to be expressed in how we talk about sex and sexual desire, in the films we make and books we write, and in the way we often act. It is a reflection, however, that engenders counternarratives, arguments, critiques.

One standard critique, not a critique of the idea of masculinity but rather of its moral legitimacy, is that it is the role of women to rein in and channel such power. Women in this scheme are the arbiters of society. They supply a moral compass because, so the story goes, they are more sensitive to social censure than are men. They are in a word more "modest"; they have a heightened sense of "shame," that emotion that requires that you are aware of and worried about what others around you are thinking of what you are doing. Because they are more modest—in Jefferson's day this propensity was thought to be literally biological and exhibited in a proper girl's tendency to blush—they resist or otherwise thwart masculine desire. Their virginity in this scheme becomes a kind of protected prize. Men want it; women keep it from them because when they lose it they lose their social value. In thwarting male desire, they are in a sense less free but they also act as standard bearers for social convention. In their modesty they are embodiments of the social.

This idea of a woman's natural propensity toward modesty in contrast to a man's tendency toward transgression is a very old idea in the West, but it could be argued that it also became a dominant one in the late nineteenth century and into the twentieth century. In this period the idea cloaked itself in modern science as scientists debated, for example, the evolutionary utility of the female orgasm. As the cultural historian Thomas Lacquer notes in his study of the development of Western sciences of the sex organs and their relationship to social trends and mores, the increasingly dominant view was that females did not need orgasm. Women's sexual bodies were made, so it was increasingly assumed, to make babies. Their biologies meant that they were more naturally nurturant and the love they felt for men was eclipsed by the deeper love they would eventually feel for children. Thus the West invented the myth of woman the mother, man the hunter, all over again, albeit in this case dressed up in the guise of modern urbanized society with men hunting women, with women, at once prey and prize, allowing themselves eventually to be caught in order to trick a man into settling down and making a family, our little micro-society. Woman in this case acted as civilizer; man in this case acted as savage.

Love in Manjaco

Given that this vision was and still is quite common in the Western imaginary, Manjaco can appear oddly familiar. Men are associated with their genitalia. They are warriors as a result. They, like us, talk of men having sex with women as eating meat. But they do not contrast male to female as savage to civilized. Rather, Manjaco acted as if both females and males would want to make families and that both males and females would be equally committed to reining in desire to make this possible. But they assumed that this would require social training. Boys and girls both would have to learn how to become committed, and this would require struggle, abnegation. Indeed, they created an institution that made this commitment the culmination of a rite of passage.

The institution is called a *baniu*—a word which literally means "group hut" but which I translate as "dormitory." A *baniu* is a large circular hut where juniors slept and ate together, while the young unmarried men worked in the rice fields of the parents of their brides-to-be. While the juniors lived in the *baniu* they went through a series of ceremonies marked by the exchange of labor and products such as palm wine. Eventually the juniors would emerge from the dormitory to marry and take up residence as adults in the Manjaco households. The girls left first. They married men of the age set of the "older brothers" of the men with whom they cohabitated in the dormitory. The men, in turn, would marry girls who had not yet entered the dormitory and for whose parents the men provided free work in their future parents-in-law's fields. It was as such that life in the dormitory was a drawn-out rite of passage marked by public ceremonial changes in labor prestations, in a variety of feasts, and the like. But the dormitory also was a place of potential sexual license. An early European observer of Manjaco, the French geographer Bertrande-Bocande, wrote that in the *baniu* young men and women "slept together, nude and pell mell," and that it was a place where youth met to drink palm wine and dance. He assumed that the *baniu* was a site of savage sex—entangled bodies hidden in the darkness.

When I arrived in Bassarel, the *baniu* was no longer a feature of the local landscape. It had been a casualty of the revolution. The Portuguese outlawed it and bulldozed the structure, fearing it would allow subversives to meet with large groups of youths and convert them to the guerillas' cause. Moreover, with emigration at its peak there were fewer young men and teenaged boys in permanent residence in the village, so it was almost impossible for them to organize the kinds of labor parties their parents and grandparents remembered from the days before the revolution and independence.

Older men and women alike talked with considerable fondness of their time in the dormitory. They described occasional furtive sexual encounters. But they also stressed that such "play" had to be kept within limits and that excessive licentiousness was scorned. Most boys and girls restricted their play, they said, to "touching" and did not have intercourse. When the girls of the dormitory left to be married, they performed a public dance, presenting themselves, their bodies glistening with palm oil, to the village as a whole. It was at this point that the girls would suddenly turn on any of their peers who had violated the rules of the dormitory not to have sex. Forming a quick circle around such a girl, they would take turns bumping into her as they danced. Even though the *baniu* no longer existed, Manjaco still performed this dance. I witnessed one such dance in a village near Bassarel. I saw the girls swarm around one of their peers and take turns knocking into her and elbowing her, pushing her body this way and that.

If the girls were supposed to keep their play fairly innocent in the *baniu*, the boys had serious but also playful work to do in protecting those same girls from the aggressions of the men in the village. It was believed that the older men—the "hyenas" as they were disparagingly called, "with their sagging rear ends"—liked to the test the youths of the *baniu* by using their contacts with spirits to try to make the girls sick. The young boys in turn would go out into the village to steal goats to use in sacrifices at the spirit shrines to enlist the spirits' aid in protecting the girls. One elder, describing this to me, said it was a "game"—a game of power and prowess that youth played as a team against older men. Doubtless it was a game made all the more passionate by the fact that these youths slept together with girls they were supposed to protect and cherish but whom they would never marry.

Yet the elders also talked fondly of the love matches they made in the *baniu*, and several had become village celebrities because of their powers of amorous persuasion. These love matches, again though innocent, were memorialized in songs. When an elder died in Bassarel, the age set of his or her peers in the *baniu* would come en masse to the funeral. There they would sing the love songs they had composed while they were young. Manjaco talked much of the bonds they had made during their youth. These were bonds that held up for life. You could trust your *baniu* companion. If men and women had friendships with those of what we too sometimes euphemize as the "opposite sex," it was with a *baniu* partner. Manjaco husbands and wives were also occasionally on very good terms, but there was not the expectation that such a relationship began with or depended on passion or love or the bonds of affection that were at the heart of the *baniu*. Manjaco, if you will, separated what we would call love from marriage, perhaps in large part because it was a relationship between groups as much as between two individuals.

That fact became obvious and indeed strangely unfamiliar to me when I attended my first wedding in Bassarel. I joined the bride's party as she and her kin made their way, taking the most roundabout way possible, from her compound to the cluster of huts of her husband's family. Her "brothers"—a category of kin that included sons of father's brothers—took turns carrying her on their shoulders. She was slick with palm oil and naked but for a strip of cloth and strings of beads around her hips. The rest of her family crowded around her, making as much noise as they could. Once we reached the husband's compound, we stopped at the entry gate, the brothers refusing to go further until they were given some chickens as gifts. They placed one such chicken at her feet. She stepped on its outstretched neck while a group of women from her husband's compound linked hands with her and pulled her into the courtyard. Meanwhile, the brothers yanked at the chicken, breaking its neck. The women then took the girl into the shadows of a hut, where after a few moments she emerged with a short broom and did a perfunctory sketch of sweeping in the courtyard, with the crowd laughing and clapping, before the women tugged at her again and brought her back into the recesses of the hut. There she would spend two or three days being fed by them. They would slaughter chickens for her and make sauce thick with palm oil. That would be her honeymoon. After that she would get to work.

In all of this the husband was entirely absent. He, like so many of his peers, was away in Senegal, working, so I was told, as a schoolteacher in a rural village. His parents and hers had arranged the marriage, they told me, and he would come back during vacation to see his wife. She may have even ended up going to live with him eventually. I do not remember. But what I do remember is that the sisters of the groom all dressed up for the wedding in the clothing of the absent men of their house. They did so in a purposely comical way. One, for example, used a purse as a brief case, and scribbled on a notepad, mimicking the gestures of the absent schoolteacher. Another blackened her face with oily ashes and carried a large fulcrum shovel, imitating a typical Manjaco male farmer. As it later turned out, such a wedding was typical. Men were often absent. Their sisters often dressed up to parody them. And even in earlier times, so I was told, it was always the sisters and father's sisters who pulled the girl across the threshold and who feted the girl during her days of seclusion. In Manjaco you marry a family. You call your brother's sisters your "husband." You call your father's and your father's brothers' sisters your "husband" as well. When or if your husband died, one of these men—your husband's brothers or other male in-laws—would become your new husband.

Manjaco marriage therefore conforms to a template we have of marriage in traditional society. It is an arranged marriage. It links a person to a group, not to an individual. Such marriages work best when love is not thought to be the catalyst for the relationship. Manjaco relegate love to childhood—an emotion one indulges in during one's time in the *baniu*, an emotion one leaves behind once one emerges from the *baniu* to marry. Manjaco seem to treat love as a Hobbesian emotion. But Lauje are also a traditional society from our perspective, and there marriages only occur because of love. Because we cannot simply contrast so-called primitive to modern, the lessons anthropologists have tended to draw from their encounters with people in societies we cannot help but think of as primitive, and therefore potentially ancestral to us, is the lesson of human pluralism, not of dichotomies. Moreover, we cannot look to them for lessons or illustrations about what is more natural about humanity. We cannot discover in them lessons about whether love is a universal emotion or whether it is good or bad, or whether love entails equality or whether male is always superior to or more powerful than female. Instead what we learn is that emotions that seem so personal and profound—love, power—are also implicated in social practices. We also learn that even the body, even those parts of the body that seem so obviously a part of a savage nature—the sex organs: the vagina, the penis—these too are always perceived and therefore felt through the prism of culture. Do we want sex because of our organs? Do men and women want the same kind of sex? These are questions always wrapped up in the question of culture; they are not questions we can answer according to the templates of nature.

These are the lessons anthropologists in the early era of anthropological exploration—pioneers in our discipline such as Mead and Malinowski—brought home. They are the lessons those of us who have followed in their distant footsteps still learn.

Savage Sex?

But we also are humbled by our own blindness and recognize how hard some of these lessons are. Sex in our society is visible because of the enabling technologies of modernity. Text made sex into a story you could use to pleasure yourself in private, but it made that story a part of an endlessly permanent and public record. Pornography is in the library of our civilization. It is not difficult find if you know where to look. What text did, image, especially its recent forms— photography, film—did even more. You can rent a DVD if you are the right age or go to a theater. With the Internet you can pretty much see everything and anything no matter how old you are. No desire is hidden from view if you are curious. Even if you don't want to see the sex act, you are exposed to it in its euphemized forms—the orgasmic look of the model selling you a car or a soda, the pair of blue jeans unzipped almost to the pudenda.

The visibility of modern sex makes us appear to our erstwhile primitive Others, without our being aware of it, like we are enacting the fantasies of savage sex Europeans in the age of exploration such Bertrande-Bocande routinely attributed to primitives societies. Manjaco, we can be fairly certain, never had orgies "nude and pell mell" in the *baniu*. But Europeans and Americans travel to places like the Gambia, the Caribbean, Bali, and Thailand to strip near naked on the beach, to hook up with each other at poolside bars or on the dance floor, and to have sex in plain view. They travel to primitive places to have brief flings with Maasai or Mandinga warriors. They do it with young boys and girls in exotic Asia. Sex tourism is the distilled essence of tourism to primitive places. The exotic is the erotic.

Because sex is so visible to us, and so entwined with our fantasy of the primitive, I was far less aware than I should have been about the invisibility of sex in Manjaco and Lauje communities. Think for a moment about how paradoxical it might be to not see sex in those places. People live together crowded into small spaces. At night you can hear them cough or roll about in their sleep. Yet I never heard sex, much less saw it. Now, I did not see people defecating there either, and this in places without toilets. Both Manjaco and Lauje are good at hiding what they find shameful or embarrassing. If we have lost our sense of shame, they are adept at the arts of modesty. There is plenty of bush near the houses to hide in and do what you do not want others to see. Lauje never strip naked. When they bathe they use their *naus* cloths like portable tents and screens. You can squat inside such a screen and urinate or defecate and no one can really see you even if you are more or less in plain view. Likewise too, if the door to your hut is closed during the day and a passerby wants to visit, that passerby will quietly cough at the base of the ladder, and it is up to you to acknowledge their presence or ignore it. If you ignore it, they too can pretend that they were only pausing to clear their throat. Neither you nor the passerby need acknowledge that you noticed each other or wanted to be noticed, or wanted not to be noticed. Lauje are perhaps, if such a word is appropriate, more private than Manjaco, who tend to knock on doors and practically barge in. While I never saw sex, I did have conversations about it. I did ask questions. And not surprisingly, my questions reflected my own sensibilities.

One such sensibility was my assumption about the naturalness of heterosexuality. If I did not see sex, I also did not imagine sex that was other than between boys and girls, women and men. Other anthropologists of my era and before have been more imaginative, less blinkered. But what they have learned as often as not does not satisfy the extreme sides in current cultural controversies about the nature of homosexuality. Take an ironic upshot of recent controversies surrounding homosexuality in the United States. Some Americans continue to assert that homosexuality is "unnatural." Many of these people even imagine that homosexuality is so unnatural that society's increasing acceptance of it as a normal public fact of life indicates that we as a civilization are slipping into chaos and destruction. By moving away from nature, we slink into corruption and decline. New York and San Francisco are modern Sodoms and Gomorrahs.

Such a view of homosexuality as a symptom and cause of decay is a pervasive view, but also increasingly a minority view. More and more Americans assume that homosexuality is not only a fact of life and accept that homosexuals have the right to be who they are. Many of these people couch their acceptance in the language of nature and biology. Gays and lesbians are born that way. Among members of the gay communities there is often the same assumption, and when some scientist can report that the hypothalamus of a gay person is physically different than that of a straight person, when a scientist can report that dolphins or birds or primates or insects have homosexual sex, these findings are causes for comfort and celebration. Likewise, it would help the cause of gay rights to discover that in all other societies around the world there were gays and lesbians. The numbers need not be large. They only need to be universal.

Such desires find only slight solace in much of what anthropologists find. Take the work of Gilbert Herdt, who studied a society, called Sambia, in the high mountains of Papua New Guinea where young boys used to undergo a long period of initiation in which they fellated older youths. Sambians believe boys have to do this because they need to swallow semen to ensure that their weak bodies will become strong and masculine. By contrast, girls grow up inevitably into women. A female is naturally, so Sambians assume, stronger and healthier than a male, in large part because women menstruate. By menstruating, women's bodies cleanse themselves and stay strong. In fellating youths, Sambians assume that the boys feel love and passion for such youths, while they assume that those they fellated also feel desire and affection for the boys. Eventually, though, every Sambian youth grows up, is married, and learns to have sexual intercourse with women. Throughout the initiation, the boys, youth, and men who were the most praised by others—who were said to be the most masculine—were active and aggressive in their sexual pursuits. They should like to suck older boys. Later they should like to sleep with their wives.

Herdt uses the ethnographic material he has gathered from his fieldwork with the Sambia to argue against the kinds of routine essentializing we do in the United States and in Western societies in general. Note that for us our sexuality is a marker of our identity. We often assert our sexual identities in the political arena and think of our sexualities as essential to who we are. To accept me or recognize me is to accept or recognize my sexuality. What the Sambian case shows though is that sex and identity are not essentially linked. Like Mead, Benedict, and Malinowski in anthropology's pioneering era, Herdt offers us a glimpse of the plasticity of the human condition. We have bodies that give us pleasure; societies shape and channel pleasure (but pain too) and makes persons experience socially channeled pleasure as if it were a part of nature. And this is because, to recall Geertz, it is the essence of human nature to be in and of culture. Sex, for anthropology—no matter who does what with whom—is always an unnatural act.

Conclusion

Tending to Nature, Tending to Culture; or, Is Anthropology History?

Modernity can be a kind of mourning—an endless lament for something we have lost and long to regain. What we have lost, we often imagine, is a profound connection to the world around us. We are no longer close to God, close to each other, or, worst of all, close to nature. If modernity is nature's anathema, then that lament of loss can also be a compelling force for radical change. When modernity is imagined as technological advance, as industrialization, as consumption gone wild, such a perspective allows us to produce warnings for ourselves that compel us to become nature's stewards. Consider for example, as one long-running television commercial had it, a swampy image of a trash-covered landscape choked with smokestacks that the camera scans until it comes to an Indian looking out over that scene of destruction. The camera focuses on his profile. As the old Indian looks at the trash-strewn world, a single tear slides slowly down his cheek. When we see that Indian, we too lament because we know that not only is the nature that ruined landscape evokes lost, but so too potentially is the Indian. The Indian is our stand-in, our superego, our conscience. His tears tell us that unless we can do something to restore that landscape—unless we can return it to a semblance of the natural and protect it from ourselves—it and he are history or are about to become history.

Anthropology too might become history, that is, no longer relevant but instead passé. If there are no longer primitive people—radically different "others"—who will anthropologists study? In the past quarter-century anthropologists have endlessly addressed this question, as often as not from the perspective of a kind of guilty disavowal of our earlier—some call it romantic, some patronizing—desire to share in the space of and celebrate the primitive. So one way anthropology has changed is that many anthropologists have literally become historians of our own discipline, scrutinizing our intellectual ancestors in order to find in their ethnographic practices and in the ethnographies they wrote traces of the prejudices of their times. When they focused on difference, this could be seen as evidence of their desire for difference. They craved, as Michel Rolph-Trouillot so brutally put it, "the savage slot," so they exaggerated difference for their own and their peers' delectation. In this historical critique, anthropology's past product can be scrutinized as a kind of pornography, the exotic erotic. Implied in such a critique is the abiding idea that there really never were any primitive people like the Indian after all. Sure, there were poor people, or people outside of capitalism, but their desires were the same as ours. Power, not cultural Otherness, is what made us different.

A second shift in anthropology in the past quarter-century dovetails with the disavowal of our collective past by stressing the inappropriate moral distance our discipline used to put between the ethnographer and her subjects. Power—the fact that we inhabited positions of relative privilege and were generally unwilling to relinquish them—meant that we were only touristically involved in the lives of our research subjects, and even less in their plight. So an increasingly compelling program for research for anthropologists beginning their careers entails some kind of explicitly political or ameliorative agenda. In such research, anthropologists investigate the loci of power itself. Rather than go to the "out of the way places" Geertz once asserted were the scholarly terrain anthropology occupied, more and more anthropologists in recent years have "studied up," following an agenda Laura Nader suggested at the end of the 1960s, an era when academia was becoming ever-more-explicitly radicalized. In Nader's view anthropology had done far too much studying down. Indeed, the whole history of anthropology as an ethnographic encounter tended toward a certain social and cultural slumming. The political agenda of anthropology was therefore eclipsed by the thrill of encounters with exotic Others.

Nader wanted to make anthropology more directly politically relevant. To study up is to treat as natives upper-level administrators who run prestigious institutions, business elites, scientists, government officials. She wanted to use the ethnographer's capacity to develop rapport and make sense of the strange to pull the curtain back from the hidden actions of the powers that be in modern societies to expose elite actors to a public gaze. Hers was to be a critical ethnography, a kind of muckraking, albeit within the genre of an ethnographic analysis. So for the current cohort of anthropologists who are following Nader's lead, their "natives" are scientists in laboratories, doctors, administrators at the World Bank or the university, hedge fund managers, advertising executives. By "studying up," anthropologists expose how power is naturalized and made normal and invisible.

Meanwhile, even for those anthropologists who continue to work in the "savage slot," they focus on, for example, NGOs, missionaries, mining companies, or national parks and nature preserves. Part of the reason for this is that erstwhile out-of-the-way places are now sites of transnational intervention. The state and the non-state are everywhere these days. You cannot study a village without also taking into account possible missionaries or tourists or development workers, or for that matter soldiers, revolutionaries, party functionaries, transnational corporations, not to mention returned migrants and media flows via Internet or satellite dish. Some of these studies reflect a predicable shift—as natives move across the world's landscape, anthropologists follow them. So it is not surprising that, say, studies of Eritreans might require close investigations of expatriate deployment of ethnically focused websites, or that to understand West Africans one might spend one's time in Amsterdam or Lisbon or New York City among prostitutes, itinerant merchants, or laborers, not to mention university students and taxi drivers. Likewise, as anthropology itself has become a discipline within a globalized world, more and more of its practitioners come from the societies and places that were once anthropology's natives. Africans study Africans, Indians Indians.

If an anthropologist studies members of a different society or those in a less empowered subject position within their own society, then it is typical nowadays that one acts (and writes) as an advocate for them, pushing for example for the expansion of human rights, gender equality, the rights of minorities, whether sexual, religious, or ethnic, or pressing for redistributive justice in the domain of national or transnational political economies. Such work—it is often known as engaged ethnography—shares a kind of relentless exposure of inequities and injustices. A guiding assumption in this literature is an image of the present in which a certain form of social practice and discourse dominates and is nearly hegemonic: neoliberalism, the power of the corporation and the state. As often as not it is the discourses of the state or the corporation that become the primary topic of this research, and so engaged anthropology blends into "studying up." The goal is to expose power for what it is: a force that limits freedom and stunts the pursuit of happiness. One upshot of some of this work is that if "natives" such as the imaginary Indian with his tear-streaked face fail to speak in politically appropriate ways, they recede in value as ethnographic interlocutors.

Marshall Sahlins quite rightly sees in such a tendency the re-emergence of a certain unacknowledged ethnocentrism. In our discipline's current desire not to pigeonhole people—not to stereotype them—and in our desire to engage in politics so as to further human rights and more universal forms of equality and freedom, we are acting out the script of methodological individualism. Culture all over again.

For Sahlins, the strength of anthropology used to be that anthropology promised that it would meet and converse with people like that Indian and learn to learn from them. I feel the same way. I believe that an anthropology that is true to its traditions has a better chance of being a force for good than one that critiques all too slavishly its collective past or one that is all too predictable in its politics of engagement and in the enemies it chooses to expose. This book, I would like to think, is a review and refurbishing of enduring anthropological lessons and themes that were so well-articulated early in our discipline's history. By finding useful lessons in that history we can avoid becoming history—that is, irrelevant.

Anthropology reached its apogee as a discipline (so the fairly accurate myth we tell ourselves has it) during the eras of Benedict and Mead, and of Malinowski and Evans-Pritchard. All of a sudden, because of the territorial scramble of colonialism, there were all sorts of out-of-the-way places to explore more or less safely if only temporarily, like tourists. Anthropologists had a mission then. It was, so goes our favorite mantra, to make the strange familiar in order to make the familiar strange. We wanted our students to learn from the savage and to identify with primitive people in order to put distance between themselves and the society that surrounded them. By writing about other societies, other "cultures," we were enacting, as Marcus and Fischer called it, "cultural critique." That critique, we hoped and assumed, would make it possible to reappraise the social world and change it to make it better—to make it more just, more equitable, more salutary.

What we wanted to critique, our compatriots in the era of anthropology's apogee clearly accepted as useful criticism. Benedict's *Patterns of Culture* and Mead's *Coming of Age in Samoa* or her *Sex and Temperament* were all bestsellers. In those days anthropologists had little trouble finding a public voice; some even became celebrities. Part of the reason anthropologists were so popular was that savages or primitives were already a compelling subject in that era—the age of modernity. Anthropologists supplied eyewitness accounts to a public already enamored of the primitive, already excited by their strange ways. Gauguin went to Tahiti and painted images of young people that represent the same echo of desires Mead wrote about, but long before Mead went to Samoa. Well over a decade before Malinowski wrote to us about his Trobrianders, Picasso painted *Les Demoiselles D'Avignon*, a startlingly creative image of prostitutes whose faces were akin to the African masks he spent hours studying in what was then the Trocadero Museum, and later the Musee de l'Homme. His was a revolutionary image. Beasts had become beauties, not by erasure or substitution but by exaggeration, and thus the aesthetic line that Kant and others had so confidently drawn between the beautiful and elevated and the ugly and debased had been transgressed, painted over, scratched away. By creating such a perfectly ugly image, Picasso created a radically modern art.

Revolutions move forward by looking backward. That, so Walter Benjamin tells us, is the way the angel of history works. So, for example, when Marx and Engels wanted to imagine what a communist society would look like, Engels reviewed what was known about savage and primitive peoples to create a composite portrait of a society where labor was not alienated and people were not exploited. That past was the future's premonition. By Engels' and Picasso's eras the savage was as far back in time as we thought we could look. The savage also pointed toward the future. For Picasso, to return to the beast would make us all more human, if not necessarily more humane.

In Jefferson's day the savage was not quite yet the protagonist in our collective history making, although when Jefferson wanted to make a case for America's place as a signpost for the future, he did remind his European readers that Indians were adepts at democracy and always against tyranny. For the most part, when Jefferson and those like him looked backwards to move forward, they saw other societies—republican Rome, for example—as worthy of creative copying. The dome on Jefferson's house harks back to a Roman temple. When he left public office it was to retire to his lands and farm as the Roman citizen-soldiers used to do. Jefferson imagined a future utopian society as a community of yeoman farmers, each tending to the soil, each working to preserve and maintain a relationship of mutual benefit with nature.

There is much I do not like about Jefferson. I do not like his ease with extreme economic inequity. But I cannot help but love his garden and his preoccupation with tending to it to make it beautiful as well as productive. Engels annoys me almost as much because he failed to imagine that exploitation can exist in so-called "classless" societies. But I like what he has to say about the problem of property. What I admire about each of these men is that they knew where to find revolutionary inspiration. They were secure in the knowledge that a primitive, more authentic place existed and that it provided a way to the future. I worry that now, when we need revolutions more than ever, anthropology has lost its ability to provide that kind of surety.

Paradoxically, it may be that anthropology no longer has a crucial voice in current debates in part because of anthropology's success at making the strange familiar and the familiar strange, its success in making us take the idea of radical cultural difference seriously. In making the concept of culture so compelling, and in arguing so persuasively for cultural relativism, we had to attack all forms of ethnocentrism. Sometimes this meant that we asserted, as Evans-Pritchard did for Nuer, that so-called primitives were just as orderly as were moderns even though such societies had no "law," that is, no explicitly recognized body of rules and regulations and no group of persons specifically designated to enforce such rules, to protect, and to punish. Sometimes this meant that we demonstrated, as Malinowski showed for Trobrianders, that so-called savages could be as savvy as any Englishman and as rational (or irrational) as any shopkeeper. But it also meant we had to argue that savages were no closer to each other, to god, or to nature than we were. We had to do this in order to make our own nostalgia for the past visible to us as a by-product of the modern condition, not as a yearning for something literal and universal. In doing this we undermined the authority of primitive people to speak for nature and to lead the way toward a better future. I have tried to illustrate that basic trajectory of cultural anthropology by describing what Lauje and Manjaco and we (by a set of contrasts, sometimes stark, sometimes blurred) imagine about god and community and the nature of what it means to be human. Following Geertz and the tenets of cultural anthropology more generally, I have suggested that beliefs and practices—about, for example, spirits, or about love and sex—cannot be compared on a scale of more true, more accurate, more realistic, but must instead be understood as parts of a larger pattern—a kind of aesthetic. The lesson we learn when we compare is that all humans are always cultural and that no society has a monopoly on the true or the good.

But of course we crave more than merely that. Thus, while it may be that we are condemned by our conditional acceptance of cultural relativism to a universalizing skepticism, we also continue to want practical solutions, usable truths. And I would say that even though we cannot expect to discover absolute truths from the experiences of any society, we can and should use what we learn from others to think in fresh ways about the dilemmas we face. Lauje and Manjaco, for example, have much to teach us about nature, but not because they are less cultural or more natural than we are. Lauje and Manjaco do not exemplify biological imperatives any more than we do—their spiritual faith and their bodily desires are as much a cultural product as are ours—but they are, in a more euphemistic sense, closer to nature in that they inevitably and routinely are made aware of their dependence on nature for their livelihoods. We may love nature, and because we love nature we go on hiking trips to the woods and mountains. Some of us might even go so far as to do our hiking barefoot, because boots or shoes get in the way of our direct experience of nature. We long to feel it, to touch it, to be immersed in it; think of that waterfall at the end of the hike that figures so often in advertisements for bucolic getaways. Meanwhile, large numbers of us might consume excessive amounts of vitamins to protect our bodies against nature's loss or buy organic because we assume it to be healthier than the unnatural foods of the agricultural industry or because we hope that in buying organic we, by helping the local farmer, help protect and preserve the world as an ecological entity. Many of us might even try to grow some of what we eat ourselves in our own backyards, turning suburban spaces into simulacra of a yeoman's farm. But few of us tend to nature daily as Lauje and Manjaco do.

Yet now more than ever before in the history of modern societies, we are aware that we must again learn to tend to nature. My students often ask me hopefully if there is anything Lauje and Manjaco might teach us about how to do that tending. Here is a sort of answer. To solve any ecological problem requires a politics as well as a philosophy. That is what I would argue Lauje and Manjaco teach us, by way of contrast. And this is because while Lauje have a compelling philosophy about tending to nature, it is Manjaco who have a politics. A philosophy guides how we think about nature; a politics points to how to solve the problems of how best to tend to nature.

Connecting to Nature

Lauje philosophy seems to address in aesthetically pleasing ways the problem of the relationship between nature and humans. Many activists in ecological movements in the West like to point out that Western civilization has developed an attitude toward nature that makes it easy for us to exploit nature as a resource and hard for us to protect it or sustain it as a living coeval system. They emphasize that a philosophical error we make is that we objectify nature as a thing (or congeries of things) apart. We imagine that we use nature— harness its power, as one phrase has it—for our purposes. We also know that we sometimes use too much of it and hurt it as a result, and yet even as we are thinking of how to protect nature we cannot help but think of it as something apart from us. The wolf is nature. The hunter with the gun is not. Nature is spatialized. Nature is there; we are here. Fences and other boundary-marking devices manifest for us the apartness of nature. We use such fences to protect and to possess. The fence keeps either the wolf or the hunter out.

Lauje do not as easily put up fences between humans and nature. Their belief in Umpute, or connection, obviates this split. For Lauje the facts of birth reveal the bodily interconnectedness of nature and human. As they say when they make rice offerings to "Owner of Land and Water" at harvest time, "We are paying tribute to our bodies." For Lauje the microcosm—the human—is always equated with the macrocosm—the earth, the world, the land, and the sea. When animals eat from the edges of a field, that is because of connection. Connection requires that Lauje plant for themselves and for the vermin. When Lauje get the cold or flu, that too is because of connection, and the symptoms they suffer—snotty nose, stuffed-up chest, cough, chills, fever, diarrhea—all these are manifestations of the "tribute" a human body must occasionally pay to connection, the congeries of spirits that made life possible.

Lauje philosophy connects humans to nature. It erases boundaries rather than drawing them. And so, in some instances at least, Lauje do what ecological activists might suggest we also should do. Take the problem of medicine in modern society. Because we have been able to split nature into its component parts, we have been able to develop drugs that kill parts of nature in order to protect other parts. Just as we develop pesticides to manage the vermin that eat our crops, so too have we developed similar poisons to manage microscopic vermin. Antibiotics are an example. They are drugs that kill bacteria whose presence in our bodies make us sick. These medicines are wonderfully effective, or at least they have been in the sixty or so years that they have been commonly available. But, like pesticides, their very efficacy may ruin them while also modifying nature in ways we will find unhealthful and dangerous. The more we use antibiotics, the more likely it is that we will develop strains of bacteria that are impervious to such antibiotics. Meanwhile too, using them inappropriately—using them to treat symptoms of a virus rather than the presence of bacteria—means that they become less and less effective. In using antibiotics we also kill off helpful bacteria in our bodies. After all, as we now know, our bodies are also ecosystems, worlds, or myriad organisms sharing the same bodily space.

Because we are these bodies immersed in and a part of nature, a radical ecologist might point out that it would behoove us to act more like Lauje—and let some illnesses have their due. We might be healthier longer, both as individuals and as civilizations and as a species, if we submitted to some illness rather than trying to conquer all illnesses and destroy them. We might realize that you cannot substitute or replace nature with a multivitamin, no matter how many exotic ingredients from far-flung rain forests it contains.

Lauje philosophy lends itself to ecological thinking, but Lauje are also aware that humans do use and consume parts of nature, and that this entails moral dilemmas and choices. Lauje recognize connection everywhere, but they also recognize that human life, even the life they live, entails making distinctions. Yet the boundaries they draw are always provisional. All young Lauje file away the sharp tips of what we call their eye teeth, what they call their dog teeth. They do so because they think dog teeth are ugly and make humans look like animals. And they treat tooth filing as a kind of religious ceremony, a rite of passage into adulthood. Underlying the ritual tooth filing is a powerfully evocative myth that stresses the inevitability of boundary marking but also its tenuousness.

The myth begins at the earth's beginning. Humans and animals and plants can all communicate with one another; they can all understand each other, so, as the myth stresses, "there is no farming, no hunting." This is because every time "a man raises up his machete to cut at a tree, the tree cries out in pain and the man stops." In this world of no distinctions, human, pig, deer, and dog are playing a game of hide and seek. At one point they are squatting together around the base of the tree at the center of the earth when pig and deer point at dog and laugh. They laugh because of dog's erect penis. Dog curses them—"Haramu! I take away your voice"—and from thence forth dog and human, still understanding one another, are allied, hunting against deer and pig, whose speech they can no longer understand. Much later, human laughs at dog, because dog, who "has no hands," is clumsy at fetching water. Dog curses human, saying, "What was yours is now mine and what was mine will now be yours." That is to say that dogs now have humans' genitalia and humans theirs. Thus the injunction I alluded to earlier (which, when we were first told it in a serious and hushed voice by our hosts, we could not understand the significance of) never to laugh at dogs copulating, lest you cause an earthquake. To do so, they told us, is to laugh at humans for their inevitable carnality. To file away the dog teeth, so the myth emphasizes, is but a conditional act. Humans are still a part of nature. By the same token, humans must carve out distinctions to live. They must eat something. To eat they must murder and cause pain.

Lauje philosophy is intensely pleasing in the way that paradoxes are pleasing. It is also wonderfully holistic, as we have already seen. Thus Lauje recognize that the rainfall connects them in the mountains to the center of the sea and vice versa. Thus too, when they gather rattan or damar (a tree resin) from the forest they imagine the reciprocal products that will be returned to them from the peoples of the center of the sea. Lauje are adept at seeing connection. They think ecologically. And they think globally.

Lauje were fairly adept at adapting to some global crises. When we first lived among the Lauje in the mid-1980s, they had just experienced a long drought brought on by what Western meteorologists were calling the El Niño effect: wind and rain patterns in the Pacific depending on where a large mass of warm water was located. When it rained excessively in coastal South America, little or no rain fell in Sulawesi. El Niño is a periodic phenomenon. Global warming, we now know, makes this phenomenon more pronounced, but we also know that such shifts in climatic conditions have been a long-standing part of the experiences of human societies such as Lauje. Over the centuries, they have had to learn to cope with drought. During the El Niño drought Lauje fields went barren, but Lauje survived by eating a wild root called *ondot*. The root is poisonous if eaten raw. It must be soaked for days, then dried, then pounded into a flour before it can be eaten. That they know this speaks to centuries of experience with ecological disaster.

In the 1980s Lauje seemed also to recognize that such disasters were becoming more frequent, more violent, and more destructive. As to what was causing such shifts in climate, recall that Lauje tended to see Umpute at work, or, more accurately, they tended to blame their coastal neighbors for ignoring the Owner of Land and Water, as one refraction of connection was called, in favor of either Islam or materialism. "They," our hilltop hosts frequently remarked, "sold" what belonged to Owner of Land and Water, rather than sharing it. In selling foodstuffs they were able to buy the things that went with living in "stone houses," but they also destroyed the vitality of the earth, and it hardened and dried up as a result. Lauje could imagine the connection between connection and ecological collapse. But thought and action are not always linked in useful ways. Lauje might have been good at thinking globally, but they were not necessarily good at acting locally. This was especially true for local processes of ecological destruction that were indirectly associated with global forces but which might have had local solutions. While Lauje found it easy to talk about how humans in general were violating what Owner of Land and Water possessed, they were far less capable of confronting individual wrongdoers because of the way they conceptualized possession and ownership among people at the local level. When Lauje looked around them at a deteriorating landscape, they, like the Indian in the commercial, resorted to lament; action was beyond their capability.

Possessions

Property—who owns it, who gets to use it, who has to care for it—is at the heart of what we define as law, and law is always entwined with politics. This is as true for Lauje as it is for us. To simplify in order to think more clearly about Lauje by way of contrast, our politics and its attendant law posits that we own things and that ownership allows us to use those things as we wish as long as we do not encroach upon similar freedoms among our consociates. If law can be conceived as a set of rules that protect persons and a way of enforcing such rules, law is also about protecting their property. We own our bodies, for example. Indeed, egalitarian individualism implies a kind of exclusive ownership of the skin-bounded self. "It's *my* body," teenagers will often say to parents as they smoke a cigarette or explain why they have gotten a tattoo, "and I can do what I want with it." The possession of the self, in our traditions at least, has also been linked to the possession of arable land. It was because they possessed property that Jefferson pictured those yeoman farmers as the embodiment of American freedom. When the slaves were freed, they were promised their "forty acres and a mule." Just as each now owned his own body, so too did each have a patch of land that was his own. Such land is a private possession and, in general, just as you can do with your body what you please, so too can you use your land as you wish. Yet society, imagined as a congeries of individuals with similar rights, can restrict how an individual (or an individual's analogue, the corporation and the state) can use that land. Think, for example, of a patch of coastal wetlands, or of a strip of beachfront. We use the "law" to restrict what you can build on your land, or to ensure that we can cross your property to reach our beach. The law we deploy is a product of conflict and negotiation among competing stakeholders.

Lauje do not own land in this way. Among Lauje, as with most horticultural or hunter-gatherer societies, land is not possessed in perpetuity by individuals or individual families. Lauje own land in ways similar to the ways many Indian societies in the Americas owned land. When people in Jefferson's era encountered such people, they were confused by what they took to be such primitive concepts of ownership of land. Indeed, Europeans in the days of colonization and empire as often as not assumed that they had no concept of ownership, or Europeans exaggerated the contrast between themselves and primitives, asserting that people in such societies owned land as a community and not as individuals. In this view they were "communists" before communism. Community took precedence over the individual; community shared and prospered.

But community is an abstraction. No matter how often we invoke it as a kind of organism, a community is made up of individual actors. Even in the simplest seeming society, community is an order verging on disorder as people within it find themselves in conflict, choose to try to resolve their conflicts, or find that conflict gets out of their control. That is what a politics is all about. It is in the often fraught but always concrete relations among members of a community around the question of ownership that a Lauje politics of tending to nature is engendered.

Lauje are what anthropologists call shifting cultivators. They clear a plot of land, ideally land that is forested, by cutting down the trees and burning the branches and leaves once they have dried. They "slash and burn" to farm. This form of farming works well as long as there is enough land to use. Burning deadfall and dried leaves supplies nutrients to the soil. Farming plots of land that are cross-hatched by fallen tree trunks lends itself well to a kind of gardening where you plant multiple crops in a single space. There is no economy of scale and no pressure to monocrop. Instead of fertilizing, Lauje farm for a few seasons and then move on, letting the land once farmed revert back to forest. Lauje even move their households, which indeed are often in or near their fields. Around their houses and in their fields they usually plant some fruit-bearing trees—trees such as mangoes that are native and wild, but over the centuries also cultivated and selected for the quality and quantity of their fruit. These trees are individually owned and they are what Lauje use to claim use-rights to land.

As Lauje see it, anyone can farm a patch of forest if they can claim that a "grandparent"—and this category extends upwards into great and great-great-grandparents and outwards to great-uncles and aunts—once cleared that patch of land. Fruit-bearing trees count as memory markers of this. Only the owner has the right to the pick the fruit of the tree he or she planted, although anyone can take what the wind makes fall and anyone can ask to pick fruit—a request that is rarely denied as there is an abundance of fruit around the homesteads. But the etiquette of asking serves as a reminder of ownership. Lauje look at the forest around them and see in the fruit trees that grow in it the signs of ownership. When I used to walk with Lauje through the forest from ridgeline village to ridgeline village, I would often get an impromptu running commentary about who had planted this or that tree and whose grandparent that person was. As we walked we would often stop to climb a grandparent's tree for fruit. We would eat it but save the pit to be planted later at the current homestead. Or my Lauje guides would venture off the path to take a cutting of a vine or of some bamboo or other fibrous plant to later plant at the house. Thus the landscape was being constantly tended as plants from the forest were transplanted to the cleared spaces of the houseyard, blurring the line between the wild and the cultivated. Thus too, a walk in the forest between ridgeline homesteads also became a history lesson about who had rights to farm where and why, as the fruit trees and stands of bamboo were invoked to commemorate who had lived and worked this patch of forest before.

By the late 1990s, when we paid a brief visit to the Lauje after a long absence, this casual way of accounting for ownership was coming under considerable stress as an indirect result of the forces of global transformation. One vector of these forces was population pressure. In the twelve years that had elapsed since our last stay among Lauje, Indonesia's population had increased by more than 30 percent. Indonesia is an archipelago nation. Most of its citizens come from the island of Java, a densely populated, largely rural, intensely impoverished, but also increasingly urbanized and industrialized core to the rest of the islands, some of which, such as Sulawesi, count as a kind of frontier. To relieve population pressure in Java, the Indonesian government began a "transmigration" project in which hundreds of thousands of rural poor were sent off to colonize forested areas in Sulawesi and the other outer islands. Forest, to the Indonesian government—the kind of landscape Lauje inhabited—was public land, not owned, not cared for, but land that was "empty" and could be filled. In this way, Indonesia, a postcolonial nation-state, followed in the footsteps of modern nation-states. Its laws, like ours, underwrote a concept of possessive individualism. With public land, the state itself acts as a giant individual, a person writ large. So the state could claim forest land, because no one owned it, and grant it to impoverished Javanese, giving them, as it were, their forty acres and a mule.

As the transmigration camps came to regions near Tinombo, the impoverished lowland Lauje were squeezed out of laboring jobs and forced to move up into the hills to make a livelihood. This migratory movement was piecemeal, as individual families would claim distant kinship to hill Lauje families in order to acquire use-rights to land from them.

Meanwhile, lowland and hill Lauje alike began planting cacao trees as a source of income. Cash cropping was a sort of gray area in Lauje practice. In recent history, hill Lauje were adamantly against selling what they defined as food owned as much by Earth and Water as by humans. Such food included rice and corn and taro. It did not include "foreign" crops such as shallots and tobacco, which were always cash crops before they were food crops. So too had coconuts been introduced to the region by the Dutch as a cash crop in the early twentieth century. In the 1990s the new crop was cacao. Then world market for chocolate was huge and prices were high.

Some hill Lauje, following the lead of lowlanders, planted the trees with alacrity, but it was usually the more sophisticated lowlanders who planted the most cacao. With trees came ownership, and soon the landscape was carved up as individual families laid claim to individual patches of forest. In a few short years a casual system of shifting cultivation had given way to a scramble for land. Cacao became a monocrop, vulnerable to disease and economic downturns. Hill Lauje, as a people, were incapable of protecting their rights to the land. They lost out to more aggressive kin from the coast, and the land lost with them.

Politics was the reason for the Lauje defeat. In Lauje, politics at the level of small communities stresses personal autonomy. Lauje count themselves as a shy people. They are adept at staying out of each other's way. They try not to inject themselves into the personal spaces of others. Recall the shy coughing that signals a visit. Think too of the silent way Lauje have of passing each other on a forest path. This tendency to avoid potential conflict is extended into what counts as Lauje law.

Among Lauje, many disputes can be resolved through the mediation of an informal court proceeding involving a traditional authority figure known as a Kepala Adat, or custom chief. To simplify a complex system, a custom chief will intervene and adjudicate a dispute if an aggrieved party is willing to put up a fairly large quantity of cash as a guarantee that the suit is not frivolous and if the ostensibly injuring party is willing to show up for adjudication. If the case goes against the plaintiff, the Kepala Adat keeps the cash. If the case goes against the injuring party, that person pays the cash to the Kepala. The upshot, as we often saw, was that potential plaintiffs lost their nerve, or even when they were felt wronged enough to bring suit, their opponent would usually fail to show up for the trial.

Here is a typical case involving a highlander from one of the more remote Lauje communities named i Robot or Mr. Robot (his name reflecting the usually random flow of words and images that is a symptom of globalization), who was accused of stealing some cloth *naus* wraps from a Lauje who lived in Taipaobal. Several people claimed to have seen Robot lurking near the hanging cloths. They saw him trotting away from the house and up into the mountains, and they saw that the clothesline was empty after he left. But it took days of debate and discussion before the aggrieved person was willing to call in the Kepala, as many of his consociates argued that either the witnesses would fail to show up for the trial or that Robot himself, a notorious sociopath, would simply run farther into the mountains. Eventually the aggrieved party did openly accuse Robot of the crime, and to nearly everyone's surprise Robot did show up to confront his accusers, and did return the cloth.

He did so because of the intervention of a kinsman, a renowned shaman who in turn had a special trade relationship with a kinsman of the owner of the cloth. Such a relationship typified Lauje social relationships, linking different communities. Called *mebembelaan,* it entailed a quasi-formal ceremony of mutual adoption where two men or women from different ridgelines agreed to become *bela*—or partners for life. As *bela* you were required to give your *bela* food. Usually those in a *bela* relationship grew slightly different things because of slightly different ecologies. The people of Robot's ridgeline, for example, grew much taro. The people of Taipaobal grew corn. Thus the *bela* relationship allowed two sets of people in two communities to benefit from each others' position in ecology of the mountains. *Bela* create and maintain a dyadic relationship. But their relationship only links individuals, not communities, as each individual in turn has a network of other relationship—as father, mother, brother, neighbor. The network itself is not a guarantee that conflicts will be resolved and the guilty punished. So the case of Robot's theft became a cause for much discussion because the accuser actually won. Usually, *sala bibi,* "false lips" or a false accusation, was the end result of trials. As a result most interpersonal problems merely were left to fester.

In the mid-1990s such problems were common. On one occasion, a lowlander set fire to brush land to clear a patch for planting, and the fire got out of control and burned some locals' gardens. Everyone knew who had set the fire. But no one had actually seen him start it. In another instance, a lowlander's goats strayed into a neighbor's garden and ate the fresh corn that was growing. Again, no witnesses were willing to come forward. Time after time, Lauje complained amongst themselves about the misbehavior of newcomers—of their tendency to fence in land that was not theirs or that they planted trees and made claims to spaces that were already claimed by others whose grandparents had originally cleared that forest. But the complaints stayed inside the huts of the Lauje; bitter and angry words were exchanged among close kin, supplemented with brave talk of revenge. Yet the Kepala Adat was not called, and the landscape around Taipaobal was gradually fenced in and transformed. Hill Lauje had usually solved most of their disputes by moving. They tended to avoid confrontation rather than encourage it. Land that was once ostensibly theirs was now slowly but surely someone else's. And this was nature's loss.

Manjaco Landscapes

Hundreds of years ago, Manjaco invented special shears to harvest rice by hand. They use it still. Like the fulcrum shovel Manjaco use to plow and prepare their fields, or the woven harness they use to climb tall palm trees to tap for wine or to gather palm fruits to make oil, it is an old and remarkable example of human ingenuity. This tool means that harvest is a highly labor-intensive activity. It takes many people working together to gather the rice from a family field. But with this tool you collect nearly every kernel. Nothing is lost or wasted.

When I first joined my companions in a harvest I learned how hard the work was and how careful they were not to let any kernel go to waste. But after two years with the Lauje I was chagrined that there was no religious ceremony that marked this moment of symbiosis between an ancient cultivar and its human cultivator. "Does rice have a soul?" I asked them, thinking that it had to, or at least should have after my sojourn in Taipaobal. "What an odd question," was the routine response. Humans had souls; rice did not.

Other things had souls too, bush spirits for example. Bush spirits looked like humans (to those who could see them), yet had features that made them odd, almost opposite. Their feet pointed backwards when they walked, for example. Some, as Manjaco occasionally reminded me, were "white like you, Eric" or had "long hair like you." Bush spirits were strange that way, but as strangers they also occasionally crossed the border from the marshlands and forests that were their ostensible home and into the village that was the home of humans. They did so by inhabiting, parasitically, the bodies of newborn human beings. Most humans contained the souls of ancestors. This is what made them human and connected each human to a long line of their progenitors. To be born in a village usually meant that an ancestor came to inhabit you while you were in the womb, demonstrating by the ancestor's actions that you had a pedigree in that village. Routinely, however, some village women gave birth to children with bush spirit souls, and while most of these children died quickly once the spirit tired of its sojourn among humans, a few lived to become members of the human beings. In doing this, the bush spirit forgets its kith and kin and adopts as its own the family of human beings that lived in the villages. Humans with bush spirit souls were especially adept at the work of curing and divination. That work entailed communicating with spirits that were generally invisible to humans.

Spirits were everywhere in the village. Almost all had been brought there at one time or another by a person with "eyes"—the capacity to see and communicate with the spirits of the bush—brought there, that is, transported from one place to another. Such spirits guarded and protected, and they could be used to injure and kill. But spirits only harmed or helped because humans asked or told them to. Every Manjaco house for example was guarded by a spirit, and in the dry season when the harvest was in and the sap flowing from palm trees made wine plentiful, there were nearly weekly celebrations at their shrines, with people gathering to give thanks to them for their protection.

All this I quickly learned, because Manjaco were quick to tell me; they wanted me to know what power they had and perhaps as a result be wary of violating their trust. "These are our police," even the village skeptics would tell me. Spirits were "police"; they resided in spaces reserved for them throughout the village, but they did not own anything. There was no Manjaco equivalent to the Lauje Togu Ogo, Togu Petu—at least none I encountered or was told about. Bush spirits were from nature. They emerged out of the swamps near the rice fields or the uncleared bush near the palm groves. That is, they were natural phenomena. But they were not owners of nature, nor were they were nature's agents, nature's refractions. Instead, they were people's agents. Housed in the villages, they enforced human laws. And if you did not believe in them yet wanted to imagine what they represented, you would say that they embodied social groups of various sizes and shapes. A house had its spirit, a kin group had its spirits, a village its spirit, a "land" its spirit, and each specialized group—the grave diggers, the blacksmiths, the aristocrats, the weavers, the women—had its spirit too.

To me at least, such spirits were far stranger than were the spirits Lauje claimed shared their mutual patch of earth. They seemed to speak to a pervasive distancing of nature from the world of humans that I found at first hard to square with my experience of the Manjaco landscape around me. From the compound where I lived you could barely see your neighbors because of the trees that grew all around us. There were groves of oil palms and palmettos interspersed with tall silk cottonwood trees; there were tall dark-leaved mangos and stands of thorn trees (acacias). In the late afternoons during my first months in the village I would sit on the veranda, marveling at the tangle of trees that made it seem as if my house was the only house in a benevolent wilderness. To me, the landscape looked wonderfully natural. It took me much longer to realize how much the landscape was meticulously managed. The mangos and silk cottonwoods had all been planted; oil palms and palmettos grew spontaneously, but they multiplied as other plants were pruned away to give them more room to prosper. None of the trees left in the landscape were without a purpose.

Even the thorn trees, which are a painful nuisance when they grow in low thickets, provided a fruit that the herds of wandering goats fed on during the dry season. Every one of the other trees—the silk cottonwoods, the oil palms, the palmettos, the mangos—had a use. You barely had to leave your compound to tap a palm for wine or to cut palm fruits for a sauce.

From my veranda I would watch groups of children roam the landscape, carrying between them a twenty-foot-long pole with which they would knock down bunches of palmetto fruit. Cutting the top off the green fruits, they would stick their thumbs into the opening and suck out the sweet gelatinous pulp. The villagers also harvested the fruit. They cleared a space on the ground and set hundreds of these fruits in a compact mass on the ground; within a few

months each would sprout a tuber-like root—the palmetto heart they called
"Manjaco bread"—a frequent snack they roasted during the busy months of
the harvest season. The silk cottonwood provided shade, and most had been
planted as enduring boundary markers between the upland fields of one house
and another. I was told that in earlier eras the straight bulky trunks of such
trees had been used to carve canoes—the transport of choice in this land cut by
brackish meanders. Manjaco would paddle as far as Dakar in them. Under the
cottonwood in my yard the women swept its leaves into a great pile between the
fin-like projections of the roots of the giant tree, mixing the leaves with other
refuse—cow dung, trash—and throughout the wet season it sat, a fecundating
compost pile to be spread over the rice fields in the dry season.

But where I saw a lush garden disguised as a forest, Manjaco also saw the
cancerous signs of decay. An older man who was paying an extended visit to
the village after a thirty-year absence remarked to me as we sat together on the
veranda, "When I was a boy, you could sit here and see Pitchilal" (a village half
a kilometer away). Remembering how it was when he was a boy, he exclaimed,
"The land was clean. Now it is dirty. The people have gone, the land is dirty."
Katama, with its scattered compounds, had about 350 inhabitants in the late
1980s. According to the official census taken in the early 1950s when this man
was a boy, there were close to 650 people living in the village then. In those
days the land was "clean" because people, houses, and rice fields dominated
the landscape, not "dirty" clumps of trees and patches of weedy bush.

Like this man, many others would point at the tree-covered landscape, or to
a patch of thorn trees and palmettos where they claimed that as children they
had "swum" in diked wet-rice fields, and tell me that "the land has broken."
They said that the land had broken in part because years of drought right after
the revolution and a flood of out-migration in the 1960s and 1970s had transformed wet-rice fields into sandy scrub lands or brackish marsh. The fields
people farmed in the late 1980s were far less extensive than they had farmed in
the past, although available arable land was more than sufficient for the current
population. Almost all the fields they currently farmed were what they called
blek, or watershed fields—wet-rice fields in sloping, swampy land above the
high-tide mark of the brackish water meanders that wind their way through
the landscape and finally out to sea.

Most significantly, Manjaco no longer farmed what they called *brik*, or river
fields—lands they reclaimed from brackish mangrove swamp by building a
dike below the high-tide mark. The dike kept the brackish tides out. Eventually,
as salt was leached out of the soil by the rains, the field could be farmed. River
fields are more productive than watershed fields. They are also notoriously

hard work. Each year a man must begin preparing such fields in the middle of the dry season rather than early in the wet season as with watershed fields. As an elder who had once farmed such fields put it, "an owner of a river field can never be far from home" because he must constantly be prepared to repair damage to the dike, which is a year-round worry. Work in the river field is also notoriously taxing. It is "heavy" work. The mounds upon which the rice are planted must be higher; the soil itself has a much higher clay content, so it is literally heavier than the more sandy soil of watershed fields. By the late 1930s many such fields were no longer in use. By the 1960s, well before the drought that began after independence and lasted until the mid-1980s, almost none of them were in use.

In the past, river fields were opened up as young men who were members of an age set initiated into adulthood as a group prepared to set up autonomous conjugal households. These men cooperated to build a dike, cutting the river so that a certain stretch of mangrove swamp would no longer be inundated by the destructive brackish water tides. The men who cooperated in the work of building a dike divided up the fields. Each man got his separate share; yet maintaining river fields also required cooperation, for once any part of the dike was breached by brackish water, the entire line of fields eventually became useless for farming.

Emigration was universally recognized as the cause of the abandonment of such fields. Much of this shared work was done as part of a series of labor exchanges that were entailed in betrothal and marriage. Young men, along with their age-mates, were obligated to work on the fields of their fathers-in-law. As young men opted not to work river fields by leaving the village, it was harder for those who remained to maintain them. Emigration meant that dikes crumbled, the soil salted up, the fields became infertile. The land was "broken" by emigration.

Reparing a Broken Land

Unlike Lauje, Manjaco did not merely lament the broken land they saw all around them. To them the broken land meant that nature was out of whack—that it no longer rained as much as it once had, and that the soil dried up and was less fertile. But more significantly they thought of a broken land as a social problem; dikes fell into disuse because people stopped cooperating. For Manjaco, any social problem potentially had a social solution. Just as spirits did humans' will and not the reverse, so too did Manjaco routinely assume that they could manage, or at least should try to manage, any catastrophe.

Thus, the year before I arrived, when Bassarel held its once-in-a-quarter-century initiation ceremony (called a *kambatch*), the men retired to the sacred forest to discuss how to solve the problems they as a people were facing in the modern world. In the end they decided that several customs that had outlived their usefulness or were becoming socially destructive should be abolished. In effect, during the initiation ceremony, the men of Bassarel had almost totally rewritten customary law. The men renegotiated custom with the spirit, and they likened this reformulation of custom to Bassarel's "Party Congress." According to them, just as Guinea-Bissau, the one-party state, held periodic national congresses to rewrite laws in the people's interests, so did the Manjaco hold periodic initiation ceremonies.

Among the customs the men of Bassarel did away with, because they were thought to be causing more community strife and conflict than helping the community work together to solve its collective problems, was the requirement of groom-service before marriage. Before the *kambatch*, young men were required to work for several farming seasons plowing and harvesting the rice fields of the parents of a wife-to-be picked for the man while she was still a child. Decades before, during the period of groom-service, the youth of the village also slept together in a large communal hut called a *baniu*, and it was from the *baniu*, or dormitory, that group work parties were also organized. In those days, households could count on the labor of not only future sons-in-law, but also, when occasion demanded it, the entire age set that shared the dormitory. More recently, however, because of emigration, groom-service had been little more than a nostalgic ideal. Moreover, increasingly youths were simply eloping, daring spiritual retribution and occasionally paying a heavy "washing" fine (called the "fine of the comb") at the central shrine. After the *kambatch*, the men of Bassarel made simple mutual consent the new law of the land; they did away with fines and ritual sanctions.

The men of Bassarel also abolished a women's divination cult, in which adepts of the cult were ostensibly possessed by spirits who spoke through them to identify those people who were causing woman to remain barren or who were killing women's unborn or infant children. As with groom-service, the men abolished the cult because they decided it was impossible to know whether it was indeed the spirit speaking or whether the women were simply using the spirit's "voice" to justify punishing and fining whomever they chose for their own selfish ends.

To have acted with such alacrity to respond to new circumstances reveals the extent of Manjaco pragmatism, but also the extent of their political organization and acumen. When I asked them what they did in the sacred grove, they said simply, "we argued, we discussed, and then we agreed." Once they had agreed, the men all swore an oath at the shrine, promising to uphold the new rules on pain of death or injury by the spirit they called the King of the Below. When I was in Bassarel I participated in the weekly meetings at the shrine of the King of the Below and saw how such arguments occurred and how they led to agreement. Life in a Manjaco village is a series of such meetings. People learn from a young age the art of quick-tongued rhetoric and the practice of standing up in front of others and speaking one's mind against opponents. Of all the Manjaco I met it was the youth who impressed me most. Cosmopolitan in their aspirations—they wanted to attend school and craved their chance to try out life in distant big cities—they were also committed to making the village a better place to live. To do this the village youth had formed the Development of Culture Club, whose explicit charter was to repair as best they could the broken land they inhabited. To help their elders and therefore the village, they organized work parties, hiring themselves out at below the going rate to harvest and plow the fields. They also planted a bean field on their own account, and then sold the harvest, again at well below the market rate, to the mothers of the village so that the women might have a cheap source of seedlings to plant in their own gardens to sell. The youth of the club spent the money they earned on parties (initially the club saved its earnings to buy a car battery to power a phonograph and recordings of the best pan-African dance tunes), and they also bought schoolbooks and supplies for their peers and juniors who were attending school in the village or in the in capital city.

In buying school supplies they hoped to resolve an ongoing conflict between elders and juniors, for the elders were, on the whole, against their children getting an education. The elders worried that to pay a child to go to school meant that they were, in effect, paying children not to work in the fields. Elders argued that they lost twice. Not only did they lose domestic help, but they spent hard-earned cash for books, clothing, and so forth. The Culture Club took it upon itself to finance education and required that those who received funds or supplies had to work in the wet season, joining the work groups they hired out to the elders.

The club's members also concerned themselves with palm-wine production, because selling wine during the dry season was more or less the only source of income for young men. In the years before I was in Bassarel, the community would convene at the beginning of the tapping season to set local wine prices. Effectively, they set up a two-tiered pricing system. Palm-wine tappers could sell to outsiders at a higher price than they could to members of the community. Costs to outsiders varied with what the market would bear; villagers could get wine at a lower fixed rate. But this "custom," itself an innovation from the late colonial era, was ripe for corruption. Youths could cheat on their obligations to villagers and sell all their wine to outsiders.

A brief look at the public debate I witnessed among the members of the club and the village elders over pricing reveals how aware Manjaco are that repairing the fissures and ruptures of a broken land requires political solutions that entail mundane and routine sacrifice. Communities are as hard to tend and maintain as nature. The youth of the club recognized that the sale of palm wine created a clear conflict of interest between particular producers and wider society. Women (mostly Manjaco) from the market center in the district capital, a town called Canchungo, contracted with tappers (mainly young men) in "bush" communities like Bassarel either to buy their product or to sell it on consignment. Many young tappers were committing their entire production in advance to the Canchungo traders in order to earn more than they could if they sold their wine to neighbors. When a member of the community would come to them with "a need" (i.e., a ceremony or sacrifice that had to be performed for which a quantity of palm wine was required), such tappers would decline, claiming that the palm wine was no longer theirs to sell.

In the debate, the members of the club were instrumental in arriving at a consensus about how to resolve the dilemma of personal interests being directly opposed to community interest that would cause the community to suffer as a result. Those in the discussion drew attention to the fact that all people would, at one time or another, and often unexpectedly, come to depend upon their neighbors to fulfill a need they could not meet alone. The de facto leaders of the club kept reiterating that every member of the community should respect and strive to meet the needs of his neighbors. The members of the Culture Club who spoke up before the assembly used the image of an unexpected death (and funeral) to characterize a typical "need." They emphasized that everyone will eventually have to ask for aid from their fellows because all households can expect to suffer a death in the family. But how to ensure that palm wine would be available?

Those who spoke offered two possible solutions. One solution (backed initially by many of the young men who did the most tapping) was to do away with two-tiered pricing altogether. The proponents of this solution—we might call it the laissez-faire solution—emphasized that even if they would agree to sell to their peers when a need arose, more and more young men were finessing the obligation by moving out of Bassarel and across the river to the forest, where they could tap palms and enter freely into contracts with itinerant traders. They argued that if the village wanted enough wine, they would have to pay for it at the going rate. They raised yet another point: palm wine prices were already unfairly low because female traders knew that the tappers would have to sell quickly before the wine turned to vinegar. This became briefly a rallying cry for several young men who began to repeat "our work is expensive; the wine is cheap"—stressing that the tapper risked injury or death every time he climbed a palm tree.

On the other side, many people asserted that to do away with the pricing system would be unfair to old people. One elder pointed out that to those who could no longer fend for themselves, everything was becoming expensive. He noted (but did not name names) that several of the most active wine producers or sellers in the village lied—claiming previous contractual agreements—when they actually had wine they could have sold. Others who agreed with the elder pointed out that if the two-tiered pricing system was abolished, then other exchange relationships in the village would also be affected. Women would begin charging more for fish or soured milk, or they would simply refuse to give them to neighbors. They also pointed out that Bassarel had obligations to neighboring communities that, in turn, depended on maintaining the pricing system. In the year that Bassarel had held its *kambatch,* the men of Bassarel who had gathered for three months in the sacred forest depended upon neighboring communities for wine, which they were sold at a low price. Now one of the communities that had furnished them wine would host a similar ceremony. If Bassarel decided to sell wine at the going rate would not they be reneging on an implicit promise to reciprocate in kind?

A compromise was reached in which the two-tiered pricing structure was abolished, but in favor of a generally lower price. It was agreed that an announcement would be made to the traders of Canchungo, letting them know the price and asking them to report to the village council anyone who attempted to charge more. There would be no more incentive to hoard wine for the traders. The young men of Bassarel also agreed to give priority first to those who had needs because of the ceremony, then to neighbors, and lastly to traders. The members of the club acted so that community interest would prevail. Prices were set to make it easier for villagers to provide for collective needs, not to make it easier for individual tappers to maximize desires.

The lesson Manjaco teach us about tending to nature is a simple one. For them the land is not separate from the people who inhabit it. There is no real, rhetorical, or imagined fence that divides nature from society. Indeed, society in the Manjaco imagination encompasses all—spirits, landscape, people. Manjaco also practice what we might call a politics of hope. There is a saying they often quote: "Burn your hand, you lick your fingers." They deploy this saying to characterize moments when the problems they face are so insurmountable that no solution seems tenable. The point of the saying is that even in the worst of circumstances, people do something. They are compelled. Burn your hands, you lick your fingers. The cool of your saliva might make the burn feel less painful. You have to try.

Manjaco teach us too that this effort is a collective one, a work of willpower where you must give in so that others—that collectivity, the land—can prosper. Youth show that they are mature by doing this. They win praise from the land—that is, their age-mates and elders—by acting against their immediate interests and for the land. Likewise, the elders did as much and more when they revised custom by giving up many of their privileges in an attempt to repair a "broken" land.

The Manjaco lesson is simple to say, hard to do. What Lauje teach is also simple, and pleasing in its simplicity. Their enchanting vision of a world in which all is "our bodies" writ large and in which in turn each one of "our bodies" is the world writ small reminds us in its conceptual elegance and incisiveness that is not enough merely to recognize and, dare I say, celebrate or love nature. Tending to nature requires the hard-headed pragmatism of Manjaco and a legal and social infrastructure that allows for "argument, discussion, agreement" that leads to personal sacrifice for the common good.

Moral Mutuality

Imagine for a moment what Jefferson would have thought and felt if he had visited the Lauje or Manjaco. Jefferson could toil in the cool of the evening in his garden and think about how wonderful it would be to live in a society where most of its members tilled their plot of soil. Lauje and Manjaco live that world. But my guess is that Jefferson would have found their conditions intolerably uncivilized. The house on stilts we inhabited in Lauje (it was about 144 square feet) was huge by local standards—a "hotel," they joked. To us too, our house felt huge by way of comparison, in part because we had very little to put into it—an air mattress, a few dozen books, a box of medical supplies, papers, a couple of pots and pans. We had more than our neighbors, but not all that much more. And we were happy with that.

Both Lauje and Manjaco have things and want things. They like clothing that looks and feels good. I recall several lazy afternoons sitting on the veranda of my hut with my Manjaco friends watching them slowly iron to perfection (with a charcoal-heated iron) a dress or a pair of trousers. I have seen young men polish their shoes and put them on to stroll the village paths in the twilight hour at the end of a hard day spent barefoot and shirtless in the rice fields. I have marveled at Lauje men squatting together on a veranda, passing around a new machete and scrutinizing the straightness and sharpness of the blade. The materiality of cherished things makes Lauje and Manjaco happy. But their work in nature limits what they can have and possess. Their material poverty makes them irrevocably Other. Few of us would consider giving up the bulk of our possessions in order to recapture a connection to nature Lauje and Manjaco seem to have as a matter of routine. That, I would guess, is what Jefferson would also quickly think. To him they would be uncivilized because of their lack of possessions.

Now imagine what it would be like to be Jefferson sitting and reading a book in his garden pavilion. That structure, beautiful in its Palladian symmetries, is bigger than almost any Lauje house. Far bigger still is his house. It is around ten thousand square feet of living space, and although it is now one of the world's official heritage sites—a priceless place—it was no Versailles when it was built. In comparison to those who lived in Versailles or even in the more diminutive Bagatelle, Jefferson—busy squandering what fortune he had left on books, fine wines, and gold lockets for his cherished children, rather than, say, better housing or more provisions for his slaves—did not feel especially privileged. In France he could imagine himself a savage. He could think of his world— with its harpsichord and its copies of paintings by Renaissance masters—as a rustic world, an aspirational place. Perhaps to him his plantation, by contrast to Parisian luxuries, was a yeoman farmer's abode.

I used to wonder when I watched the visitors come to Monticello what they thought about that huge house and the fortune in labor and wealth it took to keep it up. Some of those who visited inhabited equally large places. Ten thousand square feet is small in some neighborhoods in the richer parts of America. As I write this chapter a real estate agent in Bel Air, California, is showing a house with thirty-six bedrooms and thirty-four bathrooms. It is the biggest on the block, but its neighbors are behemoths too. Most everywhere else, new houses in America now average close to three thousand square feet and they routinely contain four bedrooms and at least three full bathrooms in a space designed for a family of four. Two-car garages are becoming anachronisms among families where three or four cars is the norm. Perhaps most of these Americans can visit a place like Monticello and learn, by way of comparison, that neither was Jefferson's relative privilege over his two hundred slaves all that excessive, nor is their current relative privilege all that excessive either. There is always a Versailles, always a house in the Hamptons or in Houston or elsewhere that is bigger. There are always people who are richer and have more. We let ourselves off the hook for wanting more too. What we fail to see is that in wanting more, and getting more, those lands that Manjaco live in and those forests that Lauje increasingly cut down to plant cacao are also our responsibility, or our shame.

Manjaco and Lauje might not have been any closer to nature than we are in an anthropological sense of the term. Like us they inhabited a world mediated by culture, contained by culture, modified by culture. But because they depended on the soil for their living, they do have much to teach us about humans and nature. Both Lauje and Manjaco had an enduring relationship to the landscape they were aware they were recreating every day. They wanted to preserve that landscape, to make it better in ways we would now call good stewardship of the land. When Lauje or Manjaco planted a mango pit, they did so for the future's benefit, not for themselves. When they ruined things, it was usually because outside forces led to that ruin: Lauje hillsides given over to razor grass; Manjaco fields turned into brackish swamp.

I began this final chapter by reviewing how anthropology has addressed the question of its relevance in an era in which so much seems to be past tense, history. Anthropology's effort to make the strange familiar and the familiar strange has largely succeeded. We're all cultural relativists now, and in fact this goal has migrated to other disciplines. Even historians and scholars of literature and of the humanities broadly conceived all seem to be ethnographers now, all anthropologists in their own backyard. Many practitioners of engaged anthropology are no longer concerned with cultural difference. To them basic questions of social justice call out much more strongly for our collective attention than do the cultural critiques of an earlier era. But the best-engaged anthropologists continue to work in the kind of interpretive tradition that Sahlins or Geertz would find congenial. Indeed, this tradition is perhaps most apparent among those anthropologists working on the problem of tending to nature. So-called native peoples all over the world often find themselves at odds with national or international projects aimed at protecting the environment. Native peoples want to hunt or to fish or to farm in ways they imagine are not only traditional, but also in tune with the natural world as they conceive it. Meanwhile, nation-states, international agencies, and NGOs see their practices as endangering the environment as defined by an image of nature undisturbed by human life. As anthropologists write about the conflicts that emerge, they remind us that nature itself is a cultural construct, and they remind us that in encounters in which science or the state or the international community confront local people, the former are usually able to overpower the latter, their model of nature trumping the local model. In this kind of engaged anthropology, the older anthropological mission and its newer mission reinforce one another. Social justice entails an awareness of cultural difference and what can be learned from listening to difference. If nature is a model, then it is possible to imagine listening to those who have different models while potentially granting them an equal stake in arriving at a mutually workable outcome.

As ethnographers explore how states and international agencies tend to nature, they demonstrate that anthropology continues to be relevant because it reminds us that those people in those out-of-the-way places are still there and that we can learn something of significance from them. Above all, what we learn is that we share a world; we do not live apart. In sharing a world, we should create a moral space as well. Both Lauje and Manjaco, as I have sketched early in the book, assert that we should indeed share such a moral space. In their versions of moral mutuality, they expect us to act like them. After all they are as ethnocentric as we are. Lauje claim to speak for nature's needs, and they speak with what sounds to us like a quiet reverence for nature's majesty. By contrast, Manjaco seem constantly to shout to each other about this person's rights and that person's responsibilities. Thus Manjaco talk in terms that are not at all foreign to us; in fact the terms are all too familiar. They attempt to effect social justice by enjoining us to share with them and sacrifice along with them, just as Manjaco sacrifice for each other, because we and they together broke their land and are responsible for repairing it. When we listen to Manjaco or to Lauje we are reminded that an anthropology rooted in egalitarianism remains relevant by always returning to the problem of moral mutuality.

Notes on Sources

In this book I have made what I consider to be fairly obvious (at least to anthropologists) points about the nature of culture, about the relationship between anthropological models of the cultural and fieldwork, and of the way these models emerge out of contrasts—far too often between a reified "us" and a stereotyped "them," but also crucially in comparisons among societies differently situated in cultural space. The points are obvious and have been made since anthropology matured as a discipline as early as the 1930s and 1940s. Because of this I have tried to allude primarily to canonical authors and canonical texts (e.g. Benedict 1934, 1946; Boas 1911, 1940; Evans-Pritchard, 1937, 1940; Malinowski 1922, 1927; Mead 1928, 1935) that I would count as making up a core reading list for someone interested in understanding the contours of cultural anthropology. To this list I would add a fairly extensive sample of the writings of Clifford Geertz (e.g., Geertz 1968, 1973, 1983, 1988, 1995), whose work I feel epitomizes anthropology's apogee (see Ortner 1999). I also refer to a handful of scholars in other disciplines—in history and in sociology (e.g., Bennett 1995; Bourdieu 1984; Laqueur 1990) who reveal the transdisciplinary nature of basic concepts and research agendas. In writing about the Lauje I draw on the work more extensively covered in Nourse (1999).

In general, I wanted to avoid the cacophony of citation and footnotes, so I keep these to a minimum. In addition to specific sources I cite and the books cited above I also add a handful of references in the notes on each chapter as a resource for students—excerpts from which would have made up a kind of reading list I am imagining I would assign for a year-long seminar for under-graduates or for a reading group composed of people with college educations who want to learn about our discipline. The list would be short enough to be manageable. But it would also cover the major issues and themes. Other an-thropologists will have their lists; there will be considerable overlap but also much divergence. We are after all an anarchic and egalitarian discipline.

Introduction: Culture by Contrast and Theory in Anthropology

"Culture by contrast" is a phrase I borrow from Deborah Kaspin, who used it in her Introduction to Cultural Anthropology course as a mnemonic to talk about the ways a theory of culture emerged in a contrastive relationship to other theories of human behavior—biology being the most salient—and that the idea of culture only exists in terms of its contrasts. She planned to write a book built around the way culture emerges out of this field of contrasting ideas. Culture, as she argued, could never be a stand-alone concept. I borrowed the phrase when I substituted for her while she took a sabbatical—and have made of it something much less sophisticated than she had envisaged.

Among the several good introductory texts I recommend to my students are Lassiter (2006) and Metcalf (2005), as well as a very accessible collection of essays by Shweder (2003). In these and other texts of the genre one will get useful summaries of holism, fieldwork, cultural relativism, and ethnocentrism, not to mention culture and society—anthropology's core concepts if you will. We all tend to say much the same things about these terms and we have not really changed our collective tune since the mid-twentieth century.

As will be obvious in this and subsequent chapters, I find many of the chapters in Geertz (1973; see also 1983) foundational to my approach. Geertz is arguably the most influential anthropologist of the late twentieth century. When scholars in other disciplines, particularly in the more humanistically oriented of the social studies broadly conceived, look to anthropology for insight, they start with Geertz. For an overview of the Geertzian concept of culture in the discipline, and critiques of that concept, see Ortner (1999) and Gable and Handler (2008). For a historical sketch of the development of the "idea of culture" more generally, see Eagleton (2000). For a good history of the development of social anthropology, see Kuper (1973). Also see Kuper (1999) for a critical appraisal of American cultural anthropology generally, especially the work of Geertz and Sahlins. But read Sahlins (1999a, 1999b) for a defense. Other works—Ortner and Whitehead (1981), Clifford and Marcus (1986), Marcus and Fisher (1986), Clifford (1988), and Handler (2005)—round out a good selection of readings on significant shifts in anthropological thinking and on general themes. These texts also offer useful bibliographies for further exploration.

Anthropologists have long been preoccupied with the intersubjectivity of the ethnographic encounter. How you feel about your subjects shapes what you say analytically about them. Some well-known examples of ethnographic studies that reveal intersubjectivity include Briggs (1970), Rabinow (1977), Stoller (1989a, 1997), Stoller and Olkes (1989), and Dumont (1992). There are many more.

1. Supping with Savages

I draw from two bodies of literature in this chapter that are creative exemplifications of anthropological holism—the anthropology of food and the anthropology of the gift. For a taste of the former, see Douglas (1966) and Mintz (1985, 1996). Taste also leads us into a host of questions raised by exploring the anthropology of the senses (see Stoller 1989b). The gift is an enduring topic in anthropology. Mauss's is an enduring classic. Innovations on the topic he defined include Strathern (1988), Godelier (1999), and Gregory (1982), not to mention recent work on such topics as blood donation (see, e.g., Reddy 2007). The list goes on, but these are a good beginning.

2. Standing in a Line

This is an extended meditation on Geertz's key insight that culture is performed, or modeled, in everyday life and ritual. I discuss, in more detail, some of the material on Monticello in Gable (2005). For "the birth of the museum," see Bennett (1995). For "distinctions," see Bourdieu (1984).

3. Jefferson's Ardor

Cultural anthropology has been in a long-standing argument with proponents of biologically determined theories of human difference. Smedley (2007) offers an excellent history of the development of the concept of race. I also find that students learn a great deal from Gould (1996) and Marks (1995). On "playing Indian" in America, see Deloria (1998).

These works on Jefferson have been especially helpful to me: Brodie (1974), Peterson (1960), and Sheehan (1974), and I have quoted from them. Very helpful indeed for thinking about Sally Hemings is Gordon-Reed (1997). At the time of writing this book I had not yet had the pleasure of reading Gordon-Reed's book (2008) on the Hemingses at Monticello, but it clearly will become a foundational text, and it is likely that her work will finally transform the terrain at Monticello, making it into a very different kind of national shrine.

The quotations from *Notes on the State of Virginia* in the text come from Jefferson (1955).

4. The Colonialist's Dress Code

The chapter draws its inspiration from Mudimbe's (1992) discussion of the "bad copy" as the quintessence of colonialism and also from Homi Bhaba's (1984) analysis of the paradox of colonial belonging—the problem of the "not white, not quite." For more examples of colonial-era visual codes and for a useful bibliography, see Landau and Kaspin (2002) and Gable (2002b).

To illustrate the specifics of the "dress code" in the region of Guinea-Bissau I have quoted passages from Golberry (1802), Lyall (1938), Meireles (1960), Mollien (1967), and Viegas (1936).

5. Taking Pictures in the Field, or the Anthropologist's Dress Code

This chapter begins with references to what are perhaps anthropology's most canonical ethnographies—Malinowski (1922) and Evans-Pritchard (1940). The latter book, from which I draw my references to Nuer ideas of time in this chapter, has prompted a number of fruitful reappraisals that, read chronologically, are a virtual history of significant transformations in the discipline (see Karp and Maynard 1983; McKinnon 2000).

The chapter builds on three articles I have written on anthropology's entanglement with an ethnocentric vision of modernity (Gable 1995, 2002a, 2006), and my arguments on modernity are inspired by Geertz's (1968), and Sahlins's (1999a) essays on cultural differences.

The chapter also ties together photography and tourism. Both have become central topics in current cultural anthropology. For an accessible excursion into the anthropology of tourism by a pioneer in this field, see Bruner (2005). For excellent discussions of the visual in anthropology, see Edwards (2001), Grimshaw (2001), Macdougall (2006), and Stoller (1992).

In this chapter I have perhaps neglected or not emphasized enough the ironic marginality of the visual in ethnographic research and writing. Most anthropologists take pictures in the field, but few are trained in thinking critically about the visual. Most anthropologists are far more adept at teasing out the nuances of the verbal or the textual. Scholars have occasionally addressed why the visual has been marginal. One thread of this story picks up on a division that occurred early in anthropology's history as it became more ethnographically oriented and more closely tied to universities, and less about collecting artifacts—a task that was relegated to an increasingly distinct museum anthropology.

In the chapter I allude to Johannes Fabian's (2002; see also 2007) trenchant critique of anthropology's tendency toward what he calls the "allochronic." In keeping our subjects in a primitive time slot, we invariably draw a boundary between us that means that we are not, again according to Fabian, "coeval"— social and moral contemporaries. Fabian argues that we need to acknowledge that we are contemporary in order to explore the repercussions of our "inter-subjectivity." Fabian's critique is central to current concerns in anthropology to write in a politically and morally "engaged" way with our subjects, a topic I return to in the concluding chapter.

If our discipline is marred by an "allochronic" perspective, it might also be argued that such a perspective also leads to nuanced reflections on what modernity destroys. Claude Levi-Strauss's *Tristes Tropiques* (1974) is a classic and beautiful essay on anthropology's entwinement with this kind of nostalgia. I remind my students that critiques of modernity that are allochronic are, despite their flaws, as is this wonderful book, compelling and powerful.

6. Beyond Belief

What counts or does not count as an anthropological study of religion is neatly encapsulated in the arguments that emerge as one reads Geertz's "Religion as a Cultural System" (in Geertz 1973) along with Talal Asad's (1993) critique. For the problem of embodiment and mimesis, see Stoller (1995) and Taussig (1993).

The quotations on mumbo jumbo come from Moore (1738) and Park (1816) and are widely cited in histories of precolonial West African religion. Sahlins (1999a) is the source for "there is no God, but don't tell the servants."

7. The Sex Life of Savages

Thomas Laqueur (1990) takes an anthropological approach to sex as a cultural concept—as a model in the Geertzian sense of the term. His approach, not to mention Martin's (1992) now classic works on the cultural roots of the science of reproduction, are inspirations for this chapter. The argument that sexuality is a cultural construct is compellingly illustrated in Herdt (2005). I have found that his work is especially revealing for students if read in conjunction with Sanday (2007), whose essay on fraternity brother masculinity is a striking example of how powerfully transformative anthropology can be when it makes the familiar strange.

In discussing Lauje sexual practices, I make extensive use of insights in Collier and Rosaldo (1981), one of the many excellent essays in Ortner and Whitehead (1981), still the best introduction I know to the anthropology of gender.

8. Tending to Nature, Tending to Culture; or, Is Anthropology History?

This chapter alludes to examples of current ethnographically grounded anthropology that explores new terrains while continuing to use the interpretive tradition (see, for example, Bernal 2005; Ferguson 1994; Ho 2009; Mazzarella 2003). Implicit in this concluding chapter is a return to the overarching plan for this book, which has been to propose that the kind of interpretive anthropology our discipline associates with Geertz and more generally with "the idea of culture" is not a thing of the past but thrives in current ethnographic work even when, occasionally, not explicitly acknowledged. I think this is especially clear in the spate of work in science studies, including work on ecology and nature as ideas or programs for action which are also at once examples of engaged anthropology and continue in the tradition of "studying up" as first mapped out by Laura Nader (1972). Good examples of ethnographies of nature include Lowe (2006), Raffles (2002), and the collection edited by Zerner (2000).

Another reason for concluding with a foray into the "culture of nature" and the politics of "tending nature" is to counter what I perceive as a current disciplinary trend. To say that Geertz is relevant today or that Sahlins is right when he defends the idea of culture (Sahlins 1999a) seems hopelessly anachronistic to some in the current generation of new anthropologists. Books, like authors, die. Geertz died as I was finishing this book; in writing it, I also was constantly made aware through conversations with colleagues and with graduate students at other departments how for them, in some senses, Geertz-as-book had already died. Graduate students of the early twenty-first century had read about Geertz and by extension the classics in general only to learn that they have nothing much to say—that they are merely iterations of the fantasy of the savage slot (Trouillot 1991). For some of these students, not to mention their teachers, culture is an idea akin to race—a reification that leads to stereotyping. To them, "culture" is a dangerous concept. It is above all else not politically engaged in that it overlooks or downplays differences, disagreement, contest, and resistance within a society while also paying scant attention to transnational relations of power and disempowerment. But the idea of culture, as Geertz and others (e.g., Sahlins 1976, 1995) use it, can and does account for these kinds of differences. As Joel Robbins (2006) has recently cogently argued, these more venerable approaches in anthropology are far more radical and useful than the current focus on power. Moreover, interpretive estrangement clearly has traction in other kindred disciplines that have sometimes explicit political agendas. Here I am thinking of that hybrid transdiscipline, "cultural studies," which borrows much from Geertz and from an ethnographically centered anthropology (see, e.g., Grossberg 1997; Grossberg, Nelson, and Treichler 1992; Hebdige 1979; Radway 1984).

For an excellent introduction to anthropology's relationship to history, see Comaroff and Comaroff (1992). When I discuss Lauje in this chapter, as in previous chapters, I refer to material covered in more detail in Nourse (1999). Here I also owe a debt to Tania Li (1999, 2007) whose insights on development and the political economy of ecology in the Lauje region and in Sulawesi more generally, have provided me a new way to think about that terrain.

References

Appiah, K. Anthony. 1992. "Inventing an African Practice in Philosophy: Epistemological Issues." In *The Surreptitious Speech: Presence Africaine and the Politics of Otherness*, ed. V. Y. Mudimbe, 227–237. Chicago: University of Chicago Press.

Appadurai, Arjun. 1996. *Modernity at Large: Cultural Dimensions of Globalization*. Minneapolis: University of Minnesota Press.

Asad, Talal. 1993. "The Construction of Religion as an Anthropological Category." In *Genealogies of Religion: Discipline and Reasons of Power in Christianity and Islam*, 27–54. Baltimore: Johns Hopkins University Press.

Benedict, Ruth. 1934. *Patterns of Culture*. Boston: Houghton Mifflin.

———. 1946. *The Chrysanthemum and the Sword: Patterns of Japanese Culture*. Boston: Houghton Mifflin.

Bennett, Tony. 1995. *The Birth of the Museum: History, Theory, Politics*. New York: Routledge.

Bernal, Victoria. 2005. "Eritrea on-line: Diaspora, Cyberspace, and the Public Sphere." *American Ethnologist* 32(4) (2005): 660–75.

Bhaba, Homi K. 1984. "Of Mimicry and Man: The Ambivalence of Colonial Discourse." *October* 28(1): 125–133.

Boas, Franz. 1911. *The Mind of Primitive Man*. New York: Macmillan.

———. 1940. *Race, Language and Culture*. New York: MacMillan.

Bourdieu, Pierre. 1984. *Distinction: The Social Critique of the Judgement of Taste*. Cambridge, Mass.: Harvard University Press.

Briggs, Jean L. 1970. *Never in Anger: Portrait of an Eskimo Family*. Cambridge, Mass.: Harvard University Press.

Brodie, Fawn. 1974. *Thomas Jefferson: An Intimate History*. New York: W. W. Norton.

Bruner, Edward. 2005. *Culture on Tour: Ethnographies of Travel*. Chicago: University of Chicago Press.

Chagas, Frederico Pinheiro. 1910. *Na Guiné (1907–1908)*. Lisboa: J. F. Pinheiro.

Clifford, James. 1988. *The Predicament of Culture*. Cambridge, Mass.: Harvard University Press.

Clifford, James, and George Marcus, eds. 1986. *Writing Culture: The Poetics and Politics of Ethnography*. Berkeley: University of California Press.

Collier, Jane F., and Michelle Z. Rosaldo. 1981. "Politics and Gender in Simple Societies." In *Sexual Meanings: The Cultural Construction of Gender and Sexuality*, ed. Sherry Ortner and Harriet Whitehead, 275–329. Cambridge: Cambridge University Press.

Comaroff, John, and Jean Comaroff. 1992. *Ethnography and the Historical Imagination*. Boulder, Colo.: Westview Press.

Deloria, Philip J. 1998. *Playing Indian*. New Haven, Conn.: Yale University Press.

Douglas, Mary. 1966. *Purity and Danger: An Analysis of Concepts of Pollution and Taboo*. New York: Praeger.

Dumont, Jean-Paul. 1992. *Visayan Vignettes: Ethnographic Traces of a Philippine Island*. Chicago: University of Chicago Press.

Eagleton, Terry. 2000. *The Idea of Culture*. Oxford: Blackwell.

Edwards, Elizabeth. 2001. *Raw History: Photographs, Anthropology, and Museums*. Oxford, New York: Berg.

Evans-Pritchard, E. E. 1937. *Witchcraft, Oracles, and Magic among the Azande*. Oxford: Oxford University Press.

———. 1940. *The Nuer*. Oxford: Oxford University Press.

Fabian, Johannes. 2002. *Time and the Other: How Anthropology Makes Its Object*. New York: Columbia University Press.

———. 2007. *Memory against Culture: Arguments and Reminders*. Durham, N.C.: Duke University Press.

Ferguson, James. 1994. *The Anti-politics Machine: Development, Depoliticalization, and Bureaucratic Power in Lesotho*. Minneapolis: University of Minnesota Press.

Gable, Eric. 1995. "The Decolonization of Consciousness: Local Skeptics and the 'Will to be Modern' in a West African Village." *American Ethnologist* 22(2): 242–57.

———. 2002a. "An Anthropologist's (New?) Dress Code: Some Brief Comments on a Comparative Cosmopolitanism." *Cultural Anthropology* 17(4): 572–79.

———. 2002b. "Bad Copies: The Colonial Aesthetic and the Manjaco-Portuguese Encounter." In *Images and Empires: Visuality in Colonial and Postcolonial Africa*, ed. Paul Landau and Deborah Kaspin, 294–319. Berkeley: University of California Press.

———. 2005. "How We Study History Museums: Or, Cultural Studies at Monticello." In *New Museum Theory: An Introduction*, ed. Janet Marstine, 109–25. London: Blackwell.

———. 2006. "The Funeral and Modernity in Manjaco." *Cultural Anthropology* 21(3): 385–415.

Gable, Eric, and Richard Handler. 2008. "Anthropology." In *Handbook for Cultural Analysis*, ed. Tony Bennett and John Frow, 25–44. London and New York: SAGE.

Geertz, Clifford. 1963. *Peddlers and Princes: Social Change and Economic Modernization in Two Indonesian Towns*. Chicago: University of Chicago Press

———. 1968. *Islam Observed: Religious Development in Morocco and Indonesia*. Chicago: University of Chicago Press.

———. 1973. *The Interpretation of Cultures*. New York: Basic Books.

———. 1983. *Local Knowledge: Further Essays in Interpretive Anthropology*. New York: Basic Books.

———. 1988. *Works and Lives: The Anthropologist as Author.* Stanford, Calif.: Stanford University Press.

———. 1995. *After the Fact: Two Countries, Four Decades, One Anthropologist.* Cambridge, Mass.: Harvard University Press.

Godelier, Maurice. 1999. *The Enigma of the Gift.* Chicago: University of Chicago Press.

Golberry, Silvestre Meinard Xavier. 1802. *Travels in Africa.* London: James Ridgeway.

Gordon-Reed, Annette. 1997. *Thomas Jefferson and Sally Hemings: An American Controversy.* Charlottesville: University of Virginia Press.

———. 2008. *The Hemingses of Monticello: An American Family.* New York: W. W. Norton and Co.

Gould, Stephen Jay. 1996. *The Mismeasure of Man.* New York: W. W. Norton and Co.

Gregory, Christopher. 1982. *Gifts and Commodities.* London: Academic Press.

Grimshaw, Anna. 2001. *The Ethnographer's Eye: Ways of Seeing in Anthropology.* New York: Cambridge University Press.

Grossberg, Lawrence. 1997. *Bringing It all Back Home: Essays in Cultural Studies.* Durham, N.C.: Duke University Press.

Grossberg, Lawrence, Cary Nelson, and Paula Treichler, eds. 1992. *Cultural Studies.* New York: Routledge.

Handler, Richard. 2005. *Critics against Culture: Anthropological Observers of Mass Society.* Madison: University of Wisconsin Press.

Harding, Susan. 2000. *The Book of Jerry Falwell.* Princeton, N.J.: Princeton University Press.

Hebdige, Dick. 1979. *Subculture: The Meaning of Style.* New York: Routledge.

Herdt, Gilbert. 2005. *The Sambia: Ritual, Sexuality, and Change in Papua New Guinea.* New York: Wadsworth Publishing.

Herrnstein, Richard J., and Charles Murray. 1994. *The Bell Curve: Intelligence and Class Structure in American Life.* New York: Free Press.

Ho, Karen. 2009. "Disciplining Investment Bankers, Disciplining the Economy: Wall Street's Institutional Culture of Crisis and the Downsizing of 'Corporate America.'" *American Anthropologist* 111(2): 177–89.

Jefferson, Thomas. 1955. *Notes on the State of Virginia.* Edited by William Pelen. Chapel Hill: University of North Carolina Press.

Karp, Ivan, and Kent Maynard. 1983. "Reading *The Nuer.*" *Current Anthropology* 24(4): 481–96.

Kuper, Adam. 1973. *Anthropologists and Anthropology: The British School, 1922–1972.* New York: Pica Press.

———. 1999. *Culture: The Anthropologists' Account.* Cambridge, Mass.: Harvard University Press.

Landau, Paul, and Deborah Kaspin, eds. 2002. *Images and Empires: Visuality in Colonial and Postcolonial Africa.* Berkeley: University of California Press.

Laqueur, Thomas. 1990. *Making Sex: Body and Gender from the Greeks to Freud.* Cambridge, Mass.: Harvard University Press.

Lassiter, Luke. 2006. *Invitation to Anthropology.* 2nd ed. Lanham, Md., New York, London: Altamira Press.

Levi-Strauss, Claude. 1974. *Tristes Tropiques.* New York: Athenium.

Li, Tania Murray. 1999. *Transforming the Indonesian Uplands: Marginality, Power, and Production.* Amsterdam: Harwood Brace Publishing.

———. 2007. *The Will to Improve: Governmentality, Development, and the Practice of Politics.* Durham, N.C.: Duke University Press.

Lowe, Celia. 2006. *Wild Profusion: Biodiversity Conservation in an Indonesian Archipelago.* Princeton, N.J.: Princeton University Press.

Lyall, Archibald. 1938. *Black and White Make Brown: An Account of a Journey to Cape Verde and Portuguese Guinea.* London: Heinemann.

MacDougall, David. 2006. *The Corporeal Image: Film, Ethnography, and the Senses.* Princeton, N.J.: Princeton University Press.

Malinowski, Bronislaw. 1922. *Argonauts of the Western Pacific.* New York: Dutton.

———. 1927. *Sex and Repression in Savage Society.* London: Routledge and Kegan Paul.

Marcus, George, and Mark Fisher. 1986. *Anthropology as Cultural Critique.* Chicago: University of Chicago Press.

Marks, Jonathan M. 1995. *Human Biodiversity: Gene, Race, and History.* New York: Aldine de Gruyter.

Martin, Emily. 1992. *The Woman in the Body: A Cultural Analysis of Reproduction.* Boston: Beacon Press.

Mauss, Marcel. 1990. *The Gift: The Form and Reason for Exchange in Archaic Societies.* New York: W. W. Norton.

Mazzarella, William. 2003. *Shoveling Smoke: Advertising and Globalization in Contemporary India.* Durham, N.C.: Duke University Press.

McKinnon, Susan. 2000. "Domestic Exceptions: Evans-Pritchard and the Creation of Nuer Patrilineality and Equality." *Cultural Anthropology* 15(1): 35–83.

Mead, Margaret. 1928. *Coming of Age in Samoa: A Psychological Study of Primitive Youth for Western Civilization.* New York: Blue Ribbon Books.

———. 1935. *Sex and Temperament in Three Primitive Societies.* New York: Morrow.

Meireles, Artur Martins de. 1960. *Mutilaçoes etnias dos Manjacos.* Bissau: Centro de Estudos da Guiné.

Metcalf, Peter. 2005. *Anthropology: The Basics.* New York: Routledge.

Mintz, Sidney. 1985. *Sweetness and Power: The Place of Sugar in Modern History.* New York: Viking.

———. 1996. *Tasting Food, Tasting Freedom: Excursions into Eating, Culture, and the Past.* Boston: Beacon.

Mollien, Gaspard Theodore. 1967. *Travels in the Interior of Africa to the Sources of the Senegal and Gambia by Command of the French Government in the Year 1818.* London: Cass.

Moore, Francis. 1738. *Travels to the Interior Parts of Africa.* London: Cave.

Mudimbe, V. Y., ed. 1992. *The Surreptitious Speech: Presence Africaine and the Politics of Otherness*. Chicago: University of Chicago Press.

Nader, Laura. 1972. "Up the Anthropologist—Perspectives Gained from Studying Up." In *Reinventing Anthropology*, ed. Dell Hymes, 284–311. New York: Pantheon Books.

Nourse, Jennifer. 1999. *Conceiving Spirits: Birth Rituals and Contested Identities among Lauje of Indonesia*. Washington: Smithsonian Institution Press.

Ortner, Sherry. 1984. "Theory in Anthropology since the Sixties." *Comparative Studies in Society and History* 26(1): 126–66.

———, ed. 1999. *The Fate of "Culture": Geertz and Beyond*. Berkeley: University of California Press.

Ortner, Sherry, and Harriet Whitehead. 1981. *Sexual Meanings: The Cultural Construction of Gender and Sexuality*. Cambridge: Cambridge University Press.

Park, Mungo. 1816. *Travels in the Interior Districts of Africa: Performed in the Years 1795, 1796, and 1797*. London: John Murray.

Patterson, Orlando. 1982. *Slavery and Social Death: A Comparative Study*. Cambridge, Mass.: Harvard University Press.

Peterson, Merrill. 1960. *The Jefferson Image in the American Mind*. New York: Oxford University Press.

Ponte, Luiz Nunes da. 1909. *A Campanha da Guiné: Breve Narrativo*. Porto: Emprenza Guedes.

Rabinow, Paul. 1977. *Reflections on Fieldwork in Morocco*. Berkeley: University of California Press.

Radway, Janice. 1984. *Reading the Romance: Women, Patriarchy and Popular Literature*. Chapel Hill: University of North Carolina Press.

Raffles, Hugh. 2002. *In Amazonia: A Natural History*. Princeton, N.J.: Princeton University Press.

Reddy, Deepa S. 2007. "Good Gifts for the Common Good: Blood and Bioethics in the Market of Genetic Research." *Cultural Anthropology* 22(3): 429–72.

Robbins, Joel. 2006. "Anthropology and Theology: An Awkward Relationship." *Anthropological Quarterly* 79(2): 285–94.

Rushton, J. Philippe. 1995. *Race, Evolution, and Behavior: A Life-History Perspective*. New Brunswick, N.J.: Transaction Publishers.

Sahlins, Marshall D. 1976. *Culture and Practical Reason*. Chicago: University of Chicago Press.

———. 1995. *How 'Natives' Think: About Captain Cook, for Example*. Chicago: University of Chicago Press.

———. 1999a. "Two or Three Things That I Know about Culture." *Journal of the Royal Anthropological Institute* (N.S.) 5: 399–421.

———. 1999b. *Waiting for Foucault*. Charlottesville, Va.: Prickly Pear Press.

Sanday, Peggy Reeves. 2007. *Fraternity Gang Rape; Sex, Brotherhood, and Privilege on Campus*. New York: New York University Press.

Sheehan, Bernard W. 1974. *Seeds of Extinction: Jefferson, Philanthropy and the American Indian*. New York: W. W. Norton and Co.

Shweder, Richard A. 2003. *Why do Men Barbecue? Recipes for Cultural Psychology*. Cambridge, Mass.: Harvard University Press.

Smedley, Audrey. 2007. *Race: The Evolution of a Worldview*. Boulder, Colo.: Westview Press.

Stoller, Paul. 1989a. *The Fusion of the Worlds: An Ethnography of Possession among the Songhay of Niger*. Chicago: University of Chicago Press.

———. 1989b. *The Taste for Ethnographic Things: The Senses in Anthropology*. Philadelphia: University of Pennsylvania Press.

———. 1992. *The Cinematic Griot: The Ethnography of Jean Rouch*. Chicago: University of Chicago Press.

———. 1995. *Embodying Colonial Memories: Spirit Possession, Power, and the Hauka in West Africa*. London: Routledge.

———. 1997. *Sensuous Scholarship*. Philadelphia: University of Pennsylvania Press.

Stoller, Paul, and Cheryl Olkes. 1989. *In Sorcery's Shadow: A Memoire of Apprenticeship Among the Songhay of Niger*. Chicago: University of Chicago Press.

Strathern, Marilyn. 1988. *The Gender of the Gift: Problems with Women and Problems with Society in Melanesia*. Berkeley: University of California Press.

Taussig, Michael T. 1993. *Mimesis and Alterity: A Particular History of the Senses*. New York: Routledge.

Trouillot, Michel-Rolph. 1991. "Anthropology and the Savage Slot: The Poetics and Politics of Otherness." In *Recapturing Anthropology: Working in the Present*, ed. Richard Fox, 17–44. Santa Fe, N.M.: School of American Research Press.

Van Allsburg, Chris. 1985. *The Polar Express*. New York: Houghton Mifflin.

Viegas, Luis Antonio de Carvalho. 1936. *Guiné Portuguesa*. 3 vols. Lisboa: Imprensa Nacional.

Zerner, Charles, ed. 2000. *People, Plants, and Justice: The Politics of Nature Conservation*. New York: Columbia University Press.

Index

Eric Gable teaches anthropology at the University of Mary Washington. He is author (with Richard Handler) of *The New History in an Old Museum: Creating the Past at Colonial Williamsburg* and a managing editor for the journal *Museum and Society.*